Louisbourg Portraits

Louisbourg Portraits

LIFE IN
AN EIGHTEENTH-CENTURY
GARRISON TOWN

Christopher Moore

McCLELLAND & STEWART

Copyright © 1982 by Christopher Moore
Afterword copyright © 2000 by Christopher Moore Editorial Ltd.

First cloth edition published in 1982 by Macmillan of Canada
First paperback edition published in 1982 by Macmillan of Canada
This paperback edition published in 2000 by McClelland & Stewart

Library and Archives Canada Cataloguing in Publication

Moore, Christopher
Louisbourg portraits: life in an eighteenth-century garrison town

Includes bibliographical references.
Contents: Louis Davory's crime – The marriage of Marie-Louise Cruchon – Charles Renaut's letter – The sea and Jean Lelarge – Sergeant Koller in peace and war.

ISBN 13: 978-0-7710-6091-5
ISBN 10: 0-7710-6091-2

1. Louisbourg (N.S.) – Biography. 2. Canada – History – 1713-1763 (New France) – Biography. I. Title.

FC2349.L6Z48 2000   971.6'95501'0922   C00-931532-2
F1039.5.L8M66 2000

Cover images from Parks Canada, Fortress of Louisbourg. Background: Soldiers and drummers marching (5-J-01-789); Insets: Fisherman cutting fish at a table (5-J-01-1577); Servant working at potager in kitchen (5-H-634); Sergeant at King's Bastion Guardhouse (5-J-01-1321); Three servants gossiping (5-K-04-303); Couple chopping wood (5-K-04-367).

Line drawings throughout by Alan Daniel.

We acknowledge the financial support of the Government of Canada through the Book Publishing Industry Development Program and that of the Government of Ontario through the Ontario Media Development Corporation's Ontario Book Initiative. We further acknowledge the support of the Canada Council for the Arts and the Ontario Arts Council for our publishing program.

Typeset in Bembo by M&S, Toronto
Printed and bound in Canada

McClelland & Stewart Ltd.
75 Sherbourne Street
Toronto, Ontario
M5A 2P9
www.mcclelland.com

3 4 5   08 07 06

Contents

A Boom to preserve the French Ships.

Explanation
1. Glacis
2. Covert Way
3. Traverses
4. Ditch
5. Parapet
6. Rampart
7. Talus or Slope of the Rampart
8. Casemate
9. Fortified Casemate
10. Guard Houses
11. Governor's Apartments
12. Chapel
13. Barracks
14. Powder Magazine
15. Fortification House
16. Arsenal & Bake House

The Profile
a. Glacis
b. Banquet
c. Covert Way
d. Counterscarp
e. Ditch
f. Parapet
g. Banquet
h. Rampart
i. Talus

General Storehouse

Quay

King's Bastion or Citadel

Parade

Place of Arms

Queens Bastion

The Hospital

The Nunnery

Rue du Port
Rue Royale
Rue d'Orleans
Rue de France
Rue de Scatery
Rue Remparts

Scale of

A PLAN of the CITY and FORTIFICATIONS of
LOUISBOURG.

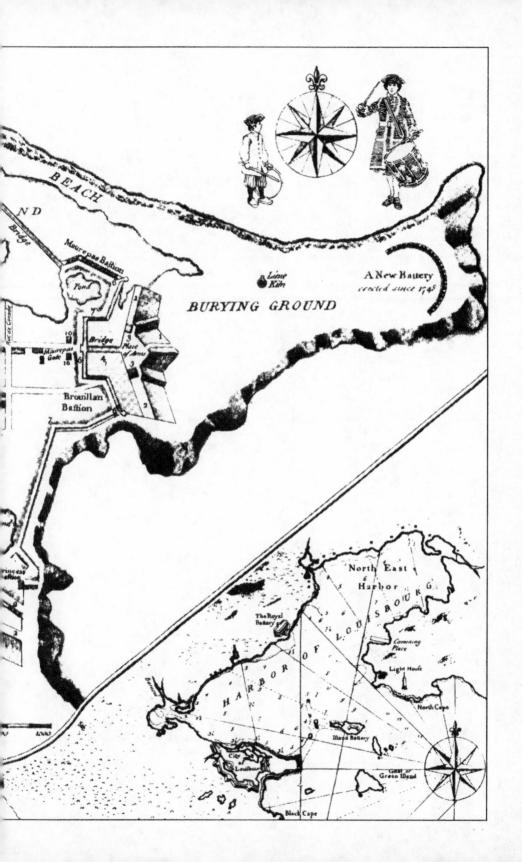

BEACH

ND

Bridge

Maurepas Bastion

Pond

Port de Canada

Maurepas Gate

Bridge

Place of Arms

Brouillan Bastion

Princeses

Lime Kiln

BURYING GROUND

A New Battery
erected since 1745

North East
Harbor

HARBOR OF LOUISBOURG

The Royal Battery

Careening Place

Light House

North Cape

Island Battery

Coast of Green Island

City
Louisbourg

Black Cape

Preface

Twice they fought sieges there. Twice armies acted out the careful rituals of eighteenth-century siegecraft there, even as they showered death by cannon fire and musket shot upon each other. It was a town prepared for the making of war, fortified on a scale unprecedented in North America, and so each siege became a slow and gruelling struggle in which endurance tended to outweigh heroism. In the end the besiegers triumphed, and at the end of their struggles a town ceased to exist. Its citizens went into exile – among them some who had come there as children or young adults when the community was being born. The fortifications were exploded into timeless rubble. After a brief half-century of activity, the town's very site was left almost abandoned for generations.

With so brief a life, so violent an end, little wonder that the history of Louisbourg has been dominated by its sieges. Some writers have found a satisfying moral in the military end of a military place, while many have been impressed by the drama of its conflicts. But gradually the military story becomes a caricature where brave Wolfe, knavish Bigot, and other one-dimensional figures fight for causes we scarcely comprehend, as if the town and fortress were only a stage set for battle epics. Surely those caught up in the combats of 1745 and 1758 had lives outside of war. What of the town behind the fortress walls in other summers and winters, and the people who lived and worked and raised their families there, engaged in more mundane struggles for survival and success?

Oddly enough, these people can speak to us if we care to listen – not just the generals and the diarists, but the merchants and the tavernkeepers, the housewives and the common soldiers. From the rich sources that survive to record the half-century of this small, lively community on the Atlantic shore of Canada, we can discover how some ordinary people lived and died in eighteenth-century Canada, how they dressed and ate and built their homes, how they earned a living and raised their children, how they fell in love and went to war. None of these people would have claimed much influence over the course of history – instead of shaping their times, they lived them – but since history usually denies us the chance to go past kings and heroes to the lives of the ordinary and the undistinguished, those rare occasions when we can make some ordinary people briefly famous are worth seizing.

Like ourselves the people of Louisbourg lived in tumultuous times. Immigrants, sometimes refugees, often pursued by economic upheaval or the threat of war, they sought with varied success to achieve a little security in a disorderly world. But they were not simply ourselves in eighteenth-century dress. Whether the issue that engaged them was the trial of a suspected thief or a quarrel between mother and son, they responded from an outlook fundamentally different from our own, one that demands to be understood within the context of their times.

In this regard the course of political and military history means less than the things that hardly seem to change. Fortunately, historians have recently been proposing novel ways to explore the nearly changeless: slow shifts in economic and social conditions, changes in the nature of the family, subtle evolutions in popular attitude and belief. Guided by such explorations, I have attempted to understand a few individuals within the time and place that shaped them, a French colonial town in eighteenth-century Canada.

A chronology of events has been included for the reader who desires an orderly sequence of the dates of Louisbourg's half-century. The note on sources provides suggestions for further reading and references to conventional historical narratives. For my part, I have followed a number of Louisbourg lives, attracted more by the quality of these people's witness to their times than by their influence on the course of history.

Andy Warhol has said that in the future everyone will be famous for fifteen minutes. It seems a comment on modern technology, but buried there is an assumption that every human life would be worthy of our attention, if we had the means to notice. If in the future, why not for the past, at least on those rare occasions where we do have the means to notice. In Louisbourg, one small community long since overwhelmed by the violence of its times, we have the chance.

As an idea and an ambition, this book began at Louisbourg. I had the good fortune to be one of the small army of researchers who have worked at Fortress of Louisbourg National Historic Park during the project to reconstruct a portion of the eighteenth-century town. Participation in that project has shaped not only my ideas about Louisbourg, but also my attitudes to the study of history and the writing of history, and I owe a debt of gratitude to all my Louisbourg colleagues past and present.

Debts of gratitude are not the only kind that writers incur. A grant from the Explorations Program of the Canada Council assisted some of my research for this book, and an Ontario Arts Council grant aided me during the final preparation of the manuscript.

My greatest debt is to my wife, Louise Brophy. Her support – financial, intellectual, emotional – touches every page.

Louisbourg Portraits

Louis Davory's Crime

n the night in question, the records show, Louisbourg was preparing for rain. At the Dauphin guardhouse by the town's main gate, soldiers of the patrol got out raingear in expectation of a wet night's work. Over the blue uniform of the colonial regular troops, they shrugged on heavy white greatcoats. For added protection those who would patrol the exposed ramparts wrapped themselves in leather capes before going out to change the guard. Shift followed shift, and the guardroom became warm and humid as returning men dropped wet gear and crowded around the fire to take the dampness from their woollen clothes, talking and complaining to pass the time. A corporal recorded the changes in the guardroom daybook – it was Sunday, August 7, 1740.

When the town clock above the citadel chimed eleven, Sergeant Dominique Bellefond *dit* LaRochelle traded the steamy, crowded guardroom for the cool quiet of the town at night. Musket slung and tricorne crammed down on his head, he marched out with his troop. The officer led a file of sentries into the Dauphin Bastion and headed up to the ramparts for the changing of the guard, but Bellefond struck out alone along the roadway. Hunch-shouldered against the rain, the sergeant began a solitary patrol through the town.

Sergeant Bellefond's patrol led him toward the heart of Louisbourg. From the gateway where his guardhouse stood, abutting the stone-and-mortar wall of the Dauphin Bastion, a narrow roadway gave access to the town. From the embrasures above Bellefond's head on his right the bastion's heavy cannon watched over the harbour waters that slapped at the wall to his left. The street widened, and as Bellefond left the bastion behind he passed heaps of sand and timber that lay on the slope below a lime kiln still smouldering from the daily burning of limestone for mortar.

Bellefond knew these materials well. Like many in the garrison, the sergeant was at least as handy with trowel and spade as with bayonet and ramrod. In his years in the ranks he had supplemented his military pay by helping to build the town's fortifications and public buildings. That work was less urgent now: around the busy town Bellefond and his fellows had built some of the most elaborate defences in the New World. Still work went on. Ahead of Bellefond as he strode east, the last large section of the rampart was a mass of scaffolding and half-finished masonry. Bellefond would return to that job site when his tour of guard duty ended.

Past the lime kiln Bellefond reached the wide quay, where the construction materials heaped on the street gave place to the goods of trade. Here a confusion of overturned boats, coils of rope, and massive anchors threatened to impede Bellefond's route across the beaten earth of the quay. Standing for a moment at the footings of the Frédéric Gate, which was soon to tower over the town's main wharf, Bellefond could look across to the lighthouse above the harbour entrance and see a hundred vessels swaying lantern-lit in the port – big traders swinging on their cables in mid-harbour, small craft and fishing schooners moored at quayside. At least one ship from La Rochelle, the fortified port that was the sergeant's home and namesake,[*] would be in that fleet, but Québec, Boston, and Martinique were just as likely to be represented, for this outpost of the French empire had thrived in twenty-five years of peace and prosperity. Bellefond's fellow soldiers and the ramparts they had built protected a town of several

---

[*] Every soldier and many civilians bore a nickname, a *nom de guerre*. Bellefond *dit* LaRochelle would have been called "LaRochelle" as often as "Bellefond," and such nicknames often came to eclipse a surname completely.

thousand and a commerce worth millions, but in 1740 the mandate weighed lightly on them. No enemy threatened; the cannon on the ramparts had never fired in anger. Patrols like Bellefond's were directed against civil disorder rather than an attacking foe.

On another night the abundance of ships might have meant a busy time for the patrol. All summer long, crews of the merchantmen and the fishing boats swarmed into a town already disproportionately young and male because of the large number of soldiers and tradesmen there. Parents chaperoned their daughters and made sure their locks were tight. Inns and taverns crowding the south side of the quay and the streets running back from it often needed the guard to quell unruly clients. But this night the town seemed quiet as midwinter. The rain and its hint of autumn had driven everyone indoors and to bed, and the streets leading up to the Place d'Armes and the citadel were silent and dark. At the busiest part of the town Bellefond spoke to no one but the sentry posted at the entrance to the colonial Treasury.

Sergeant Bellefond moved on through the streets, perhaps casting a builder's eye at the homes he passed. The imposing Treasury building was a two-storey stone-and-mortar edifice, with cut granite shaping its corners, doorways, and sills. Bellefond had passed other stone structures in his route along the waterfront, but the quay was unusually favoured. Its masonry buildings made a pleasing array for a viewer arriving by sea, but wood was the commoner building material in the town behind. Small timber-frame houses predominated. The shuttered dormers poking through shingled roofs suggested the householders' need to use all available space, and decorative iron grilles on basement windows testified to their concern for security. Bellefond caught the scent of woodsmoke that still curled from many chimneys, but even where the occupants might still be awake, neither noise nor candlelight penetrated double-shuttered windows. The silence of the darkened town was accented by sounds of waves and the drip of rainwater running from eaves and drains.

Bellefond's solitary progress brought him undisturbed to the pillory pole at the eastern end of the quay. When the fortress was complete, two guardhouses would provide sentry routines for this side of the town, but for now Bellefond's was the only patrol in the area, and he still had a lengthy march ahead. He should check that the warehouses along Rue du Port were undisturbed, ensure that no nocturnal prowler was raiding the chicken coops of homes along Rue Royale, perhaps have a word with the sentry at the hospital. Then he in turn could trudge back to hang his wet coat by the guardhouse fire. But this tranquil prospect was about to be shattered. Just as he reached the pillory, Bellefond was startled by a cry. In the next street a man shouted out: "On me tue! They're killing me! On m'assassine!"

"This obliged me," reported Bellefond laconically the next day, "to turn my steps in that direction." Turning into Rue de l'Etang, he stumbled up the narrow, unlit street toward the disturbance, hearing the shouting fade even as he ran. By the time he crossed Rue d'Orléans to reach the house of the stonemason LaPierre, Bellefond found the street deserted, the houses quiet, no murder in progress. Only someone rearing up belligerently from the rubble of the adjoining lot to challenge him: "Who's there?"

The policeman did not intend to be interrogated. Ignoring the man's question, Bellefond returned one of his own. "What are you doing there?"

"I've been in a fight," answered the man. "A soldier kicked me in the face, but I beat him for it."

"Why are you here, and what's your name? Where are you from?" pressed Bellefond, adding a final question redolent of his century's social hierarchies: "Who do you belong to?"

He got less than a full response, learning only that the man had arrived by ship the previous day. When he told the man he should be back aboard, the man replied that he was only awaiting his captain.

The fight and the shouting were clearly over, and the man showed no guilty defensiveness in the face of the law. Concern fading, Bellefond left the man standing in the street and turned back toward the quay. There the incident might have ended, except that as the sergeant made his way back down Rue de l'Etang, he stumbled on something. A roll of tobacco lay loose beside a heap of boards in front of widow Lelarge's home. Bellefond picked it up. This was not the pouch or tin a smoker might have dropped. It was a substantial roll of leaf tobacco, carefully pressed and tied for shipment, worth more than a workman's daily wage. Bellefond took the find with him, puzzling a bit, and by the time he reached the Treasury his suspicions were growing. Leaving the tobacco with the sentry there, Bellefond hurried on to the Dauphin guardhouse, but not to dry out and rest. Collecting four men from among the soldiers there, he returned to Rue de l'Etang.

A quarter-hour had passed, but Bellefond soon found the man to whom he had spoken. He now lay huddled among the stones of a demolished house. His red coat pulled over him to keep off the rain, he dozed, oblivious to the soldier regarding him. He had obviously had a lot to drink. Even as Bellefond confirmed his presence, the patrolmen scouring the vicinity found a heap of tobacco rolls cached within thirty feet of the sleeping man.

At this discovery, Bellefond pressed his men into the shadows, making them freeze against the dark fences and walls of the silent houses. They waited in hiding for a few minutes in case a theft might still be in progress near by. But the street was silent. No accomplice returned for the sleeper, no one came looking for the valuable tobacco cache. Soon Bellefond gave orders to rouse the sleeping man.

As they carried their prisoner and the tobacco toward the guardhouse, the soldiers questioned the man, but he was unresponsive, dulled with drink. Looking closer at the wet and muddy prisoner, Bellefond began to recognize him. Was this the street vendor who had offered him a half-roll of tobacco earlier that evening? When they reached the guardhouse and the men gathered to inspect the new arrival, Bellefond went to report to the officer of the guard. A theft had been discovered, it seemed. And a likely suspect taken into custody at the same time.

II

Sergeant Bellefond's encounter in Rue de l'Etang was referred to the *bailliage* the next morning. The *bailliage*, Louisbourg's general court for civil and criminal cases, was a repository of odd stories of all kinds. Before the *bailli*, a middle-aged man named Joseph Lartigue, townspeople fought over inheritances, settled their property disputes, sought satisfaction for insults real and imagined. Merchants brought

Judge Lartigue their claims against debtors, tradesmen sought arbitration of their business disputes. Anyone willing to pay court costs could bring his griefs and angers to the little courtroom in Lartigue's house, and the judge would listen gravely and render judgment. Suspected criminals were also hauled before him. Lartigue meted out sentence on minor transgressors who sold a bottle during hours of mass or shot a partridge out of season. Thieves and murderers found themselves facing the *bailli*, and some had gone out from his court under sentence of death. As plaintiff, witness, or defendant, almost everyone in the colony came sooner or later before the *bailliage*, and their testimony gave the judge a window on all the world of Louisbourg. As he listened or spoke, his clerk scribbled every word, adding to a transcript that gradually became its own witness to the life of the community.

This morning Joseph Lartigue listened and his clerk wrote as Sergeant Bellefond reported the arrest of a loitering stranger and presented fourteen rolls and two half-rolls of tobacco. Summarizing his night's work, the soldier added that the same stranger had offered him a lump of tobacco the previous evening, between six and seven. Bellefond said he had declined the purchase, suggesting the man try at widow Laumonier's down the street. With that detail, the guard sergeant concluded his statement, content to leave the incident to the civil authorities – another routine assignment for *bailli* Lartigue.

If the *bailliage* transcripts were an unparalleled record of the deeds and misdeeds of his town, Joseph Lartigue was himself representative of Louisbourg's brief history. He had arrived in 1714, part of the first small migration of refugees creating a new home on the unspoiled shore of Cape Breton Island. Louis XIV's last war had just ended, and the failure of the Sun King's grand design was forcing change upon his North American empire. At the heart of New France, Canada survived, its agricultural population quickly filling the shores of the St. Lawrence, its westward expansion scarcely checked by the British annexation of Hudson Bay. Far south, Louisiana and all its Mississippi hinterland was intact. But the French presence on the Atlantic coast was shaky. Acadia was lost, and so were France's fishing outposts in Newfoundland. Lartigue came to Louisbourg as part of the search for a replacement.

In the quarter-century since Cape Breton Island had been selected as France's new maritime settlement, Lartigue had seen the island become the colony of Ile Royale, with a string of towns along its rugged east coast, a thriving cod fishery supporting its people, and an imposing garrison to assert the authority of the Sun King's heir. He had seen Louisbourg transformed from a cluster of huts at the edge of the spruce forest to a handsome town, a flourishing outpost of French civilization and the permanent home of some two thousand men, women, and children. Shaped by encircling ramparts, crowned by the spires of its royal buildings, the town sloped gently down to a harbour full of ships. Sturdy homes filled the town and surrounded the harbour, and each day the new streets were busy with soldiers, sailors, and fishermen, mothers and children, merchants and royal officials. Undoubtedly the young colony had prospered.

Lartigue had shared in the prosperity, for he had not come as a stately judge. Born in Gascony, he had learned the fishing business in French Newfoundland and he came to Ile Royale already a leader among those who owned fishing boats and employed men. Louisbourg soon confirmed his ascendancy. While some of his competitors staggered under the strains of resettlement, Lartigue adapted quickly. His wife, nine children, and several servants were soon installed in the crowded comfort of a quayside home in the lee of the Dauphin Bastion. His fishery prospered and he diversified into ship chandlery and merchant trade. Apparently a gregarious man in the Gascon tradition, Lartigue moved easily among the military men, royal officials, and senior merchants who dominated Louisbourg. He knew the colony intimately, he was deeply involved in its economic life, he wielded daily authority over its working people. His prosperity and social stature confirmed, he began to accept official duties, and these he found congenial enough that he let his businesses wane in favour of royal service. In 1734, when the court of *bailliage* was established, Lartigue became its first judge. He was not trained for the law, but no trained *avocat* would have come from France for the small pay and mundane caseload it offered. Lartigue was sound, literate, and well connected. The fisherman became an officer of the law, charged with protecting his community from wrongdoers.

Having gained much in Ile Royale, Lartigue and men like him had much to protect. The immigrant's insecurity was strong in all of them. Most had come to Louisbourg as refugees from war and conquest, and even in peaceful times, with Boston traders welcome in Louisbourg harbour and international amity surrounding the court of Louis XV, there were other positions to be defended in the colony. Ile Royale was a royal colony in a time of absolute monarchy, and men were expected to know their places. Members of the elite expected unquestioningly that those of lesser birth and circumstances would accept their leadership. As a man of newly acquired property in an age when most men were propertyless, Joseph Lartigue obviously shared this commitment to order. But not only the rich had something to conserve. In a society that offered little shelter to the unfortunate, any upheaval in society threatened the fragile security of the working poor. An accepted hierarchy backed by stern authority offered a bulwark against economic disaster as well as military ruin. Ile Royale had thousands of transient single men – fishermen, sailors, soldiers – bound to the community only by their jobs. To protect his home, his family, and his reassuringly structured society, every settled citizen had reason to uphold royal authority by keeping such people respectful of property and the established order. The courts and the police – *bailli* Lartigue and patrolman Bellefond – bore special responsibilities to enforce stern standards. And so Bellefond's story triggered protective instincts in the judge. Rolls of valuable tobacco soaking up rain on a muddy street suggested misplaced loot from a crime against property, and the mere presence of a drunken stranger drifting about the town offended against good order. Joseph Lartigue attended closely to the sergeant's tale.

With a nameless prisoner and an ownerless heap of tobacco Lartigue could do little, but the next visitor to his courtroom brought in the outline of a case.

Louis Delort was well known to the judge. Since his first successes as a young fisherman, Lartigue had prospered side by side with young Louis's father, Guillaume. Delort senior still ran a large trade, but like the judge he had many other interests. Wholesale trader, moneylender, speculator, Guillaume Delort also sat with Lartigue on the Superior Council of Ile Royale. Now each man's large family was beginning to enter the life of the town. Young Louis Delort's marriage to Barbe LeNeuf de La Vallière had been one of the social events of 1739 for the small, interwoven Louisbourg elite. The bride's father and her two brothers were officers of the garrison, and the family roots went back to a seventeenth-century governor of Acadia. Confirmation of the new prestige of the Delort clan, this alliance with nobility had commercial as well as social consequences. Shortly after his marriage, twenty-six-year-old Louis Delort acquired a house and warehouse from his father-in-law and left his father's firm to set up independently in trade.

Louis Delort's plea to the court was brief. That morning before seven he had opened his warehouse at the corner of Rue Royale and Rue de l'Etang to find part of a wall dislodged. Inside, a door had been forced, a padlock snapped. Delort had made a quick inventory: twenty-two rolls of West Indian tobacco were missing. He had been robbed, and so he came directly to the *bailliage*.

With the source of the tobacco cache revealed, Lartigue set off for his usual inspection of the scene of the crime. Hurrying without ceremony to Delort's premises, following much the route of Bellefond's nocturnal patrol, the judge allowed Delort to lead him to the rear of a long, windowless warehouse. Calling out details to his clerk, Lartigue examined the damage to the warehouse, a simple structure built from rows of logs standing vertically and chinked with mortar and clay. Its several rooms were stocked with Delort's trade goods. One room was reserved for stacks of dried cod. Another was heaped with barrels stamped with Delort's initials and filled with wine, salt beef, and other commodities. At the main door, scales and cooperage tools adjoined a desk for the recording of sales.

The room Delort wanted the judge to see was the one that held boxes of candles, barrels of brandy, and sacks of bedding feathers. Here at the end of the building, where taller pickets rose up to the roof ridge, someone had wrenched two of the vertical poles loose from their foundation and swung them sideways to leave a substantial gap. The thief had entered here, then smashed a lock to reach the valuable and portable tobacco. His method was obvious, but the warehouse offered no further clues to Lartigue's investigation.

Before leaving, Lartigue confronted Bellefond's prisoner, for soldiers had escorted a squint-eyed, long-haired man in a red coat from
the guardhouse. Pointing to the damage, Lartigue challenged the man
to confess his responsibility, but the scene of the crime, stocked with
more wealth than a common labourer could possess in a lifetime,
elicited no confession from the suspect. He stoutly denied all knowledge of the theft. He claimed never to have visited the warehouse
and rejected all knowledge of what had occurred there. Lartigue
ordered him searched: the pockets of his baggy woollen breeches held
only a jackknife. Then, leaving the merchant to set about the repair
of his premises, Lartigue returned to his court. With his aides and the
prisoner in attendance, he began to draw up documents for a criminal investigation.

To solve this crime against property and good order, the judge
commanded no elaborate apparatus of criminal investigation. There
were no detectives among his officials and no fingerprint kits shelved
beside his lawbooks. Lartigue would rely almost wholly on oral testimony. Few events went unnoticed in a small and crowded town, even
on a wet, dark night, and a community respectful of the law usually
brought forth what it knew. Interrogation was the tool Lartigue would
use to expose the alibis and untruths of the guilty party. Justice
would be the product of a meticulous examination of the day of
the crime.

First among Lartigue's three assistants, a stark contrast to the
judge, was Jean Delaborde, a man in his late thirties who had been
attorney to the *bailliage* for less than a year. He had accepted the job
while a legal trainee in Paris, and the career opportunity had
required some sacrifices. Delaborde had elected to leave his wife
and family in Paris rather than bring them to the small, remote colonial town. The decision underlined his lack of commitment to the
colony, and though he would hold his office until 1754, he seems to
have maintained an aloof professionalism. It was his duty to lead the
investigation of crimes, seeking out witnesses and information for
Lartigue to evaluate. He would also provide the legal expertise that
Lartigue lacked. The law empowered the judge alone to render sentence, but the Crown Attorney who advised him on legal procedure
was a counterweight as well as an assistant. Was a judge harsh or

unfair to a prisoner? The attorney was a public defender to remind him that the King's justice must be tempered with understanding. Did the judge show weakness or sentiment? Then the attorney became the spokesman of implacable justice.

Delaborde may often have found it hard to square his own concept of the judiciary with Lartigue's self-taught law, but he saw nothing unusual in the pairing. He had observed the same system working on the two highest officials of Ile Royale when they had crossed from France in 1739 on the same vessel as Delaborde. Governor Isaac de Forant, a career naval officer, expected to command in Ile Royale as surely as he had aboard his ships. He would be governor, military commander, ceremonial and titular head of the colony in the King's name. Yet much of the authority would lie with the chief administrator, François Bigot, an official of the colonial service on his first overseas assignment. Personally compatible, the aging de Forant and the ambitious young Bigot co-operated from the start, but each was the other's guardian in much the way that Delaborde balanced Lartigue. Long experience had convinced the royal service that divided authority and overlapping jurisdiction best guaranteed the upholding of central authority. A headstrong local official could not easily ignore directives from Versailles if he shared authority with a colleague who, like himself, was in constant correspondence with their Minister. In the same way, Delaborde's professionalism and Lartigue's practical knowledge were expected to balance the scales of justice.

The third official was Laurens Meyracq. A Gascon like Lartigue, Meyracq had come from France just a year before Delaborde. He too had trained in France, but he was adapting to Louisbourg as Delaborde never would. Through his cousin, a merchant who was Joseph Lartigue's son-in-law, Meyracq would quickly find commercial commissions to supplement his clerk's pay. He was soon to marry another of the judge's daughters, and eventually he would rise past Delaborde to succeed Lartigue. But in 1740 he was still court clerk, endlessly transcribing legal documents and reading law.

A minor court functionary was the bailiff. As the man who served warrants and collected court-ordered payments, the bailiff was the scapegoat of the townspeople's occasional resentment against intrusive authority. Neither popular nor remunerative, the job changed hands frequently. At the time of the robbery at Louis Delort's warehouse, the bailiff was Jean-Jacques Chantrel.

There was no defence attorney at the *bailliage*, for its trials were not adversary processes. Scorn would have greeted the suggestion that justice might be achieved by the balancing of defence against prosecution before an impartial judge. Could poor, inarticulate, and often illiterate defendants be expected to hold their own against a trained prosecutor? Better by far to put the burden of investigation on men of quality like Lartigue and Delaborde. Experienced, intelligent officers of the court were surely better qualified to determine the truth than the defendant, and the balance between the judge and the attorney assured that neither the prisoner's needs nor the King's justice would be neglected. It would be the court's responsibility to solve the crimes committed in its jurisdiction.

With few resources beyond his own wits and Delaborde's legal advice, Joseph Lartigue would try to solve the crime committed at the Delort warehouse through a patient exploration of circumstances. Evaluating clues and witnesses gathered by Delaborde, the judge would slowly amass supporting testimony and demolish false witness. His investigations would become an oral history of the day of the crime, every detail meticulously rendered in Meyracq's transcript. If enough strands of testimony could be woven on the loom of the investigation, Judge Lartigue would assemble a tapestry of evidence fine enough to reveal somewhere in its folds a glimpse of the culprit at his guilty deed. Few incidents would be put aside unexamined.

Already, the morning after the arrest, as he set his crabbed signature beside Delaborde's name and Meyracq's swirling clerkly autograph on the documents that would set the investigation in motion, Joseph Lartigue nursed preconceived suspicions of what his tapestry was going to show. For if Judge Lartigue personified the determined immigrant who had found security and intended to preserve it, Sergeant Bellefond's prisoner seemed the image of his foe, the feckless, dissolute stranger whose presence was a threat to the ordered society the Lartigues and the Delorts liked to see surrounding them. Already Sergeant Bellefond's evidence hinted that a recreation of events leading to that rainy evening encounter would confirm the judge's prejudice. Though at first the prisoner would be little more than one witness among many, he had already acquired a special position in the investigation. And so his name joined those of the court officials on Meyracq's transcript. In a large, open scrawl at the foot of the page, the prisoner inscribed his name: Louis Davory.

III

An interrogation of the prisoner opened the investigation. At seven on Tuesday morning soldiers removed Louis Davory from a damp, straw-strewn cell and escorted him to the other end of the barracks building in the citadel, to a sparsely furnished room over the chambers where the colonial council sat. There were no benches full of spectators, neither jury nor lawyers, just an armoire for law books and tables and desks for the only occupants of the room, Judge Lartigue, attorney Delaborde, and Meyracq bent over his papers. At a lectern designed for the purpose, Davory raised his right hand and promised before God to answer truthfully. Then the judge launched into the prescribed phrases of his opening question: "What is your name, surname, age, profession, origin, residence, and religion?"

"My name is Louis Davory," said the prisoner. "I am twenty-four years old, or about that. I am a navigator. I was born in Saint-Grégoire near Rennes and I am of the Roman, catholic, and apostolic religion."

Lartigue pressed for more details. Davory acknowledged that he had reached Louisbourg only the previous Saturday. Before then he had lived in Canada, having emigrated from Saint-Malo in 1738 aboard one of the vessels of Dugard and Company, merchants of Rouen. Another merchant vessel, Sieur de Boucherville's brigantine *Saint-Charles*, had brought him from Canada to Ile Royale. He had joined the ship at Ile-aux-Coudres downriver from Québec, where he had briefly been employed as a domestic servant.

"When did you disembark and with whom?"

"The morning after we arrived, with the ship's cook, a fellow named Pierre."

Lartigue told the prisoner to describe the day he had spent in the town. Davory answered briefly, referring to hearing mass, running an errand with the cook, and drinking for much of the afternoon. He had passed the evening drinking at another tavern with several companions, mostly nameless. Finally, unable to find the ship's boat to take him back to the *Saint-Charles*, he had retreated into the town in search of shelter. Here, he said, he met a soldier who seized and kicked him, provoking a fight that caused someone to shout at them and eventually brought the sergeant. When the sergeant left him, he sought out a place to sleep, until the same sergeant and more soldiers came to arrest him and haul him off to a guardhouse. There, Davory added vigorously, the soldiers bullied and threatened him for fighting with their comrade.

Lartigue reversed direction, going back over Davory's voyage to learn the prisoner had been a charity passenger on the *Saint-Charles*, not a crew member. Then the judge attacked, disdaining Davory's denials. "Do you know of the theft of tobacco from Delort's warehouse? If it wasn't you who stole it, who did these damages? Do you know? Weren't you with them?"

"I know nothing of this," cried Davory. "It wasn't me who did it, and I don't know who did."

"Didn't you have a piece of tobacco under your coat on Sunday at six or seven, and didn't you try to sell it?"

"No."

"Didn't the man you tried to sell it to send you to a housewife in the town?"

Again the prisoner denied the accusation.

"Did you know your sleeping place was just two hundred paces from a stack of stolen tobacco, with more tobacco just twenty feet from you? Where did you get them? Do you know who put them there?"

"I don't know about any tobacco, near or far. I took no one's tobacco. I don't know who put it there."

"Hadn't you heard 'On me tue, on m'assassine!' being cried out from near by?"

"Well, I yelled 'Guard! Guard!' myself. That's what I remember."

Lartigue turned to some new information Delaborde had uncovered. "Didn't you sell some tobacco at seven on Sunday evening to Pierre Barrau, a labourer who was at Pichot's?"

"No," said the prisoner, and on his denial the first interrogation ended. Davory's statements were read back to him, and he reaffirmed them all, adding that while he was in the guardhouse, the soldiers had taunted and abused him. Leaving this note of grievance in the air, the prisoner was led away.

The *bailliage* turned to other responsibilities, leaving judge Lartigue's preconceptions reinforced by the interrogation. Two nights in a damp cell had done little for the prisoner's appearance. Unshaven, dishevelled, still clad in a red suit borrowed from one of the sailors, Davory looked precisely the man fallen out of the bottom of society who might attempt a clumsy robbery. Interrogation confirmed him as a drifting, rootless alien set against the taut structure of Lartigue's community. His status was virtually a motive, though Lartigue's bullying had elicited no wavering and no hint of a confession from the man. Soon witnesses uncovered by Delaborde's inquiries would add evidence to motive, proving that despite all his denials Davory had been in possession of stolen tobacco before his arrest late Sunday evening.

The first witness was the gravedigger of the parish cemetery, a thirty-six-year-old soldier named Pierre Pichot, subpoenaed at his rooms on Rue Saint-Louis and brought before Lartigue three days after the crime. After taking the oath and hearing Meyracq read Bellefond's report and Louis Delort's complaint, Pichot presented what he knew of the matter.

On Sunday evening, Pichot told the judge, he had dined at home with his wife and two friends, Pierre Barrau and René Saint-Amant, a drummer in Pichot's company. As the four sat at dinner, a stranger entered. He was, by Pichot's estimate, thirtyish, with long black hair, and he was wearing a coat of red cloth and a hat and carrying a roll of tobacco under his arm. He asked Saint-Amant if someone might buy his tobacco. "Look, I'm not a tobacco merchant," responded Saint-Amant rudely, but Barrau expressed interest and took the roll for inspection. Pleased with its quality, Barrau bought the tobacco, a full roll cut in two pieces, for a *demi-écu*.[*] After Barrau fetched money from his own residence and paid the man, Pichot expressed an interest in sharing the tobacco, but the stranger said they needn't share.

---

[*] The unit of value in French currency was the *livre*. A *livre* was divided into 20 *sols*, a *sol* into 12 *deniers*. The principal French coin was the *écu* or crown, though many foreign coins also circulated in France and its colonies. At this period the *écu* was valued at six *livres*, the *demi-écu* at three *livres*. The *demi-écu* traded here might have been Pierre Barrau's wage for one day's labour.

He would come back later with another roll for Pichot, for he had fourteen for sale.

"We went to bed not long afterward," said Pichot, "but we were awakened by the same man knocking at the door. He thrust two rolls of tobacco at me, promised to return the next day for his money, and went away."

So ended the incident, except that the next morning when Pichot joined the crowd watching the judge inspect Delort's warehouse, he saw that their prisoner was the red-coated tobacco-vendor. Of course, said Pichot, he and his friends had accepted the tobacco in the belief that it belonged to the vendor. Pichot read and signed his deposition, accepted the witness fee, and left the courtroom.

Cued by Delaborde, the bailiff ushered in Pichot's friend Pierre Barrau. A paver and a mason, Barrau was one of the soldier-labourers who had built Louisbourg. In 1738 he had won one of the rare *congés d'ancienneté*, the military discharges granted to the soldiers with the longest service in the colony. Now he was a civilian employee of the fortification contractor. A bachelor at forty-one, Barrau lodged in the Rue de l'Etang house of another stonemason. His testimony recapitulated Pichot's: the group at dinner meeting the stranger and agreeing to buy his tobacco. Barrau remembered the fellow to be "tall enough," perhaps twenty-five, wearing a red cloth coat and a hat that covered long, stringy hair. But where Pichot remembered only that the man had departed suddenly, Barrau reported leaving Pichot's home in the stranger's company. In fact, the two had spent an hour at Lajoie's tavern drinking wine purchased by the stranger, finally parting around eight.

With accusations from Pichot and Barrau in hand, Joseph Lartigue was ready to begin constructing his tapestry of the day of the crime. The two men's testimony, which seemed to convict Davory of complicity in the tobacco theft, also suggested a focus for Lartigue's subsequent interrogations. How had a stranger in the midst of an inebriated pilgrimage through the town discovered and looted Louis Delort's warehouse? Had accomplices drawn him in? To pin his prisoner to the crime, Judge Lartigue embarked on a reconstruction of Louis Davory's day in Louisbourg. His first guide would be

Pierre, the ship's cook with whom Davory claimed to have spent much of his day.

Pierre Charas, summoned into court to hear Meyracq read the depositions of Bellefond and Delort, at first denied all knowledge of the matters they raised. He had only heard people say that the passenger from his ship was suspected of theft. But Lartigue was determined to learn all that had led to the theft, and under his questioning, the thirty-three-year-old cook began to recreate a day in the life of Louis Davory.

Anchorage among the ships and schooners in Louisbourg's spacious harbour completed a voyage of about two weeks for Pierre Charas and the brigantine *Saint-Charles*, and the prospect of a day off cheered the crew. They were fortunate to arrive on Saturday evening, for Captain Boucherville wanted his cargo unloaded as soon as possible. This was his second trip of the summer down the St. Lawrence and across the gulf to Louisbourg. Canadian wheat and flour for Ile Royale's winter stores had been his cargo each time, and Boucherville hoped for a third trip before winter. Monday morning he would be sure to have his crew and the working passenger, Davory, busy unloading *Saint-Charles*. The men would hoist barrels of salt pork and sacks of grain and dried peas out of the hold and into barges and boats clustered about to take the cargo ashore. Everyone would work long hours, choked with flour dust in the hot, dark hold, soaked with spray in the boats. But first there was Sunday. Boucherville needed only a few men to keep the ship secure at its anchorage. He gave shore leave for six men.

The town that had revealed itself as Captain Boucherville brought *Saint-Charles* past the fortified island guarding Louisbourg's narrow harbour channel was familiar to Pierre Charas. Like most of the crew he had seen Louisbourg on previous voyages. With the brigantine safely anchored among the fishing boats and traders, Charas began to prepare for his chores in town. Davory was new to Louisbourg and offered to help him, perhaps to be sure of winning permission to go ashore. Though he was not close to the indigent passenger, Charas accepted the offer, and Boucherville agreed readily – why should he want his least-experienced man tending the ship? Davory had Saturday night and Sunday's dawn to study the town, possibly his new home.

Unlike Québec, perched on and under Cap Diamant, Louisbourg sprawled over a low peninsula, a triangle defined by the harbour and the open sea. The style of its buildings and ramparts would have reminded Davory of Saint-Malo and other towns of northern France, but this one showed its youth in the morning sunlight – in the orderly pattern of its streets, in the new construction to be seen everywhere. Along the water's edge all around the harbour stood the wharves, sheds, and drying racks of the fishing industry. These Davory could scrutinize professionally from the ship, for he had worked briefly in that trade. The threat of rain had prompted the workers to gather the drying cod into huge piles sheltering under sailcloth. All along the shore, ship's boats, lighters, and small craft lay tied up at the wharves, some even pulled ashore and overturned. Few of their owners were at them when *Saint-Charles*'s crew lowered a boat for the shore party.

They went ashore at seven in the morning, Pierre Charas, Louis Davory, and four sailors rowing a shallop from *Saint-Charles*'s mid-harbour anchorage to one of the wharves projecting from Louisbourg's unfinished quay. After securing the boat and unloading their belongings, the group split up. Charas and Davory strode up the gentle slope of Rue Toulouse, lined on one side with inns and homes, on the other with the bare side wall of the royal storehouses where they would soon be delivering most of *Saint-Charles*'s cargo. Time enough for that on Monday, Charas might have implied as he pointed out the building.

They were approaching the citadel. Where the fortifications crossed the peninsula from harbour to open sea, military works crowned the highest of the town's low hills. Stone walls facing the countryside and grassy earthworks facing the town made this enclosure a fort within a fortress, theoretically the defenders' last resort in time of war. In truth it was a residence more than a stronghold: no one would propose a last stand in this citadel, where a long, three-storey edifice housed the colonial governor's residence and the barracks quarters of some bachelor officers and most of the private soldiers. A slim bell tower rose from its black slate roof, for the barracks also sheltered a chapel, the parish church of Notre-Dame-des-Anges.

As the bells chimed eight, Davory and Charas joined a few townspeople entering the citadel under the idle observation of the sentries. Their path curved across an open courtyard to a draw-bridge, and they entered the barracks and the chapel. A Récollet chaplain offered low mass beneath the portrait of Saint Louis, while Charas and Davory stood and knelt among the soldiers and citizens on the bare wooden floors.

At the end of mass, Charas and Davory retrieved the merchan-dise they had stored at the guardhouse during the service, for it was time to work. Charas intended to sell the townspeople baskets of Québec cheese, gaggles of trussed turkeys, and jugs of medicinal syrup. As he explained to Davory, he had learned on previous trips how eager Louisbourg was for farm produce. A fishing and trading community, it had no agricultural population to provide fresh produce for a farmers' market, so an enterprising sailor could do well by bringing such merchandise with him. Charas probably brought a private cargo on every voyage. With Davory's help he began to lay out his merchandise where the outer slope of the citadel earthworks levelled into a parade ground and public square, the Place d'Armes.

From this vantage point, Charas could watch the town coming to life. Smoke would be curling up from most of the houses around him to be blown eastward across the shingled roofs by the breeze, but most of the people moving about were servants at their morning chores. In someone's backyard behind a high fence of vertical posts, a goat would demand to be milked. A girl might come by chasing stray chickens. Before spreading grain in her yard, she had to be sure that no raiding fox or hungry soldier had stolen any of her flock. Counting on her fingers, she would pass the vendors without a word. Close behind her might come two black women, slaves, one with a barrow, one with an armful of laundry, heading for the washing stream outside the Dauphin Gate. A servant might examine Charas's cheeses briefly before pursuing his course toward one of the town's bakeries, which was already sending the rich smell of baking bread over the neighbouring houses. A boy with a pair of wooden buckets would idle back from a well. Looking over the rooftops toward *Saint-Charles's* anchorage, Charas could see more boats moving across the water, pulling for the quay or for fishermen's wharves along the north shore. Some kind of drill was underway aboard the naval vessel in the harbour: Charas could see officers ordering the crewmen up and down the catlines of its three masts. Further off, a pair of coastal schooners might pass in succession between the surf-washed cliff of Lighthouse Point and the tiny island fort. Perhaps a cloud bank driven by the shore breeze and shrinking in the sunlight receded before the fast-moving vessels, but as Charas watched, the ships would fade and disappear in the fog.

Eventually the bells announcing a second mass brought a crowd of worshippers across the Place d'Armes toward the chapel. Men would outnumber women in this crowd, but there were many family groups. Middle-aged soldiers in threadbare uniforms escorted their simply dressed families. Prosperous, bewigged civilians and resplendent military officers strolled by with their coiffured wives and daughters, all freshly powdered by a servant or a wigmaker. Children would swarm around, as if to prove to the visitors that this community was not merely one of soldiers and transient sailors.

As music came faintly across the earthworks to mark the progress of the high mass, more people began to circulate on the square. Stocky, dark fishermen, some wearing their heavy leather aprons, might come by, talking together in a language Charas could guess was Basque. Soldiers in blue would drift past, waiting for the end of mass to signal the opening of taverns. One group of soldiers training as artillerymen emerged from the citadel in formation and marched east on Rue de France, pursued by shouting children. Soon the noise of their gunnery boomed from the Princess bastion, clouds of white smoke billowing seaward at every firing.

The end of mass would bring the gentry back to the Place d'Armes – Judge Lartigue and his family might have been among them. Senior garrison officers, civil administrators, and merchants strolled homeward making conversation. Among the officers in particular, a favoured topic must have been the appointment of the new governor. Isaac de Forant had died suddenly in May after less than a year in office, and news about a successor was expected imminently.

Meanwhile François LeCoutre de Bourville, second-ranking officer since 1730, was once more the interim commander. Once again he had requested promotion to the governorship.

A man of seventy, Bourville had served in the local officer corps since 1718, and the prospect of his accession to governor's rank drew mixed reactions from the corps. On one hand, his promotion would move all the officers upward. Michel LeNeuf de LaVallière, town major, would become *lieutenant de roi*, the senior company captain would rise to the majority, and all the others would increase their seniority. Bourville, moreover, was one of their own; he would surely look after the local officers' interests. Yet some officers pointed to Bourville's age and implied that his cautious interim administration was barely adequate. Better perhaps to hope for another de Forant, an active man out of the navy. Promotion would come in any case, for Bourville's retirement could not be far away.

Functionaries of the colonial service also awaited news of the governorship, but their prime loyalty lay with their own superior, administrator Bigot, now securely established in office. Perhaps the functionaries preferred to gossip about the imminent *accouchement* of the widow Desmarest. Her husband had been one of them, for he had held the post now filled by attorney Delaborde, and their daughter had married Lartigue's counterpart in the Admiralty Court, Louis Levasseur. Yet his widow had abandoned propriety and social standing to live with a blacksmith in the *faubourg* beyond the Dauphin Gate. Their second bastard child would soon be born.

Merchants talked business, worrying over poor fish catches and speculating about the adequacy of the colony's grain stockpiles. Their children might discuss an expedition to Rochefort Point or the outer earthworks in search of wild strawberries, while the younger men considered a hunting trip across the boggy ground toward the Gabarus shore. Couples would arrange to walk the ramparts in the afternoon if the weather remained fine, and invitations to luncheon would be tossed back and forth.

None of these doings, so familiar to Judge Lartigue, would have concerned Charas greatly had he had the leisure to eavesdrop. In any case, the crowds now mingling on the square provided an abundance of customers to keep the vendors busy bargaining and selling. A gang of Boston schoonermen, gesturing to explain their meaning, might buy cheese to munch as they explored this foreign town. Perhaps the wife of a fishery proprietor from the north shore came by with her daughter, only to decide after inspection that their own chickens would suffice. The best customers were the innkeepers and taverners. Always interested in new sources of food for their boarders and clients, they crowded in to see the Canadian's wares. One had already asked Charas to keep some cheeses until noon, then deliver them to his tavern to collect payment and take a meal. Now, close to noon, another innkeeper, Nicolas Deschamps, was pointing out his establishment just across the square. Could they deliver some chickens and a basketful of cheeses there in mid-afternoon?

By the time the bell in the tower behind them began to ring noon, Charas was well pleased with his sales. The mild, dry morning had brought out crowds, and sales had been quick. Now he and Davory were ready for a drink. They gathered up the merchandise that remained and sought directions to the tavern where their meal awaited them.

Their host, Pierre Morin, had invited them to his house on Rue de l'Etang in a typically spontaneous gesture. A master stonemason, Morin was already well established in Louisbourg at the age of twenty-six. He led an *atelier* of masons for whom the enormous job of fortifying Louisbourg provided steady work. The job had led Morin without conscious effort to the proprietorship of a tavern, for the tradesmen who worked with him often spent their spare time in the kitchen of a house Morin and his wife rented. With a wife and a servant to help with the routine work, Morin found innkeeping a congenial sideline. Some of the men now roomed with him, preferring the rowdy companionship of Morin's busy premises to life alone in cramped lodgings elsewhere. Morin had guessed that several of his guests would become customers for Charas's cheeses. If the two vendors spent some of their earnings on his wine and rum, so much the better.

At Morin's tavern, Charas and Davory found themselves in a drinking house of a type familiar to Judge Lartigue. Though the town offered several large inns where hotelkeepers attended to transient guests and long-term tenants, many of the townspeople patronized taverns as informal as Pierre Morin's. In these houses the tavern was just an ordinary kitchen dominated by a stone fireplace and cooking hearth, a rendezvous for friends and co-workers of the owner. The small room was jammed with tables, benches, and a few armchairs, and already several of Morin's fellow craftsmen and a few soldiers were lunching on bread and sausage or pulling on their long clay pipes. Bottles of rum graced most of the tables. Dice, playing cards, and other amusements were stacked on an armoire.

After the servant had shown Charas a storage cellar where he stacked the cheeses Morin wanted, the two men learned Morin was not there to pay for them. After inviting them to his tavern, Morin had accepted an invitation to lunch elsewhere, and he had not yet returned. Unperturbed, Charas said they would have a drink.

Soon the two vendors were starting conversations with other customers and finding more buyers for Charas's dwindling stock of cheeses. The topic monopolizing discussion, they probably discovered, was the recent murder of three sailors aboard a schooner on the fishing banks. One of the crew had taken a knife and begun stabbing his sleeping fellows, killing three before he was subdued. With the help of another schooner, the survivors had brought their ship back to port, and the trial of this madman, a Basque named Detchepart, was still in progress. Stories of the killing and the quarrel that had provoked it hummed through every tavern in the colony. Since the trial was not public and since the Basque fishermen tended to keep to themselves, Charas and Davory would have been treated to several versions of the story.

When interest in the murder was exhausted, the men could continue a desultory exchange of news about events in Québec, about the fortification work that employed many of them, about the unusually dry summer Ile Royale had seen. In June, a month known for cool weather and fog, drought had led to a grass fire at the Miré valley where the colony's few farms were located. The blaze had consumed the entire cattle ranch recently started by François DuPont Duvivier. Duvivier, a captain in the garrison troops, whose family led one of the cabals of the colonial elite, had been so angry over his loss that he pressed charges against a boy he held responsible. Scornful about the trial, the men at Morin's tavern would nevertheless have taken the fire seriously. Duvivier's ranch had been meant to supply the butchery from which a civilian associate of the enterprising officer provided much of Louisbourg's fresh meat. Loss of the herd made the town once more dependent on the few cattle imported aboard the trading schooners from New England and Acadia. Prices would rise, and salt beef brought across the Atlantic by Davory's compatriots of Saint-Malo would once again be the only meat for the winter's meals.

Charas and Davory spent two hours in this pleasant, gossipy company. Davory drank faster than his companion, who remained intent on collecting his payment. By two, Charas decided he had better complete the rest of his errands. They could return later to await Morin. So, with Charas toting several chickens and Davory carrying a quarter-cheese on his shoulder, the two made their way up Rue de l'Etang and along Rue d'Orléans to Nicolas Deschamps's inn.

Here their business was quickly concluded. Deschamps's was one of the larger inns of Louisbourg, fully occupying the time of the innkeeper, his family, and their servants. Deschamps's businesslike wife counted the cheeses, examined the poultry, and closed the bargain. Davory had time for no more than "un grand coup de vin" before Charas was closing his money pouch and preparing to return to Pierre Morin's.

At Morin's, Charas was pleased to find the stonemason-turned-tavernkeeper at home, and the two men sat down to settle their transaction. Just as they were joined by one of the sailors from the *Saint-Charles*, a Provençal nicknamed "Saint-Louis," Charas heard Louis Davory being hailed by a friend. A man who had known Davory in Canada was sitting at one of Morin's tables waving at him with a bottle of wine. Leaving Charas with Morin and the Provençal sailor, Davory happily crossed the room to renew acquaintance over a bottle or two.

His goods sold and his money secure in his pouch, Pierre Charas had begun to think of the ship. Morin was too busy to talk for long, and the sailors were eager to go back aboard. Shifting breezes were bringing the fog banks back from the open sea, threatening rain for the evening. Finishing his drink, Charas called to Davory, urging him to drink up and come along, but the passenger preferred to sit discussing Louisbourg with his friend. A little concerned over Davory's drunken state, Charas repeated his advice not to be late returning to the ship. Then he left Morin's tavern and set off for the wharf with the other sailor, leaving Davory pouring wine with his friend. Pierre Charas saw no more of Louis Davory, and here he ceased his testimony to the judge.

Charas's narrative had taken Lartigue down familiar streets. The judge knew this sunlit side of his town – the Sunday strollers on the Place d'Armes, the workmen and soldiers idling away their day of leisure in taverns and canteens. Charas's account of the prisoner's progress had told Lartigue little of the more sinister issues in question. The witness's closest reference to stolen tobacco was his statement that Davory had not had any tobacco all day. Charas seemed to share the judge's opinion of Davory as a drifter, a heavy drinker on the fringe of the *Saint-Charles*'s crew, but he had revealed nothing of Davory the thief. It was time to enter less innocent territory, to follow the prisoner toward dark night-time streets where thieves had planned their crime and Sergeant Bellefond made his solitary patrol.

After Charas signed his papers in Meyracq's transcript, the bailiff called another witness. Attorney Delaborde had located the man from Morin's tavern who had known the prisoner in Canada, and Pierre Charas was replaced in court by Armand Clavier, a thirty-one-year-old tailor, nicknamed Angevin for the regional accent he had carried from his native Anjou.

When he entered Pierre Morin's tavern, Louis Davory had unwittingly walked into the home of the only person he knew in Louisbourg, the man whose departure for Ile Royale may have led Davory to consider the same voyage. In his evidence Clavier gave no explanation of what had brought him to Louisbourg, where a bachelor tailor might have expected a smaller market for his trade as well as limited social prospects. He merely testified to being a tenant at Pierre Morin's Rue de l'Etang tavern. There, where Morin's lively household offered a convivial atmosphere, Clavier had been drinking with friends when Davory and the ship's cook returned from Deschamps's inn. Clavier hailed his friend, and Davory came over to join the group. By half past five, when the bells began ringing for vespers and all the clients left the tavern, three men had consumed three bottles of wine.

Clavier's testimony about the vespers service was vague enough to suggest he preferred to avoid the subject. Davory and Clavier should have completed their Sunday obligation by attending the vespers service, either at the barracks or at the smaller chapel near Morin's house, but Clavier was circumspect. When the vespers bells rang, he said, the three men left Morin's tavern together. Unwilling to say that their exodus had been prompted mostly by the law requiring taverns to close during hours of divine service, Clavier hurried on to say that though he had left Morin's with Davory, they returned there separately when it reopened after vespers. When Davory returned, Clavier was already seated with a soldier and a cannoneer. Davory bought a bottle of wine and joined them, dropping some Canadian cheeses on the table for payment.

This time, said Clavier, Davory stayed only long enough for a drink and a pledge to meet Clavier again when he was free of his shipboard duties. Then Davory departed, neglecting in his drunken condition to pick up a copper tobacco tin. Seeing it on the table, Clavier pocketed it for safekeeping. Concluding his testimony with this point, the witness gave the tobacco tin to Meyracq, who entered it as evidence. Unable to read or write, Clavier accepted the witness fee without signing his deposition. Later in the trial, Pierre Morin would confirm Clavier's testimony. He recalled the short, squint-eyed fellow in a red coat who carried a basket of cheese. Davory had left the tavern about five-thirty, said the stonemason.

With the account of Louis Davory's day given by Charas and Clavier leaving the accused alone and inebriated on Rue de l'Etang near the onset of evening, the court could advance into the period already partially exposed by Pichot and Barrau. A woman now entered the courtroom to swear the oath and give her name as Jeanne Crosnier, widow Laumonier.

When death could strike people at any age, and an adult could foresee being widowed and remarried two or three times in a long life, Jeanne Crosnier's use of her maiden name was routine and practical. Her use of the term "widow" was slightly more unusual. She had been married in 1719 to Jean Laumonier, a stonemason who, like Pierre Morin, led a group of workers in Louisbourg's building trades. It was a turbulent marriage. In 1731 Jeanne Crosnier sought legal protection

from the beatings inflicted by her husband, asking the courts to authorize a separation. Reconciliation was made, and the couple reunited,
but by 1738 the marriage had collapsed, and Laumonier sailed off to
the West Indies. He would eventually die there, but Jeanne Crosnier
had already covered her ambiguous status with the term "widow." At
the time of Louis Davory's trial, she maintained the Rue de l'Etang
property they had acquired in 1728, supporting her family at least partly
by the revenues from a small tavern or rooming house. A year later,
after learning of her husband's death, she would marry a carpenter. A
vulnerable minor citizen of Louisbourg, she was probably nervous in
the presence of the powerful judge.

The widow had a single incident to relate. She had been at home
between five and six on that Sunday evening – no, perhaps a little
later – when one of her daughters called her into the front room. She
went through to meet a man of medium height, wearing a red vest
or coat, who demanded to speak privately to her. She allowed him to
follow her into the adjoining room and he announced he had some
tobacco to sell. Oh no, she said, she didn't need any, but the man
insisted it was fine tobacco, she must sample it. Eventually she
accepted the halved roll he displayed. As she turned to grate a little
of the tobacco, which did appear to be of good quality, she noticed
the man drop the other half of the roll from under his coat. At this,
something in his manner made her suspicious. She abruptly refused
all interest in the tobacco, even though he insisted he had chosen it as
the best among several. Adamant, she hustled the man into the main
room, where he offered the tobacco to her guests before she drove
him out the door, unwilling to tolerate the fellow's furtive manner
and insistent peddling. The man tossed a few rude remarks back as
he left, and that was all she could tell the court.

Another part of the story came from a garrison sergeant, forty-
five-year-old Pierre Jovin *dit* Lajoie, who lived with his wife in
cramped quarters in the town. Lajoie recalled Pierre Barrau's visit to
his house that Sunday evening. Barrau arrived about eight o'clock,
he testified, with another man – about five foot three, red coat, long
and straight dark hair. Lajoie was already in bed, but either because
guests had taken his bedrooms or because his quarters were so small,
he was lying in the main room which the visitors had entered, perhaps

in a curtained four-poster. Unperturbed by the intrusion, he referred the men to his wife and went to sleep. His wife told him the next morning they had eaten bread and cheese washed down with brandy that she drew from a barrel. They left after their meal. Tobacco? The sergeant knew nothing about that.

Thus far none of the witnesses had taken the judge into unfamiliar territory. Rue de l'Etang he would have known well even if he never entered Morin's working-class tavern or the poor widow's home. In Louisbourg, as elsewhere at the time, the gulf between classes was not expressed by where they chose to live. Rich and poor lived crowded together throughout the town. The widow Laumonier's poor household adjoined the home of a military officer. Commercial warehouses abutted homes and inns, and soldiers lounged in taverns adjacent to the residences of the wealthy Delorts and close by the nuns' convent. Such mingling even occurred in individual buildings: the ill-paid Sergeant Lajoie probably rented his rooms from a much more prosperous householder, and of course servants and slaves slept where they could in the kitchens and attics of their masters. Visiting aristocratic friends along Rue de l'Etang, Joseph Lartigue would simply have declined to notice who his hosts' neighbours were, but he would have had no trouble recognizing the quarters described by his witnesses.

Now he wanted guides to a hostile landscape, someone to show him the deserted streets patrolled by Sergeant Bellefond after decent people had slammed their shutters on the night and the rain, preserving propriety and candle tallow by an early bedtime. Someone had been skulking among the houses and fencerows of Rue de l'Etang. Sergeant Bellefond had heard a fight and arrested Louis Davory. Who could lead the judge from Lajoie's kitchen to that moment, perhaps by way of Louis Delort's warehouse?

The witness was another soldier, twenty-nine-year-old Private Desjardins of Captain d'Ailleboust's company. On the night in question he had been to dinner at the home of his friend Philibert Pineau *dit* Lajeunesse, along with another member of d'Ailleboust's company, nicknamed Sanschagrin, and a soldier called LaRose. The meal was late, and the group continued to drink and talk afterwards, putting off the return to barracks. When the wine ran low about eleven, no one wanted to retire, so Desjardins got into his military greatcoat, found a wine jug, and ran down Rue de l'Etang to seek some wine from LaPierre's tavern. Reaching his destination, Desjardins was surprised to find a man lying in the mud, face down on his arms in front of LaPierre's dark and shuttered house. The soldier felt he should assist the poor fellow out of the rain. Picking the drunk up in his arms, Desjardins propped him in a sitting position against LaPierre's wall. As he did so, he saw the man was not lying directly in the mud. Underneath him were five or six rolls of tobacco.

With the man under shelter, Desjardins was ready to return to his friends. But he had roused the sleeper. The man he had just helped seized him by the hair and, taking advantage of Desjardins's astonishment, began to pound him with a rock. Taken completely by surprise, Desjardins screamed as the man flung him down and dragged him by his hair. He lay gasping in shock as the man drew a knife and demanded that his victim ask quarter. Still unable to believe what was happening, Desjardins hesitated, but when the man waved his knife, the soldier said hastily that if it was a life-and-death matter, he would rather ask quarter than die. This submission satisfied his attacker. The man released him and the bleeding soldier was able to stagger back to his friends.

Could Desjardins describe his assailant to the judge? Only partially. He had seen that the man had long hair and wore a red coat.

Two witnesses added to Desjardins's story. The host of the party remembered Desjardins's departure with the wine jug. During his friend's ordeal, he had been in his garden relieving himself. He had actually heard Desjardins's cries, but he had not understood them until his friend reeled back to the house. According to Lajeunesse, Desjardins had stammered out a story of how two men had attacked him in the street, beating him until shouts from a nearby window drove them off. Lajeunesse put the injured soldier to bed and took him next morning to the town hospital on Rue d'Orléans, where he had needed seventeen days' treatment before he could testify.

The other witness with evidence about the fight was André Villefayau *dit* LaPierre, the married soldier whose Rue de l'Etang house had been locked when Desjardins arrived in search of wine. LaPierre recalled that one of his lodgers, Baptiste Dion, had spoken of being disturbed by noise in the street that night. Dion had opened an attic window and told the noisemakers it would be the guardhouse for them if they kept up that noise.

This hearsay was only part of LaPierre's testimony, for he too had witnessed dealings in tobacco earlier in the day. He told the court how his lodger Pierre Barrau had come in while he and some friends were eating. Barrau carried half a roll of tobacco that he said he had just purchased at Pichot's from a man who had himself bought the tobacco from a merchant on the Place d'Armes. LaPierre and his friends inspected Barrau's purchase, and one of them, a sergeant called Lepine, bought some of the tobacco. LaPierre put the time of this encounter at roughly one in the afternoon. Sergeant Lepine later confirmed this estimate.

Judge Lartigue's orderly pursuit of Louis Davory's nocturnal prowls had lost some of its sequence, but there was one more witness to be heard, and it seemed his story would at last shine a lantern's glow over the time and place toward which Lartigue's questions aimed. Jean Delaborde may have been saving this witness to culminate the hearings, but it seems just as likely that the attorney had hesitated to bring him forward, for some of the details he would tell further disturbed the ordered presentation of the evidence linking Louis Davory to his crime. It was long after the testimony of his two friends that René Saint-Amant, the drummer who had been eating with Barrau and the Pichot family, appeared before the court to weave new material into the judge's tapestry.

At twenty-two, René-Antoine LeMoine *dit* Saint-Amant was in his fourth year as a soldier of the colonial troops at Louisbourg. After enlisting in Paris, he had been sent directly to Ile Royale to become a drummer in the same company as Pierre Pichot, whose guest he was on the day of the crime. He had been the one who at first rebuffed the man with the tobacco, and his description of this encounter echoed those of Pichot and Barrau. However, the drummer went on to describe a prior meeting with the vendor. That morning at nine, he said, he had been approached at his barracks by a civilian, a young man wearing a red coat, with his hair tied back. The observant young soldier noticed a detail only one other witness had mentioned: the red-coated man had a squint in one eye. This fellow asked Saint-Amant to direct him to a washerwoman who could clean the shirts he carried. As it happened, Saint-Amant knew that the wife of his friend Pichot took in washing to supplement the family income. He led the civilian from the barracks across the Place d'Armes and down to Pichot's rooms, where he left him talking to Pichot's wife.

The civilian in the red coat had turned up at Pichot's again that evening, just as Pichot and Barrau had said. There was more. Saint-Amant claimed he himself was the one who left with the man and together they had gone to see the source of this tobacco. They went directly from Pichot's to the warehouse recently acquired by Monsieur Delort *fils*. There the red-coated man led Saint-Amant into a lane between the building and a neighbour's garden. Despite the gathering darkness, the man easily found and dislodged a loose post and climbed inside. Inviting the drummer to join him, he offered tobacco, wine, brandy, whatever he liked.

Saint-Amant understood the offer only too clearly. "You're a thief," he said, "You will have us both arrested." He obliged the man to admit the tobacco was not his, then forced him to leave the warehouse and replace the dislodged post. This done, testified Saint-Amant, he had left this dangerous man and headed for the citadel guardhouse, where he had night duty. He had mentioned something about the incident to his corporal.

Did Saint-Amant's story fit the final details on Judge Lartigue's tapestry of evidence? His evidence about Davory – surely the identification was easy – could be the final crucial link to cap all the accounts of his tobacco-selling, yet the testimony was two-edged. Neither Pierre Charas nor Pierre Pichot had mentioned Davory's search for a laundress, and Barrau and Pichot had failed to mention that Saint-Amant had left Pichot's with the red-coated tobacco vendor. If they had lied to protect their friend, should the omission invalidate all they had said? Lartigue evidently thought not. Witnesses often muddled the mundane details, and Pichot later acknowledged he might have been mistaken. Saint-Amant's description of the site of the robbery outweighed all the complications. It was all the more believable for being close to self-incriminating.

Judge Lartigue's methodical rebuilding of the day of the crime from innocuous morning travels to sinister street violence seemed to have been justified once again. The suspect's character stood exposed: a drifter from place to place, chronically between jobs, amiable but irresponsible, and at war with loyal, hardworking colonists of every sort. From Sergeant Bellefond to the widow Laumonier, witnesses had portrayed a man matching the prisoner's description selling stolen tobacco up and down Rue de l'Etang. Finally, sworn testimony had taken the judge directly to the scene of the crime and revealed Louis Davory in his criminal act.

There were no important witnesses after Saint-Amant. With a solid case against the prisoner Louis Davory, Lartigue prepared to let the suspect face his accusers and hear the evidence against him. Each witness was recalled to the courtroom to hear his testimony read out in the presence of the accused, who now heard their evidence for the first time. Each stood by what he had originally testified. Among the witnesses who had met the red-coated tobacco vendor, only Jeanne Crosnier failed to identify Louis Davory as that man. Davory, permitted to "reproach" anyone whose testimony he doubted or denied, could only protest that the others were mistaken, that their evidence had nothing to do with him. Saint-Amant's testimony provoked an angrier response. Davory denounced the drummer to his face, calling him a liar and a rogue. He claimed Saint-Amant had come to his cell promising to seal his fate and see him hanged. False testimony was surely the product of this vindictiveness. "How could his story be true?" asked the prisoner desperately. "If I had led a soldier to the scene of a robbery, any soldier would surely have arrested me." Saint-Amant shrugged off the attack and declined to change anything in his deposition.

Lartigue's tapestry was complete. The bailiff cleared the court and the judge began to consider a verdict.

IV

S uspected criminals brought before Joseph Lartigue rarely languished through interminable delays before hearing a verdict. The judge had heard of Louis Davory's arrest on the morning of August 8, and by noon the next day he had heard several depositions, inspected the scene of the robbery, interrogated and charged the prisoner, and issued subpoenas for several witnesses to appear before him the following day. Yet this auspicious start had not given Lartigue the satisfaction of a quick conclusion. Under interrogation the prisoner had obstinately protested his innocence and denied every suggestion that he knew anything about the matter. His refusal to co-operate increased the importance of other testimony. Delaborde needed time to seek witnesses. The judge himself had pressing duties in other court cases and administrative functions. Within a week of opening the case, the judge and the attorney had agreed on a month's postponement while inquiries were made into Davory's background. Eventually a second delay was approved. Having heard the first witnesses within days of the crime, Lartigue heard no others until late September. The last witnesses appeared on October 25 and the confrontation of witnesses was not complete until November 4. A lot had happened in the meantime.

The brigantine *Saint-Charles* had not remained long at Louisbourg. True to his word, Captain Boucherville had driven his men hard in the unloading of his cargo. Though many other ships also sought the service of barges and lighters, *Saint-Charles* was reloaded and ready to sail before the end of August. Pierre Charas and the rest of the crew left without learning the fate of their shipmate. Nor were they soon to return to Louisbourg, for Boucherville did not attempt a third voyage that season.

Early in September Pierre Barrau, the stonemason and retired soldier who had bought some of the red-coated man's tobacco, was married. His friends Pierre Pichot and René Saint-Amant attended the wedding and signed the priest's register as witnesses. A few days later, Barrau set out in a small boat for the outport called Fourché, perhaps intending to visit his new in-laws in the small fishing port. But the weather was bad, and the shoals and currents were treacherous. Not far from Fourché the boat capsized and Pierre Barrau drowned.

In the prisons of the citadel barracks, Louis Davory had found the cells crowded. Most of his fellow inmates were soldiers serving a few days for breaches of military discipline, but there were also civilian prisoners awaiting trial or sentence. As the time approached for Judge Lartigue to render judgment in Davory's case, several prisoners went out to face their punishment.

Another theft suspect arrived in the cells on September 21. A young soldier named Pierre Prevost *dit* Lafleur had been doing sentry duty the previous evening, quite without criminal intent until he realized he was alone beside the house where one of his officers had sometimes brought him to do chores. Entering and leaving the house without difficulty, Lafleur returned undetected to his post with a pair of gloves and a handful of money. He was to be less successful in concealing his loot. When the loss was noticed, suspicion turned quickly toward the soldier-servant, and a search of his mattress revealed the goods. Admitting his offence, Lafleur was quickly convicted. On the afternoon of October 11, Meyracq came to the cells to read the soldier his sentence. Lartigue had ordered him publicly whipped "at the crossroads and customary places of the town" with six lashes at each stop. Then, at the quay, Lafleur's shoulder would be branded with a large v for *voleur*, thief. His belongings would be confiscated to cover a fine and costs, and he would be deported from the colony forthwith.

Attorney Delaborde caused a delay in the execution of this sentence, but not to give Lafleur any relief. He appealed Lartigue's ruling to the Superior Council, protesting on behalf of the King's Justice that the sentence was insufficient punishment. Nine days later the appeal court brought down a harsher sentence. Learning that Lafleur had once been punished by the military authorities for another theft, the Council ruled that instead of being banished, the prisoner should spend the rest of his life as a bound oarsman in the King's Mediterranean galley fleet. Within a month Lafleur went aboard the naval transport *Orox* for the voyage to France and the prison fleet, along with another soldier, René Roch *dit* Laterreur, convicted by court martial for threatening his sergeant with a musket.

The day Lafleur first entered the cells, a seventeen-year-old fisherman, Nicolas LeCasteloir, ended his detention with a trip to the quay for two hours in the pillory. Brought in from the Gaspé coast charged with desertion and theft from his employer, LeCasteloir was fortunate to suffer only the humiliations of the pillory. Disobedient servants were usually punished severely to deter their fellows from mischief. Young LeCasteloir had saved himself by aggrieved eloquence, convincing the court that only the maltreatment practised by his master had induced the boy to steal a shallop and flee toward

Québec. Louis Davory might have wondered if his own protestations of innocence could be so effective.

The third prisoner punished during Davory's detention was the Basque who had killed his shipmates. Since Davory spoke no Basque and Bernard Darospide *dit* Detchepart no French, the two had had little contact. The prisoners would be glad to distance themselves from Detchepart, for no one could doubt his fate.

Death sentences were automatically reviewed by the Superior Council; the Detchepart case ended with such a review on August 23. That day or the next, the royal executioner and a group of soldiers led the condemned man from his cell to the quay and broke him on a wheel. Executioner Antoine Banc lashed Detchepart flat, face to the sky, on a scaffold built earlier that day by a carpenter named Lamusette. Then Banc used an iron bar to smash the legs, arms, thigh-bones, and ribs of the murderer. In accordance with a modification approved by the appeal court, Banc was authorized to strangle his victim two hours after the breaking of his limbs. The corpse lay on its scaffold for the rest of the day.

The sentences meted out to his cellmates gave Louis Davory blunt notice of the punishment Lartigue might choose for him if he were convicted. Detchepart's grim death had been a foregone conclusion, but Delaborde's appeal of Lafleur's conviction had been *a maxima*: Delaborde believed the soldier deserved to hang. The *bailliage* had accepted Lafleur's pleas that his theft had been a foolish, spontaneous act, and the coins he had snatched were of little value, yet the attorney still called for his death. By comparison, the thief who had stolen Delort's tobacco had taken a valuable commercial commodity, damaging the merchant's warehouse in the process. And the victim of the crime had been Louis Delort, part of a colonial elite intent on protecting its position and property from the insults of the rootless and the unruly. Neither Delaborde nor Lartigue had much incentive to be merciful. At the least, a man convicted of the tobacco theft could expect a sentence to match Lafleur's, sending him to a short, harsh life pulling an oar in the galley fleet. He would never be free again.

Before he recommended a verdict in the Davory case, Jean Delaborde came to Joseph Lartigue with a proposal. Convinced that the witnesses had proven Louis Davory's guilt, Delaborde still

regretted the court's inability to put the case beyond doubt by securing a confession from the accused. To fill this last gap, Delaborde asked
Judge Lartigue to order Louis Davory put to the question.

The question meant torture, a normal, even essential, tool of
eighteenth-century justice. The law which understood the inability
of a defendant to handle his own defence, and therefore put the duty
of investigation on judges and attorneys, also acknowledged the
difficult task they faced. Witnesses would not always be available, sus-
pects could not be trusted to reply honestly, and the courts had limited
means of investigation. Yet the law could not permit judges to convict
merely on the basis of their own suspicions, no matter how well-
founded. The law required proof, and an admission of guilt was the
best possible proof.

Without absolute proof – and Delaborde acknowledged it was
lacking – sentencing Louis Davory would be difficult. A prison sentence was out of the question. Only late in that century would
enlightened thinkers argue for the reform of criminals through long
isolation from their corrupting environment. In 1740, jails were only
detention centres for men awaiting trial or punishment: no
Louisbourg judge imagined sentencing anyone to years of imprison-
ment. Punishments were swift and stern, and if errors were made
there was little chance to make restitution to the victim.

Since guilt had to be certain before such punishments could be
imposed, the law gave courts one additional means to reach the truth.
When a suspect refused to confess his crime in the face of compelling
evidence of his guilt, the law permitted the use of torture to extract
a confession. Let Louis Davory be put to the question, urged
Delaborde, and be compelled to answer honestly, that we may hear
the truth of the matter from his own mouth.

Lartigue was willing to sign the torture order, but Louis Davory
never felt the searing pain of wedges being pounded into his legs.
The judge had no one to carry out his order, for though society might
accept torture, it was less tolerant of the torturers. After executing
Bernard Detchepart in August, hangman Antoine Banc had been subjected to such abuse and contempt that he collected his wages and
left the colony. Capital punishment itself was not the object of

popular wrath – it was only the men who sank so low as to earn their living that way who were shunned. With no one willing to become a pariah by accepting the *maîtrise des hautes oeuvres*, Louis Davory escaped torture.

Thwarted, the judge ordered more interrogations. The prisoner had already been obdurate in two sessions, so the judge decided to make the next questionings particularly solemn and serious. In two more interrogations of Louis Davory, Lartigue was joined by a panel of interrogators, while the prisoner found his low and dishonourable position emphasized by the *sellette*, a tiny stool on which he was obliged to sit.

Lartigue had more than a stool to ridicule and an interrogation team to intimidate his prisoner, for the court's inquiries to Québec had finally borne fruit. A late grain ship from Canada had brought a revealing report on Louis Davory's Canadian career. Lartigue learned that Davory had been planning to marry in Canada and had received a copy of his baptismal certificate for that reason. He also discovered that since 1736 Louis Davory *dit* Dassaudray had been a soldier of the colonial troops in garrison at Québec. He had received a conditional discharge in 1739 on the basis of physical infirmities and his intention to marry and settle in Canada. Since the prisoner had chosen to conceal these facts in his previous statements, Lartigue might now have a weapon as effective as the torturer's tools for exposing Davory's penchant for lying under oath.

The judges' first questions set the theme of the interrogations. As soon as Davory had been sworn and seated on his ridiculous stool, the judges began to investigate his past.

"Why did you come to Ile Royale?"

"I sought work as a navigator on the vessels going to the islands."

"Then why not do so at Québec, where there are always vessels?"

Davory explained that Louisbourg had seemed to offer a greater choice. If he could not find work on a vessel bound for the Caribbean, there would be a Saint-Malo ship to take him home to Brittany. It was a plausible reply, perhaps pleasing to the pride Louisbourg took in its commercial success, for Louisbourg did have more diverse trading links than Québec. Québec attracted ships of the big merchant houses of La Rochelle and Bordeaux, but traders from many ports in France and the Americas stopped at Louisbourg.

Asked why he had left France, Davory replied simply, "C'est pour voir les pays" – to see the world. One might wonder if his answer evoked any sympathetic response in the judges. Certainly it typed him as an irresponsible drifter, and yet how different had been the motives that brought Joseph Lartigue to the New World? Had they been sufficiently introspective, many of Louisbourg's most successful men could have given much the same answer. Pondering the sorry state to which Louis Davory's dreams had brought him, Joseph Lartigue might momentarily have bridged the gulf of outlook and station that divided him from his prisoner by recalling the risks that had attended his own ambitions. On the whole, however, a suggestion of similarity between judge and prisoner would have been more likely to offend the successful immigrant's touchy pride. Davory probably won no sympathy.

"In what circumstances did you emigrate in 1738?" Always the concern for hierarchy: an employed sailor was worlds away from an indentured servant or a charity passenger.

"I came as a passenger. It cost me twenty *écus*."

"And what work did you find in Québec?"

"I taught reading and writing to children and some adults . . ."

Lartigue cut him off. "Were you not a soldier in the troops? Where are your discharge papers?"

The question was intended to shock. An ex-soldier without discharge papers was a deserter, and unconditional discharges were rare. Soldiers in the colonial service served until the King saw fit to release them from his service. To recruit, transport, and train a man for Louisbourg or Québec was costly; only a year before, the colonial governors had been told to restrict the number of retirements severely. In Québec, Governor de Beauharnois had made even medical discharges conditional on the soldier's agreement to settle in the colony. The population would increase and malingering would no longer be rewarded by passage home. Lartigue now knew that Louis Davory, claiming a bad eye and an intention to marry in Canada, had won discharge under these new rules. But since Davory had concealed his military past,

Lartigue's abrupt question was calculated to shake the truth out of him by adding desertion to the list of his crimes.

The prisoner might have proved himself a perjurer by denying he had been a soldier, or he might have broken down under the shock of learning that the judges knew all about him. Instead, he admitted Lartigue was correct, claiming to have received a discharge in 1739 after three years in the ranks. He had left the certificate with his other papers aboard the brigantine that had brought him to Louisbourg. After three months in prison, he no longer knew where the ship or his papers might be.

"Tell us how long you spent on the Ile-aux-Coudres," said a judge.

"Just a month."

"Have you ever been to Ile Royale before?"

"No, but I made three trips to the Gaspé coast, twice to fish and once on a trading voyage."

"Then explain how you spent three years in the troops up to 1739, when by your previous testimony you only arrived in Canada two years ago, in 1738."

Again Louis Davory slipped out of his contradictions. He had meant to say 1736, not 1738. To support his claim, he named several officers of the ship that brought him. When one of the judges suggested he must have fled from France, a fugitive from justice, the prisoner pointed out that his baptismal certificate had been sent to him in Canada. The authorities would not have done that for a fugitive. Since Davory did not know that the judges had a copy of the certificate before them, it was a convincing reply.

Still there were inconsistencies. The judges asked if his military discharge was absolute. "Yes," he said, "absolute and without limit."

"No conditions whatsoever?" prompted the judges, and Davory weakened. The discharge obliged him to remain in the colony.

"Yet you came to Louisbourg."

"I thought Ile Royale was part of the one colony of Canada." Ile Royale was in fact part of New France, though the two regions were largely autonomous of each other. Davory's belief could have been honestly held.

"Nevertheless you intended to sail to the Caribbean or to France."

"I counted on getting permission here. If not, I would have returned to Canada."

"Why leave Canada at all when you planned to marry there?"

"I needed to earn money before I returned."

Stalemate. The judges returned to the theft, and Davory began once more to deny his involvement. No, he had not sold tobacco. No, he had not gone to Rue Royale with criminal intent; he did not even know that street. He had not broken into a warehouse. The theft had nothing to do with him.

"Where did you spend the afternoon?"

"At Morin's tavern, until the time for vespers."

"What did you do between six and seven?"

"I am not very sure where I was then," said the prisoner ruefully. "I spent the afternoon with Clavier the tailor. Then, near nightfall, I went down to the quay to look for the ship's boat. I couldn't find it, and as it was raining heavily, I went back into the town. But I couldn't even find the place I had left. So I lay in the shelter of a house somewhere and slept. I was drunk."

The prisoner added one detail. Stumbling along some street whose name he did not know, he had asked a man to show him to a tavern. "They won't serve you, drunk as you are," the man had said, but he took Davory to a house where a woman and two girls served Davory with bread while the man had a drink.

"Why did you not stay the night there?"

"I only had ten *sols*. I was afraid they would throw me out."

"Where had you come from when you met this man?"

"I had been at the waterfront, calling for the ship's boat."

"Didn't you sell this man a roll of tobacco?" By this time Lartigue knew further interrogation was pointless. As the other judges accused Davory all over again, searching vainly for a confession, Lartigue recognized that the prisoner would admit nothing more than drunkenness. He had been evasive about his career in Canada, but his response to the revelation of his military service had been smooth, even persuasive. Could the man's confidence mean he had nothing to feel guilty about?

Failure to extract a confession denied the court the highest and finest proof, the accused's admission of guilt. Without that proof Delaborde could not blandly advise the highest punishment, and Lartigue's choice of sentence became subjective. With these facts in mind, Delaborde presented his recommendations to the judge on November 8.

It was Delaborde's formal advice, based on his legal knowledge and his position as defender of the King's justice, that Louis Davory should be duly convicted of theft, on the evidence of the arresting officer and several witnesses. In reparation for his offence, the prisoner should be whipped at the intersections, squares, and customary places of the town. He should be fined the costs of investigation and trial and banished in perpetuity from Ile Royale. Delaborde probably thought such punishment mild reparation for a man who had damaged a warehouse, stolen valuable property, and gone brazenly about the town selling his loot. Only the man's defiance under oath and the lack of a torturer to smash through his denials had enabled him to escape fair punishment.

In the early afternoon of November 14, Judge Lartigue sat in the Superior Council chambers considering verdicts, fingering Delaborde's written advice and the eighty-eight large folio sheets of the trial dossier. The top page, Sergeant Bellefond's report of the arrest, brought back the warm August days when the case moved so rapidly and the verdict seemed clear. The long sheets filled with the witnesses' depositions maintained that certainty, as page after page confirmed the prisoner's possession of stolen tobacco. Doubts appeared as Lartigue leafed through late October's hearings. The drummer Saint-Amant was particularly troublesome, contradicting the testimony of his friends. Would Davory have risked either arrest or competition for the loot by taking a stranger to the building he had robbed? And why had Saint-Amant not come forward sooner? These suspicions remained unresolved as Lartigue reviewed the plausible responses Davory had given under interrogation. Lartigue was used to guilty men who confused themselves and collapsed under rigorous questioning, but Davory had been calm and logical, even when confronted with the military record he had tried to conceal. Perhaps the judge took one final look at the witnesses' stories of the red-coated tobacco vendor before calling Meyracq to take down the sentence.

"*A tous ceux qui ces présentes lettres verront, Salut.*

"We have found the said Louis Davory the accused to be vehemently suspect of the theft of tobacco from Sieur Delort *fils* on Sunday the seventh August last, and in consequence we have condemned and do condemn him to be banished in perpetuity from this colony and sent at the first opportunity to Canada to be disembarked into the authority of Monsieur le Marquis de Beauharnois, governor at Québec. A copy of the present judgment and the discharge certificate of the said Davory together with all his papers will be sent to Monsieur de Beauharnois."

Lartigue considered a moment and added a codicil.

"And considering the rigours of the season and the harshness of the prisons, we order the prisoner freed until his banishment." He went on to set regulations for Davory's movements until his deportation, ordered the convict to pay court costs, and then signed the sentence: "Given at the *bailliage* in the chambers of the Superior Council this Monday fourteenth November 1740, Joseph Lartigue."

Lartigue's sentence, neither conviction nor acquittal, must have been almost equally distressing to the prisoner and to the King's attorney. Though the sentence seemed mild, it meant the ruin of whatever ambitions Davory held: to sail, to return home, to earn enough money to marry. Despite its hedging, the verdict effectively labelled him a felon and a deserter. When he returned unwillingly to Québec, the military authorities might make an example of him, charge him with desertion. His links to the society of honest men, tenuous as they were, were gone for good. To be out of jail and free of the noose was consoling, but his troubles were not much reduced by Lartigue's ruling.

Davory had cause to be distressed by the verdict, but Jean Delaborde found it no verdict at all. It was a pure product of Joseph Lartigue's pragmatic approach to the law. "Vehemently suspect" might rid Lartigue's community of the wastrel who threatened order and decorum, but as a decision in law it was wholly unacceptable to the legal expert and a rebuke to his careful advice and investigation. The attorney immediately appealed the sentence to the Superior

Council, taking "vehemently suspect" as a guilty verdict and appealing the inadequacy of the punishment.

V

T he Superior Council of Ile Royale, highest court of the colony,
sometimes showed pretensions to parliamentary status. Like a
provincial *parlement* in France, it registered royal decrees, inspected
the certificates of newly arrived officials, and could be asked to advise
on major decisions of the colonial government. Though these were
privileges rather than powers, the council in its early years had been a
cockpit of factional contests for authority, with the governor and his
military subordinates ranged against the administrative branch of the
colonial service. Eventually reprimands from above and the growing
professionalism of the administration had curbed these squabbles. By
1740 the council generally kept to its role of appeal court, and the
power struggles found other forums.

In its membership, however, the court still resembled a governing
council. The governor, his military second-in-command, and the
senior civil officer were members by virtue of their office, and most
of the other councillors bore major administrative duties. They were
all busy men, and they were particularly busy in November 1740, for
the new governor had finally arrived. The appointment of another
naval officer had dashed the hopes of Bourville and his supporters.
Jean-Baptiste-Louis LePrévost Duquesnel, a peg-legged veteran in
his fifties who reached Louisbourg on November 5, kept his aides
and administrators busy as he inspected and investigated his new
command. Parades, dinners, and celebrations in honour of the
new commander preoccupied the colonial elite.

Faced with Delaborde's appeal of the Davory case in the midst of
this activity, administrator Bigot used his authority to delegate the
case to a one-man committee, a councillor who could investigate on
his own and recommend a decision to the whole council. Looking
around the table, Bigot rejected most of the potential investigators.
With a new governor to be briefed and all of the year-end reports

for the Ministry looming up, none of the officials on the council could easily be spared. Bigot proposed the one councillor not deeply involved in administrative responsibilities. To investigate the appeal for a harsher sentence on the man who had robbed Louis Delort, the Superior Council appointed Guillaume Delort, the victim's father.

Well into middle age, Guillaume Delort stood among the wealthiest and most influential of the merchants of Louisbourg. Like his contemporary Joseph Lartigue, he had emigrated from Gascony to Newfoundland as a young man without notable wealth or connections and had transferred a thriving business to Louisbourg in 1714. Now his wholesale and retail trades placed his big quayside warehouse at the commercial hub of the town, and marital alliances and commercial ties linked his clan to wealthy and powerful names in and beyond Ile Royale. Wealthy enough by 1735 to be a financier making loans to his fellow merchants, Delort had been the first civilian named to the Superior Council, winning special dispensation to share office with his brother-in-law André Carrerot.

If his oldest son's decision to leave the family firm and strike out on his own had disappointed him, he had not shown it. With younger sons to maintain his firm, he had even given Louis five thousand *livres* with which to begin. Father and son now operated similar businesses. Neither employed many men directly, but the debts of the colonists they supplied placed them in positions of comfortable authority. Neither man could be much inclined to leniency when his rights were infringed. Like Joseph Lartigue they had cause to stand for order and authority, particularly when they themselves were the victims of crime. Whatever Louis Davory thought of Judge Lartigue's sentence, he would not have been happy about the man on whom the appeal depended.

Nevertheless, Guillaume Delort's reactions were not entirely predictable. For one thing, he probably assumed he knew at least as much law as Joseph Lartigue. If he held fewer appointments than the judge, it was largely due to his greater concentration on his business. Lartigue had retained some business interests, but he never neglected the friendships that brought titles and sinecures. Delort was more inclined to stick to his warehouse. Still, he had five years' experience on the appeal court, and the methodical traits that served him well amid the endless complications of his commercial negotiations applied as well in the analysis of tangled legal problems. Delort took up the Davory case intending to make his own judgments. He had no cause to favour Louis Davory, but he need not passively accept the opinions of either Lartigue or Delaborde.

The Davory case seems to have interested Delort. His son's warehouse lay just across Rue Royale from his own premises, and several of the witnesses were his neighbours. He had worked in that neighbourhood since 1714 and had never once been robbed, yet his son had been victimized in his first year of business. The case would have piqued Guillaume Delort's interest even had he not normally been a careful arbiter.

A methodical man, Delort undertook several readings of the bulky dossier delivered to him by Laurens Meyracq. Then he reached for several sheets of paper and drew wobbly vertical lines down the centre of each page. Only after preparing a stack of these did he begin to take notes. In the left column, entitled "Proofs against the Accused," he began to summarize the testimony most damaging to Louis Davory, making comments opposite each point in the "Remarks" column to the right. Pierre Barrau's testimony prompted him to observe the differences between Barrau, Pichot, and Saint-Amant on the circumstances of the tobacco purchase at Pichot's house. Reading the widow Laumonier's evidence, he remarked that she had been offered tobacco, apparently by Davory, between five and six in the evening. Further on he noted how other witnesses established Davory's movements until he reeled out of Morin's tavern around five-thirty. How could the accused have found time to wreck Louis Delort's wall, smash a padlock, and remove the tobacco in daylight, even had he possessed the knowledge and sobriety to attempt the theft?

Delort went on noting small inconsistencies in the evidence until he reached the testimony of Saint-Amant, at which point his comments became longer than the summary of proofs. Pichot, Delort wrote, does not mention the visit that Saint-Amant claims Davory made to his house on Sunday morning. Pichot has the group eating when Davory returns in the evening, but Saint-Amant says they were awaiting dinner. Saint-Amant refers to a whole tobacco roll being offered; his friends describe a halved one. Consider the tobacco-vendor's departure, continued the investigator. According to their sworn testimony, Pichot saw him leave the house alone, yet Barrau left with him and went to Lajoie's tavern, and Saint-Amant left with him and went to Delort's warehouse – all at the same time. "Beaucoup de contrariété!" scribbled Delort in the right-hand column. Abruptly he abandoned his careful comparison of testimony and began to spread his argument right across the page, ignoring the vertical lines he had prepared to divide Proofs from Remarks. Over this section he put a new heading: The Acquittal.

On December 1 the Superior Council assembled to consider the report from Guillaume Delort, investigator in the matter of Louis Davory *dit* Dassaudray.

"Note," began the report, "that the accused arrived in this port on August 6, 1740. He arrived in the evening aboard Sieur de Boucherville's brigantine and had never been in this colony before. He did not go ashore until August seventh. As the combined testimony of Pierre Charas, Armand Clavier, and Nicolas Deschamps shows, he came ashore early and was busy until evening, first on the Place d'Armes, next at Morin's tavern, then at Deschamps's, finally leaving Morin's in a drunken state about five-thirty. Despite this, the testimony of André Villefayau *dit* LaPierre, supported by Sergeant Lepine, shows that while the two sergeants were dining at LaPierre's home at one in the afternoon, Pierre Barrau came in to display and offer to sell a half roll of Dominican tobacco, at a time when Davory and Charas had barely left the Place d'Armes."

Delort's conclusion was blunt. "All this with the contradictions and variations in the depositions of Pichot, Saint-Amant, and Barrau regarding the halved tobacco roll sold that evening proves, I say, that the theft occurred before the evening of August seventh to eighth, since Barrau sold some of the loot at noon." Since the theft had been committed before Davory could have become involved, Delort ignored the red-coated man's identity and Davory's drunken wanderings. He may have sold the tobacco, but he could not have been the thief.

Louis Davory found himself in the council chamber again, hearing the same questions and making the same responses. This time he was spared the stool of dishonour. The questioning was milder. And when the interrogation was over, the report was different. "The council acknowledges that a misjudgment has occurred," read the clerk. "In consequence we acquit and discharge the said Davory Dassaudray and order his release from prison." For the last time Louis Davory set his now shaky signature to a trial document. After four months of detention he was free.

As Davory departed from the chamber and the case, the councillors ordered a new investigation. In the next few days René Saint-Amant would be arrested and interrogated. The chest stowed under his bunk in the barracks would be searched, as would the home of Pierre Pichot. More neighbours would be asked about a particular Sunday in August. But the trail was cold. Pierre Barrau was three months dead. Nothing suspicious turned up in Saint-Amant's trunk or Pichot's rooms. The young drummer proved as adamant under interrogation as Davory had been, and there was still no torturer. Saint-Amant was released for lack of evidence.

Two weeks later François Bigot wrote an epitaph to the case in a letter to his superiors in France. Referring to a crime gone unpunished for want of a torturer to put the question and extract the truth, he asked the Ministry to send the next slave condemned in the West Indies to fill the job. No one in the colony would accept it.

Joseph Lartigue had little incentive to dwell on closed cases. He was a busy man, and he still had to work with his attorney, his fellow councillors, and his old associate Guillaume Delort. Recriminations over a closed case could only cause trouble, and the Davory trial had not been his best work. Nevertheless, he may have mulled over the Louis Davory affair a few times before his death in the spring of 1743. Guillaume Delort's reasoning was irrefutable, it was true, but Lartigue could remember some testimony Delort had not explained. It stretched credulity to believe that some drunken, street-fighting vagrant *other* than Louis Davory had been selling stolen tobacco up and down Rue de l'Etang that summer evening. It was just as well the man was gone and the case forgotten, but Joseph Lartigue never fully repented his original verdict finding the man "vehemently suspect."

And Louis Davory? Ushered out into freedom on the first of December, he learned that two tardy merchant vessels, delayed by storms in November, were preparing to leave for the Caribbean. Davory must have boarded one of them as crew member or charity passenger, and he never came back, for he was not seen again in Ile Royale or in Canada. He had spent less than a day at liberty in Louisbourg, and his memory of it must have been hazy with drink. Still, he had explored its streets and sampled its taverns, and he had certainly discovered the powers by which the town was run. Even if most of the life of the town was still strange to him, he had learned more of it than it had learned of him.

What had Louis Davory done that night? Was he an accomplice to theft who escaped punishment by luck and perjury? Or was his crime only that of being a poor, powerless stranger, drunk and vulnerable in a rainswept street, victimized first by the town's lawbreakers and then by the law itself?

There is no answer. Louisbourg may have offered him little but its jail cells, but Louis Davory had successfully concealed his own secrets from its scrutiny. From the rail of his southbound vessel he looks back at Ile Royale sinking into winter isolation behind him, and he laughs.

The Marriage of Marie-Louise Cruchon

ut for chance Jacques Rolland might never have heard of Louisbourg. He might have spent his life peacefully in Hédé, the village in the Breton countryside where he was born about 1720, where the Rollands lived comfortably on Joseph Rolland's income and on the small rents from land he owned in the nearby countryside. Young Jacques could expect that after a slow maturing under parental guidance he would inherit his father's career and property, take over as head of the Rolland family, and begin raising sons of his own to follow him. In that serene procession of events, the tumultuous risks and prospects of a colonial career need never have troubled his mind.

Instead, chance cut Jacques Rolland adrift early in life, when the death of his father shattered the Rollands' placid prosperity. Joseph Rolland died before his children were old enough to take over their father's business or provide a substitute income, and without his income the family could not be held together. The widow soon retired to live quietly in the nearby city of Rennes, and her teenaged son Jacques was left to seek work on his own. He had a patrimony – a plot of land called Duverdé that entitled him to style himself Sieur Duverdé on formal occasions – but its value was small and it would not truly become his until he gained adult status at twenty-five. Fortunately young Rolland had a more valuable asset in the beginnings of a commercial education. With that he took his search for employment to Saint-Malo, the seaport not far from his home, then in the full vigour of its eighteenth-century growth.

Home to merchants and sailors for centuries, Saint-Malo had lately prospered in the surge of oceanic trade inspired by a quarter-century of peace with Britain. Any young man seeking work there was likely to be swept into the colonial trade. From Saint-Malo Jacques Rolland might easily have passed to a French merchant's counting house in Cadiz or a sugar plantation in Martinique. The young Breton could have taken his chances in one of the disease-ridden slaving ports of West Africa or might even have travelled to Pondicherry, the Indian outpost where France traded for Eastern spices and fabrics. As it happened, the merchant house where Rolland found work looked westward for its business, and Rolland found himself apprenticed to the Louisbourg trade.

The new apprentice learned it was codfish that attracted the Saint-Malo merchants to Louisbourg. Cod not only helped to feed Saint-Malo and to employ its fishermen but was also an export product that Malouin ships could haul to the West Indies, Spain, and the Mediterranean. And Louisbourg was also a hungry market for Saint-Malo's own exports. Cod and the supply trade it generated had put Louisbourg on Saint-Malo's commercial map, one more destination for its busy fleets, one more opportunity for its merchants. It was soon a familiar name to the country boy from Hédé.

Jacques Rolland's new employer was the firm of Mervin *et fils*, wholesale merchants and shippers. Typically, Mervin *et fils* was a family enterprise, the partnership of a father and two grown sons. Tanguy Mervin senior, family patriarch and head of the firm, directed the company's affairs from its Saint-Malo headquarters, using a Europe-wide network of correspondents and the reputation he had built over years in trade to combine farm produce from the Breton and Norman countryside with manufactured goods from textile towns and artisan centres all over Europe. These goods became the firm's cargoes, to be marketed by Mervin's two sons. Louis-François Mervin, a sea captain, commanded one of the firm's vessels, carrying

Mervin goods and paying cargo to distant markets. The other son, Tanguy *fils*, was the specialist in colonial trade, spending most summers and some winters in the colonial ports that bought Saint-Malo's goods and sold fish or furs or sugar for European markets.

Jacques Rolland spent several years in the Mervins' counting house in Saint-Malo. As an apprentice *commis*, one of the clerks who performed the routine tasks of the firm's business, he began to learn the basics of merchant trade. As he worked to perfect a clerkly writing hand by copying and recopying the correspondence that kept Saint-Malo in touch with markets, clients, and financiers, Rolland began to grasp the intricate networks of the eighteenth-century business world. From the daybooks and ledgers that recorded the Mervins' bewildering variety of transactions, the young clerk learned commercial mathematics and the art of bookkeeping. And as he ran errands, collected debts, and began to socialize among the mariners and merchants of the town, Rolland picked up more subtle skills. A witness to endless calculations of risk and potential profit, to assessments of potential clients and partners, to applications of commercial law and theory, the young apprentice gained a hard-won appreciation of the arts of trade.

Even as he learned Saint-Malo's trade, Rolland was tantalized by its rewards. As clerk in a prestigious merchant house, he had a certain precarious status. Living under the Mervins' guardianship, boarding in their home, and dining at their table, Rolland tasted the comfort and security that commerce had brought to fortunate traders like the Mervins. Far-flung assets and valuable cargoes had set the Mervins well on the way to wealth. Securing their gains with property investments and the purchase of royal offices, the Mervins held an assured position in the shipping and trading society of France's western ports, a society that was almost a separate world from the hierarchical rural society of most of France. Himself displaced from the meagre security of rural society, Rolland grew keenly aware of the rewards of commercial success.

Yet despite its privileges, Rolland's clerkship gave him no assurance of entry into the proud society of the established merchants. Mervin *et fils* was a family business: the only partners it would be likely to consider were the social equals who might marry Mervin daughters. As an unrelated apprentice without funds or family, Rolland hardly qualified. The Mervins would employ him for decades if he performed well, but they could neither offer him significant promotion nor be eager to see him form a rival firm. Rolland probably knew enough propertyless, penniless, and dependent old clerks to recognize how limited his prospects were. Clerking for the Mervins assured his daily wage, but he had not rebuilt the solid prospects shattered in the breakup of his family.

In 1741, when Rolland was twenty-one, still a comparatively junior clerk, but one with spirit and ambition, a chance to better his circumstances arose when the firm proposed that he accompany Tanguy Mervin *fils* to Louisbourg. It was a significant advance: though Rolland would remain subservient to Mervin, he was moving out of the accounting room into the firm's major commercial venture. The promotion showed the Mervins' confidence that Rolland had mastered the fundamentals of trade. He might even be considered their protégé. Further progress suddenly seemed possible to Rolland as he boarded a merchant ship in Saint-Malo for his first Atlantic crossing.

Merchant and clerk disembarked in Louisbourg some time in early summer, and Mervin secured his usual rooms in the home of a military officer. As he set about his summer's trade, Mervin also began to introduce his clerk to the business world of the colony.

The Ile Royale trade rested on the needs of the cod-fishing industry. At Louisbourg and in smaller harbours up and down the coast, scores of small proprietors each employed a few men in a few open boats to catch and dry cod. These proprietors needed salt to dry their catch, lines and tackle to equip their boats, food and drink to feed their employees. It was the wholesale merchants' business to supply these staples and all the other commodities for which they could find customers. Competing in this lively market, Tanguy Mervin would advance the fishermen's supplies on credit, contracting to collect his payment in the fall when the cod catch came in.

Jacques Rolland had come out to Louisbourg to free Tanguy Mervin from the routines of this business. Mervin spent only a few summer months in Ile Royale, and it was vital that he use this time to extend the network of clients and informants he had developed over the previous decade. Personal contact and sound commercial intelligence were essential, and Mervin would devote much of his time to cultivating his associates. Over a bottle of wine or a game of cards, he might edge out a less persistent competitor to secure a major sale. News overheard at a formal dinner might persuade him to turn his shipments from an about-to-be-glutted market in Europe to the fast-growing plantations of the Caribbean. A fortuitous acquaintanceship with a visiting sea captain might open prospects for a profitable shipping speculation. Such associations could be crucial in the vigorously competitive trade of Ile Royale, and while Mervin pursued them, Rolland was left to handle the routines.

He did the books. He arranged deliveries of merchandise from fishing-station warehouses and supervised the loading of great heaps of dried cod. He kept up his employer's correspondence and followed the smaller opportunities Mervin uncovered. On such tasks the young clerk spent most of the summer of 1741, extending his knowledge of the business even in mundane chores. Occasionally he seized a more exciting opportunity. During that summer, Rolland advanced three hundred *livres* – half his annual wage – to an officer of the garrison, perhaps committing part of his small inheritance to a potentially profitable speculation.

It was probably Mervin who made this venture possible by introducing his clerk into Louisbourg society. Under his employer's tutelage, Rolland discovered that Louisbourg had merchant houses and commercial circles reminiscent of those he knew in Saint-Malo, but the colonial city was far smaller than Saint-Malo and its merchant community less self-contained, so Rolland also met military families, royal officials, and other propertied people of the colony. Among the acquaintances he made as he began to move in this society was the émigré Malouin family of the widow Cruchon, who clung to the margin of the colonial elite on the strength of her late husband's reputation.

Late in 1741 Mervin and Rolland returned to Saint-Malo. Evidently Mervin was pleased with the season's business and content with his clerk's performance. He had already decided to revisit Ile Royale in 1742 and to take Jacques Rolland back with him. For his part, Rolland seems to have been eager to return. Already he may have been considering a permanent commitment to Ile Royale, for his actions in 1742 suggest that he had quickly perceived how Louisbourg could offer an escape from the impasse of endless clerking and a chance at wealth and security.

When he returned to Louisbourg in the spring of 1742, Rolland's duties with Mervin *et fils* were no different from what they had been, but now he began to advance a more ambitious proposal to Mervin and a few other confidants. Rolland intended to stay in Louisbourg, not as Mervin's employee but as an independent correspondent of the Saint-Malo firm. Settled in Louisbourg, he could purchase Mervin cargoes and retail them locally, paying his suppliers out of the profits. Through his agency, Mervin goods would sell year-round and penetrate to the retail markets that only settled merchants could tap.

For Rolland the incentive was independence. If he were industrious and fortunate, he would find new clients and suppliers and diversify into all the commercial dealings Ile Royale could offer a skilful merchant. The career that eluded him in France might blossom in the New World.

Tanguy Mervin was interested, perhaps even impressed, by the proposal of his precocious clerk. The firm had consigned merchandise to local retailers in the past, and had found it a useful, profitable operation. In the early 1730s Joseph Dallemand, a bachelor Marseillais with a shop in Louisbourg, had handled many Mervin consignments, saving Tanguy Mervin from several lengthy trips to Ile Royale. Since Dallemand's death, Mervin had increased the length and frequency of his visits to Louisbourg, and though these visits had strengthened the family's position in the Louisbourg trade, he might now consider divesting himself of some of these responsibilities to devote his energies elsewhere.

The prospect of finding a new representative in Louisbourg was particularly appealing in 1742. That summer, a crop failure in the St. Lawrence valley had prevented the merchants of Québec from exporting Canadian grain to Ile Royale, and in Louisbourg flour prices were soaring. Among the first to benefit from the price rise was Tanguy Mervin, who was well provided with European wheat. If Rolland stayed in Louisbourg, the Mervins might continue to reap windfall profits from the winter market they normally left to the resident traders.

Mervin may also have considered Rolland's proposal as a way to begin reducing his firm's commitment to Ile Royale. Since 1739, business in the colony had been disturbed by a decline in fish catches. The fishermen predicted imminent improvements, but an experienced merchant could see that if production continued to fall, fishing businesses would soon be hard pressed to repay their suppliers. It was, typically, a situation requiring flexibility and judgment from the merchant, but the shrewd Mervins may have thought it prudent to shift some of the risk from Mervin *et fils* to a resident business agent.

If Tanguy Mervin hesitated, it was not over the idea of using a middleman in Ile Royale. The questions he posed himself mostly concerned Jacques Rolland's suitability for that role. After only a few months in Louisbourg, Rolland could not claim the range of business contacts Mervin enjoyed, and few colonists knew the young clerk well enough to give him their business. Even backed by Mervin *et fils*, a business novice would need well-connected patrons to smooth his path in the colony. Reputation was everything in the merchant trade, where global dealings demanded rock-steady confidence in one's associates, and reputation was a delicate thing, slowly acquired, often based on what the older merchants said to each other about their juniors. Mervin had introduced the young clerk to many of his business and social acquaintances, but he doubted that Rolland could have established a reputation that would carry his business through its growing pains.

Rolland's youth added to the problem. Though he had probably started work at twelve or fifteen, twenty-two-year-old Rolland was thought inexperienced by a society that greatly valued maturity. Despite his clerk's ability, Mervin probably hesitated over giving Rolland responsibility for merchandise far more valuable than all the young man's assets, and his hesitation was compounded by Rolland's legal position. Until he was twenty-five, Rolland would be a legal minor, limited in his authority to hold property, prevented even from exercising full control over his parental legacy. Unless he were emancipated – given majority status prematurely by a difficult legal process – Rolland would not be accepted in law as an adult for three more years. Until then his authority to sign contracts or accept legal liability for goods consigned to him would be closely circumscribed. No matter how much Mervin wanted to turn over the bulk of his Louisbourg business to a local agent, Rolland seemed disqualified by his youth and his lack of standing in the local business community. Mervin surely advised Rolland to postpone his plans for a few years.

Delay was intolerable to Jacques Rolland. The temporary commercial advantage offered by the wheat shortage seemed a unique opportunity, and after a decade of striving, the prospect of running his own affairs was irresistible. Hoping to overcome Mervin's objections, Rolland began to seek allies among the friends he had made during his two sojourns in Ile Royale.

During his second summer in Louisbourg, Rolland had become a regular guest in the Rue Saint-Louis home of the widow Cruchon, appreciated for his news of Saint-Malo and his attentiveness to the widow and her young daughters. As his friendship with the family grew, the young clerk began to discuss his ambitions and his frustrations. Before long, the widow Cruchon had become his strongest advocate and his principal adviser. She had begun to see Jacques Rolland as more than an occasional dinner guest.

II

T he widow Cruchon – Thérèse Boudier was her given name – seems to have been a sharp and calculating woman, and indeed her well-to-do urban background was one likely to instil respect for intelligence and education. The husband who had brought her to Ile Royale had been an educated man, his family wealthy enough to support him through extended studies at Saint-Malo's school of hydrography. As a professional in hydrography, Jean-René Cruchon LaTour practised "that branch of geography that studies the sea and its navigation"; the family lived by the sale of this knowledge. It was one of Cruchon's professional judgments that had brought his family to Ile Royale in 1726. When he visited Louisbourg to assess the opportunities the new colony might offer an hydrographer, what he saw impressed him enough that he acquired a home and sent for his wife and infant son.

Cruchon had found that, a decade after its foundation, Louisbourg was a busy port. Each year it attracted up to two hundred fishing and trading vessels to its spacious harbour, already home port to a host of local craft. These ships had transformed the foggy and surf-battered coast of Ile Royale from a little-visited and uncharted shoreline into a busy and crowded but still uncharted highway of ocean commerce. It was a *côte ferrée*, an ironbound coast; inevitably disasters struck as inexperienced pilots tried to outguess the tricky waters. The new colony and its sailors would pay a high price in lives and ships until the local waters were made familiar by marine surveying and navigational instruction. These were Cruchon's skills, and he soon found his niche.

Cruchon surely came to Louisbourg seeking appointment as *hydrographe du roi*, royal hydrographer, with the prestige of an official title and the security of a royal wage. But when the Ministry refused to fund the hiring of a hydrographer for Ile Royale, Cruchon did not return thwarted to France. Instead, he made a business of his skills. He charged fees to teach theoretical and practical navigation to aspiring sailors. He persuaded the local admiralty service to hire him for the surveying and charting of coastal waters. He sat on boards of examination when seamen applied for their captain's papers. He offered mathematics courses to garrison officers who watched the cannon-bearing ramparts encircle the town and considered how the science of artillery could further their careers. Soon Cruchon found that private practice would bring enough earnings to support his family, and he sought no other occupation during his years in Louisbourg.

As a trained scientist whose knowledge was vital to the community, Cruchon merited the success that came to him in the 1720s and 1730s, but merit was not the essential organizing principle of eighteenth-century careers. Since a hierarchical society inevitably affirmed that status was itself a kind of merit and a justification for promotions and favour, Cruchon's achievements in Ile Royale were naturally social as well as professional. Fortunately, as members of an urban, educated elite – Cruchon a scientist, his wife from a propertied family of Saint-Malo – the Cruchons were well placed for social success. Cruchon's professional contacts were soon reinforced by social links to some of the most influential people in Louisbourg's little society.

For the wealthy, the powerful, and the distinguished of the colony, society in Louisbourg modelled itself on the distant royal court of Versailles. Personal devotion to the King rather than to the abstract idea of nation was the touchstone of loyalty, and so the colonial elite imitated the lavish and luxurious display with which Versailles reflected the glory of the Bourbon monarchs. Where Versailles revolved around the person of Louis xv, Louisbourg made do with the vice-regal figure of its governor, a bachelor military man. The places of the great lords and ladies of the French court passed to the military families of Ile Royale, men and their wives who were undoubtedly of the nobility but generally came from a minor provincial aristocracy that would scarcely have gained entry to Versailles. As at Versailles, where the administrative *noblesse de robe* claimed its place alongside the military *noblesse de l'épée*, an important place in Louisbourg's high society went to the royal officials who administered the colony. In the French court, vulgar trade could expect no place at all, but business rather than landed wealth was the foundation of prosperity in Ile Royale, so entry to the governor's circles could not be denied to the prosperous merchant families, who in any case were often linked by marriage to the military elite and the royal officials.

As head of the colony and its personification of royal authority, the governor gave the lead in the ceremonial and social life of Ile Royale. A colonial governor would commit his personal fortune to this duty, entertaining lavishly to demonstrate his distinction. His beneficiaries were expected to respond with deference and respect, and so the governor's hospitality sustained his authority. A governor's largess went far beyond invitations. To reward those loyal to him (and hence to the king he served), the governor and his aides would dispense royal patronage: promotions and bonuses for his corps of officers, career recommendations for civil officials, supply contracts for deserving businessmen. Hierarchy was built on this network of patronage and loyalty, and so the social life of the colonial elite was also a forum where all its members gathered to demonstrate their loyalty and validate their claim to preferment.

The elite pursued this quest amid the governor's frequent entertainments at his quarters in the citadel. In winter, fish might dominate the menu, but the governor could always offer a selection of fine wines and liqueurs, rare condiments and spices, and smaller treats such as brandied fruit and superb tobacco. He always had the finest service in the colony, displaying his personal china and silver, his fine linens, and his array of liveried servants. The influential danced and chatted at balls and costume parties, and they gathered for soirées of cards and gambling at each other's homes. These were the circles Jean-René Cruchon had to enter if he hoped to make a career in Ile Royale. Social distinction and career advancement went hand in hand, and someone unacceptable in society would obviously be unworthy of professional respect. Once within the charmed circle, the hydrographer needed to advance himself carefully, gaining the favour of one well-placed official without antagonizing rival powers.

It seems to have been easily done. Cruchon soon found favour with Louis Levasseur, who, as senior official of the admiralty service, controlled a source of patronage vital to Cruchon's advancement. Levasseur could provide work for the hydrographer, and he was the intermediary who might secure Cruchon's appointment as royal hydrographer. In 1729 Levasseur gave his blessing to the Cruchons' social aspirations by standing as godfather to their daughter Marie-Louise. Etienne Verrier, senior royal engineer in the colony, also advanced Cruchon's standing by accepting him as a fellow scientist, for the designer of most of the colony's public architecture ranked among the most important men of the community. When men of the standing of Verrier and Levasseur accepted the Cruchons, the hydrographer's social and professional ascendance was assured.

The Cruchons also made their way into the society of sea captains and businessmen. One of Cruchon's close working associates was port captain Pierre Morpain, who managed the daily administration of Louisbourg harbour. Renowned for his privateering exploits in the late war and for his quick temper – he had killed at least one man in the course of his quarrels – Morpain was the colony's leading sailor and a respected figure on the quayside. Morpain and his servant became tenants in the Cruchons' home, and the port captain smoothed Cruchon's entry into the company of shipowners and sea captains.

By 1733, when Morpain stood as godfather to the Cruchons' second daughter, the hydrographer's family had settled comfortably in Louisbourg. Cruchon's career flourished, and his income proved sufficient to support his growing household, though like many in his position he shouldered substantial debts. The elite patrons he had cultivated remained vital, but the family found more of its friends among mercantile circles. In this milieu, comfortable rather than rich, and including several former Malouins like themselves, the Cruchons were at home. They were among people who lived by skills, mostly in business but also in medicine or practical science or administration. They were owners and proprietors, valuing education and enterprise and more likely to employ men than to be employed. Though their number included some master artisans risen into trade, a gulf separated such people from the ordinary labouring folk who worked with their hands. Rather they followed and imitated the aristocratic elite – but at a certain distance. The elite based their lavish display on inherited private incomes that these people could not match, so the style of the Cruchons' kind was modest by comparison, and they were more likely to live within their means. Their ideal was *bon ménager*, prudently to manage their affairs and accumulate wealth with the aim of finally establishing a *rentier* family able to live on its investments as did the aristocracy.

Typically, the Cruchon household included a servant, who may well have been a black slave. Slaveholding was hardly essential to the local economy, but it was easily accepted by a hierarchical society used to setting men over men. The sensible, calculating men of Cruchon's circles could appreciate the value of slaveholding, and trade with the Caribbean provided the few slaves Louisbourg needed. A fortunate slave might be freed by his master, and one Louisbourg slave became a married, settled landowner. More typical was the life of one slave, an African-born fifteen-year-old who slept under a table in his master's kitchen and lived in constant fear of casual kicks and canings. The propertied bourgeois might not expect the power and prestige of the hereditary elite, but he entertained few doubts about his standing above the mass of men.

Unfortunately Jean-René Cruchon's security was not quite complete, his dignity not quite beyond rebuke. Despite his prosperity and social acceptance, a crucial weakness placed a question mark against Cruchon's good management of the family affairs. As long as the hydrographer had no official title and stipend, he would depend entirely on his earnings. He had not yet been able to ensure that the position he had won for his family could outlive him. Indeed, his death or disability would surely leave his wife and young family unsupported, and what his social and professional successes had brought them would quickly erode.

The remedy was his official recognition as a salaried *hydrographe du roi*. Then, if he died in service, his widow could hope at least for a modest pension and his son might win help in the form of official patronage. Without the title Cruchon lacked these safeguards, and as he aged, his thirst for an official appointment grew. By the late 1730s, presumably after discreet inquiries among his local patrons, Cruchon determined to take his campaign for official recognition to France. Local officials showed their support by securing his passage on the visiting naval frigate *Héros*, and Cruchon sailed in November 1737, leaving his family in Louisbourg.

The outcome of his trip was a tragic irony. Not only did Cruchon fail to obtain his cherished appointment as *hydrographe du roi*, but during the early months of 1738 he died alone at Saint-Malo, plunging his wife and children into the crisis he had been seeking to avert.

News of Cruchon's death reached Louisbourg at midsummer, and the family had scarcely faced its grief when creditors descended on his estate. An inventory satisfied the creditors, but it showed the family to be barely solvent, its only significant asset the house and property Cruchon had acquired in 1726. With Cruchon's earnings gone, the widow's only income was a small inheritance and some rental income. She had still to support herself and her three children. René-Charles was now thirteen and ready to be apprenticed to a craft or profession, but the two Louisbourg-born girls, Marie-Louise and Marguerite, were only nine and five years old.

Jean-René Cruchon's death, suddenly burdening his widow with sole responsibility for the Cruchon family, left Thérèse Boudier more completely abandoned than most Louisbourg widows. The family had been reaching toward the professional and administrative elites, but now the widow Cruchon found she lacked the access to royal patronage that widows of that class could take for granted. She had less protection even than a bereaved family of the working class. In that milieu wives often participated in the running of a tavern or a workshop or earned income as a seamstress or a laundress, so the loss of a spouse rarely meant the loss of all the family's income.

Even in the Cruchons' own educated milieu there were usually safeguards against the sudden death of the household head. As a rule, these men were proprietors, and their widows could often take an active part in the management of the properties left to them. Louisbourg always had several enterprising widows running fishing properties, shipping businesses, and other commercial ventures. In their husbands' lifetimes such women had generally deferred, but no social prohibition kept a woman from the world of work. In case of need, a widow left in charge of her family's destiny could plunge into the full range of business responsibilities. The widow Cruchon would not have demanded a life of leisure, but her late husband's specialized skill was not the kind of business she could take over and run, and Cruchon had left little property for her to manage.

Just how the widow and her children lived in the years after Jean-René Cruchon's death is unknown. Well into middle age, the widow probably nourished an edgy pride in her now-vulnerable social standing. Too proud to marry beneath her, too poor to be sure of acceptance by one with whom she had formerly been equal, she appears to have renounced the idea of remarriage as a solution to her family's straitened circumstances.

The family still had a rent-paying boarder in their home, there was a small legacy from Saint-Malo, and neighbours and friends probably gave them help. René-Charles Cruchon soon ceased to be a burden, for he left the household much as Jacques Rolland had left Hédé a few years earlier. Perhaps the boy was apprenticed aboard a merchant ship, an appropriate profession in light of his father's career but not one from which he would soon be able to support his mother and sisters. Through the late 1730s and early 1740s the widow Cruchon and her two small daughters probably struggled on in genteel poverty, earning a little money from lacemaking, sewing, and other crafts appropriate to their status. Living on her wits, frugally doling out the limited resources available for the support of her family, Thérèse Boudier must have been acutely sensitive to the complicated social consequences of Jean-René Cruchon's death.

Beneath her she could see an abyss of indigence threatening to engulf her family. Recently there had been the sad example of Judith Pansart, a woman hardly so dignified as the Cruchons but still the daughter of a fishing proprietor with a property near Louisbourg and a crew of labourers. As a young girl, Judith Pansart had even caught the eye of a noble Canadian officer, Picoté de Bellestre. Marriage had been mentioned, but the suitor went back to Canada and a more appropriate alliance. Probably seduced and definitely abandoned, Judith Pansart had never married, and the seeds of her misfortune were sown. When her father died, his widow and spinster daughter were unable to maintain his fishing business, and they began to support themselves as laundresses. They ran a little tavern as well, and the living was enough to keep a servant in the household, but the pace of decline increased after the mother died. Judith Pansart was still a householder with title to a potentially useful piece of property, but without an income such possessions represented empty status. She raised poultry and goats, and may even have rented her fishing shore, but the servant who stayed – through family loyalty or lack of alternative – regularly scoured the shoreline for shellfish and discarded fishheads they could eat. Judith became an object of Récollet charity, her house declined to a ruin almost bare of furnishings, and in her forties her once-able handwriting deteriorated into illiterate scratchings. Eventually driven afoul of the law – she connived in a minor theft by her servant – she unsuccessfully begged forgiveness, describing her "sad and dolorous situation" in a petition she signed "la malheureuse Judith."

Without a certain minimum amount of income, the Cruchon family might easily be overwhelmed by a similar train of events. The widow's precious girls would then be fortunate to find servants' positions in the homes of their former equals, and her own future would be bleak and probably brief.

Yet the widow could see that if a certain minimum could be scraped together, disgrace need not be the family's fate. She was not the only householder in Louisbourg trying to preserve high status against low income. Indeed, income problems were chronic among many of the military families at the apex of colonial society. As aristocrats, military officers were expected to live on private incomes rather than on their small military pay, but families that had provided generations of colonial officers had often lost all claim to landed revenues from France, and the Canadian estates that now provided their titles tended to consume rather than produce revenue. Some military clans like the DuPonts, newly out from France and still supported by estates in the fertile county of Cognac, could be lavish with their private incomes, building further wealth and prestige by their colonial investments. But several officers of the Louisbourg garrison eked out a living on their pay, their patronage, and what they could borrow. Such officers lived simply, not from choice but from the lack of means to do otherwise. To maintain their social standing, they presented an aristocratic façade and depended almost totally on the hospitality and benevolence of their commanding officer, the governor.

The presence of such poor-but-proud families at the heart of colonial society obliged Louisbourg to show tolerance for social pretension unsupported by wealth. If the Cruchons could scrape together enough income to maintain a façade of gentility, a blind eye might be turned to their scrimping, and they could remain part of the society in which they had always moved. To preserve that façade seems to have been the widow Cruchon's overriding concern in the years following her husband's death.

The struggle to keep the family together and its dignity intact demanded the exercise of a careful guiding intelligence. Though there was scarcely an estate to manage, Thérèse Boudier had still to accept a heavy responsibility as head of the Cruchon household in a time of family crisis. With some help from friends who had rallied around in the difficult aftermath of Cruchon's death, she achieved her limited aims. The little family of three remained intact, and stress honed the widow's shrewdness and calculation without exacting the permanent sacrifice of her aspiration to something better. In 1741, when she was introduced to the personable young clerk Jacques Rolland at the social functions she still managed to attend, the widow swiftly summed up his potential value to her hard-pressed family.

Despite the evident disparity between the declining and impoverished Cruchons and the ambitious young businessman, the widow perceived shared interests that could draw them together. Each was attempting to recover the security shattered by a premature death in the family. To the widow, always seeking to defend the social standing she had enjoyed in her husband's lifetime, the young clerk symbolized that prosperous wider world in which Jean-René Cruchon had once been important: the world of traders who visited Ile Royale, merchants who dealt with them, and the captains, clerks, and clients who supported their endeavours. To young Rolland, keen to settle and establish himself in the colony, the Cruchons could provide an entrée into Louisbourg society. The widow could still boast friends more affluent than herself, and each time she secured Rolland an invitation to one of their soirées, she helped to erode Tanguy Mervin's doubts about the young clerk's ability to make his way in Louisbourg.

No matter how well he was received, Rolland had still to face the fact that as a minor his right to hold property was limited. From remarks he made later, it appears that the widow Cruchon was the first to calculate how the law might permit Rolland to escape the limitations imposed by his youth – and simultaneously advance the interests of the Cruchons.

The age-old civil law sternly denied anyone under twenty-five full freedom to manage his own estate because it was concerned above all to preserve family lineages from the youthful mismanagement that could quickly dissipate a family's laboriously acquired patrimony. Until he reached his majority, a man was kept subservient to his family's needs, as determined by the mature head of his household, whether that was his father, his widowed mother, or even a relative. The one exception the law made was for a married man: to manage a household and support a family a man had to be considered an adult even if he were under twenty-five. Marriage did not give a young man absolute control of his patrimony, but any goods he and his wife might accumulate would be legally untrammelled. Here lay the key to Rolland's freedom. If he took a wife, hinted the widow to the young clerk, his problem would evaporate. The patrimony awaiting him would not yet be his, but if he were married, the goods he handled in his trade would be free of the limits imposed on minors.

With the marriage idea planted in his mind, Rolland must quickly have perceived the other benefits of allying himself to a colonial family. By mid-1742 Rolland was becoming known in Louisbourg, but he was still a newcomer and a transient. A local marriage would win him a circle of patrons and friends and announce his commitment to the colony. Once he had acquired adult status and social acceptance by marriage into a Louisbourg family, the Mervins should no longer hesitate to support his plan to settle in the colony.

If Rolland wavered, the widow must have gone on to hint that he really had no other choice if he seriously desired to rise from his clerkship. Her logic was unassailable. Marriage and a colonial career would give him the opportunity he craved. Refusing to marry would send him back to the Mervins' counting house, perhaps for years. Rolland proposed.

The Cruchon–Rolland alliance was one of perfect symmetry. Marriage freed Jacques Rolland from his legal minority and gave him the Cruchons' friends as the potential first clients of his new business. Even weakened by the strains of the previous four years, that social network could still bring an ambitious businessman a good haul of prospective clients. The Cruchons might not provide Rolland the upward step taken by another Louisbourg clerk, Blaise Lagoanere, who had married the eldest daughter of his wealthy employer, Michel Daccarrette, but Rolland hoped to do better than another Daccarrette clerk, Jean-Baptiste Lascorret, who, having left his job without any marital tie or social connection to sustain him, had failed utterly in his business venture. Lascorret had recently died on his way to attempt a new start in the Caribbean, leaving a vivid example of the novice merchant's need to find staunch backers in the colony.

In return for his entry into the social and commercial world of Ile Royale, Rolland offered the Cruchons a chance at financial security. In Rolland the needy family would once more have a wage-earner who might soon be able to support his wife and relations in the manner to which they had once been accustomed. If, as a novice merchant in a depressed season, he was not so exciting a prospect as one of the better-off military officers or civil officials whose lifestyle the Cruchons knew but did not share, still his prospects were good. The alliance worked out between the widow and the clerk during the summer of 1742 promised to save each party from the insecurities that plagued them both.

Rolland's bride was not to be the widow Cruchon. In urging him to marry, Thérèse Boudier had never implied to the twenty-two-year-old clerk that such a relationship might form between them. Instead, the alliance turned on Rolland's marriage to the widow's elder daughter, Marie-Louise Cruchon, who had turned thirteen in March of that year.

III

Quite naturally, young Marie-Louise Cruchon deferred to her elders, first to her mother, later to her husband. Just as she was expected to, she affixed her signature to documents drawn up at the instigation of one or the other. Nowhere did she leave any statement of her own opinion of the marriage arranged for her. To guess at the feelings of the girl who may have been the youngest bride ever to wed in Ile Royale, our guide must be what we know of childhood and adolescence in the eighteenth century.

Marie-Louise Cruchon was born in Louisbourg on March 15, 1729, almost certainly at her parents' Rue Saint-Louis home. Had she been a sickly child, she would instantly have been given conditional baptism by the midwife or medical brother who administered at the birth, but her good health was so apparent that on the very day of her birth her father was permitted to take her for formal baptism at the parish church. The *curé*, Récollet Father Zacharie Caradec, baptised her in the presence of her father, her godparents, and other friends and patrons of the family. Probably there were no further celebrations: too many children died in infancy to encourage premature festivities for a newborn child.

The good health Marie-Louise showed at birth carried her through her first year. That was the critical test, for the high childhood mortality typical of Ile Royale and every other society of its time struck mainly at the newborn. Once she reached her first birthday, Marie-Louise's chances of reaching adulthood were much increased. She was aided by the small size of the Cruchon family, for the Cruchons did not emulate their neighbours by producing a child nearly every year, or by losing every third or fourth in infancy.

Marie-Louise's brother was several years older than she, and she was over four at the birth of her sister. These spacings, which enabled each to receive undivided maternal care in their early years, helped strengthen them all. When smallpox scourged the colony in 1732 and 1733, tripling the annual death rate and taking children under ten as half its victims, the epidemic would claim neither Marie-Louise nor her brother René nor even their newborn sister Marguerite, who was born at the height of the crisis. Either a fortunate or a careful mother, Thérèse Boudier was spared the grief that many wealthier Louisbourg families faced that year.

Louisbourg's children, at least those who survived the first perilous months of life, were valued members of the community. In the small, crowded, neighbourly town, mothers traded advice and shared responsibility for each other's children. That Louisbourg's mothers cared for their children is not an entirely obvious statement, for in many parts of Europe maternal affection was less firmly established in the eighteenth century than in more recent times. Many working women left their small, swaddled children untended and alone while they worked, without incurring the disapproval or concern of their communities. More affluent parents routinely sent newborn children to hired wet nurses miles away, evincing no interest in their offspring until those who survived the nursing years were returned home weaned, toilet-trained, and amenable to discipline.

At Louisbourg discipline was firm and corporal punishment common – one woman interrupted her complaints of maltreatment by her husband to "discipline" her crying infant – but the parental obligation to care for children was established. Brutal parents were criticized by their neighbours, who would even intervene between a mother and her child if they felt that punishment was being carried too far. To say to a mother, as one Louisbourg woman did, "You enjoy conceiving children but you don't like to raise them," was to be viciously insulting. The mothering "instinct" was hardly unknown.

The fondness Louisbourg felt for its children is suggested by the abundance of their playthings. Most households seem to have had the rattles, tops, boats, and dolls that amuse children in every century, and local merchants did a busy trade in children's clothing and shoes. Families bought prayer books, story collections, and spelling primers to assist in the education of their children. It was thought proper to punish children who forgot a line of catechism or shirked their lessons, but parents who neglected their children's education were a source of scandal. Without strong bonds of parental affection, Louisbourg's children would scarcely have been the objects of such time and expense.

Marie-Louise Cruchon may have been particularly fortunate. While most mothers probably breast-fed and tended their own infants, many women had to put their work first, leaving their children in the crowded multifamily households that became more common as Louisbourg grew. The Cruchon children, on the other hand, received the nearly undivided attention of their mother and a household servant in the security of their family home.

The house their father had built in 1726 was a comfortable timber-frame edifice on a busy town block facing the citadel and also enjoying a southern view across the ramparts toward Gabarus Bay. Insulated with board siding and a tight, double-planked roof over the attic, the home was heated by a double fireplace that divided the family quarters from a smaller apartment. The comfort of the Cruchon home, the affluence the family enjoyed in Jean-René Cruchon's lifetime, and the affection for children seemingly typical of Louisbourg all suggest that Marie-Louise Cruchon and her brother and sister enjoyed a secure and nurturing environment in their formative years.

Somewhere between the ages of five and seven, Marie-Louise probably enrolled as a pupil at the Louisbourg convent. Ile Royale's only school, the convent was the creation of Soeur de la Conception, a headstrong nun who had come to Louisbourg from Québec in 1727. Her transfer had been caused at least partly by her inability to live in peace with the other sisters of the Congrégation de Notre-Dame de Montréal, but as the founder of Ile Royale's convent, Soeur de la Conception found her niche, earning unstinted praise from local officials impressed by her energy and dedication. Within a month she and her two lay companions had twenty-two pupils, and by the time Marie-Louise was old enough to attend, six nuns were housed in a large home on Rue d'Orléans for which Soeur de la Conception had confidently mortgaged the convent's future revenues. There the sisters cared for a score of girls orphaned by the smallpox epidemic. They assisted the Récollet missionaries in religious instruction and ran a school for perhaps forty young girls of the town.

The convent taught only the female children of the elite – none of the colony's sons and only a few of its daughters ever attended. For most children, primary education went on at home, with religious indoctrination the major subject. Further education depended on the vocation chosen for the child. Boys in particular learned on the job. Even reading, writing, and arithmetic could be part of job training, taught to an apprentice clerk or young artisan who needed a measure of literacy, but rarely to a fisherman or day labourer. Though the convent taught only girls, these vocational opportunities probably meant that more boys than girls received much education.

The convent school offered a special kind of vocational training, giving the daughters of the elite the deportment and manners they would require as adults. Girls whose parents could afford to pay up to two hundred *livres* annually to see their daughters board at the convent would enter at the age of five, six, or seven and might stay to the age of twelve or thirteen. Judging by the social and professional success of Jean-René Cruchon in the mid-1730s and Marie-Louise's confident literacy in later years, it seems likely that the elder Cruchon daughter was one of these resident pupils. Perhaps she withdrew at her father's death, when she was nine, but the sisters were known to be charitable, adjusting fees and accepting payment in goods or service when necessary.

The convent education had a strongly devotional basis, but religion was not the only subject taught. Convent pupils learned to read and write and may also have learned some arithmetic. Latin was taught in some convents, and music, art, and crafts were probably important. There were also intangible lessons to be learned in behaviour and deportment, for culture and refinement were at least as important as practical education. Some well-to-do Louisbourg parents desired this refinement so much that they sent their daughters to the more aristocratic Ursuline convent at Québec, and a few of Ile Royale's children were educated in France. Nevertheless, the Louisbourg convent of the sisters of Notre-Dame was respected. During Isaac de Forant's brief tenure as governor of Ile Royale, he was disturbed to see that some of his garrison officers, despite their noble lineages, could not afford to educate their daughters at the convent. In his will, de Forant left the sisters funds to provide places for eight daughters of officers every year. Evidently the Governor had been impressed with the standard of education attained by the local school.

Schooling for all of Louisbourg's children seems to have ended between the ages of twelve and fourteen. The end of education and the onset of puberty were intended roughly to coincide: one girl whose guardian had neglected her education was sent at court order to a convent "to be educated until she reaches puberty." For Marie-Louise Cruchon the rites of first communion may have been a form of graduation ceremony to mark her transition from childhood to something more mature.

A glimpse of young women in this transitional stage of life emerges from a court case fought with great vigour in 1755 over a girl a decade younger than Marie-Louise Cruchon. A merchant who had left his daughter in the care of an associate named Duboé while he made a voyage became convinced on his return that the girl had not been treated as befitted her bourgeois station. He took his complaint to the courts. Sued, Duboé brought forth a crowd of witnesses to describe the girl's life in his household. Her religious education was still in progress – "the only work required of her," claimed Duboé, "was that she learn the principles of the Catholic religion" – yet the child dined nightly with the adults, unless the company was thought unsuitable for her. She was always immaculately dressed and powdered: "dressed as for Sunday even on working days," said one admiring witness. Duboé claimed his ward spent her days in graceful activities, often promenading with other young ladies of the town. He even hired the garrison drum major, a fortyish sergeant named Bozeac, to teach the girl to dance.

On the other hand, the plaintiff's witnesses had seen the girl helping Duboé's servant in a variety of household chores, and following the servant's orders. Before the transition signalled by puberty, it was natural for children to help in such menial tasks as feeding chickens and carrying laundry or going out in groups to gather shellfish and wild berries. Duboé's young houseguest seems to have been in a transitional stage, its boundaries the subject of dispute. In some ways the girl behaved as an adult, but with her education incomplete she had not quite graduated into the full dignity of young womanhood or completely escaped the supervision of household servants.

The step out of childhood attained at puberty and marked by first communion and school-leaving brought Marie-Louise Cruchon into a time of preparation for adult status. In this stage, which could last a decade or more, young people were introduced to adult careers and adult society. Young men were now apprenticed to a trade or brought into the family business. Sons of military officers became cadets, serving two years with the enlisted men before receiving commissioned rank. Girls took on greater responsibility too, joining the older women in dressmaking and sewing or beginning to share in the family occupations. In all these careers, however, young women and men remained under close adult supervision. Parents vigorously assisted their children's advancement, and in exchange the young were expected to serve and promote their families' interests without yet sharing in the defining of those interests.

As they joined the work force, young people also began to enter adult society. Their signatures began to appear on the church registers that testified to attendance at festive and ceremonial occasions. They began to dine in adult company, though whether this was at a formal dinner or at a casual drinking session in a soldiers' tavern depended on their place in society. As in the world of work, young people were being introduced to an adult world, not as equal partners but as junior members expected to follow the lead of their elders.

This apprenticeship stage differed from full adult status by the degree of supervision under which young people lived and worked. Whatever their career, young people remained under the tutelage of an adult, whether this was a parent or an employer. Jacques Rolland, for instance, when obliged to leave his parent, had moved into the home of his employers the Mervins, who wielded parental authority over their young apprentices. This close supervision of young workers was matched in social situations by close chaperonage, and in a society without a distinct youth culture, young people accepted the moral and cultural lead of their parents. These values were reflected in the civil law that placed such importance on maturity and experience, for young people were only slowly accepted as equal adults. The influence of parents and elders remained strong, and, if the parents survived, a close parent–child tie could be maintained well into the child's twenties.

One consequence of the slow apprenticeship to adulthood was a tendency toward late marriage. From puberty, when they left childhood behind, young people were expected to contribute materially to their parents' household, to which they remained legally and emotionally bound. Without a strong youth culture, young people were slow to form independent relationships that might have led them to break from their parents and form their own households. Instead, the parental family remained the centre of the young person's loyalties and responsibilities. Guidance and direction came from the family head, who continued to wield both moral suasion and legal authority over sons and daughters, even as they left their teens behind.

It is in this context that Marie-Louise Cruchon's impending marriage may be evaluated. Among the working poor, marriage often awaited the groom's slow accession to maturity and financial independence. Even in wealthy or prosperous homes, where no vital economic need bound adolescents to their parents, marriages were often delayed until brides were in their twenties and grooms even older. Yet no taboo prohibited early marriage. Marriage plans were shaped by family priorities, and youthful marriages became plausible whenever they seemed to serve a family interest.

Marie-Louise Cruchon's marriage was one of these plausible early marriages, for it could mean the very survival of her family. Given the Cruchons' pressing need for financial security, Marie-Louise was now old enough to begin contributing to her family's support. Her marriage to Jacques Rolland would not merely relieve the widow of one dependent child; it would bring the hard-pressed family a young, ambitious, and energetic wage-earner who might eventually restore all their fortunes. Marie-Louise's view of her impending marriage was surely shaped by the same sense of family loyalty and family responsibility that often kept children single and at home for many more years. Rather than splitting her from her family, her early marriage expressed the extent of the girl's commitment to its welfare.

One need not assume, however, that family loyalty was her only sentiment. She had already entered adult society, equipped by her upbringing and convent schooling with the skills and attitudes of a

well-brought-up young woman of her time. She was ready for marriage. And Jacques Rolland should have been an attractive spouse. He
was young, by local standards sophisticated, and personable enough
to have impressed both business associates and social acquaintants,
most notably the widow Cruchon. Mutual attraction between the
bride and groom may not have been the cause of the marriage, but
its presence should not be dismissed.

Once the deal had been struck and the marriage arranged, the
mother of the bride turned her attention to the one obstacle that
could interfere with her plans. Since marriage could free young
people from parental supervision before the age of twenty-five, the
law required parental approval for the marriages of underage children. The widow Cruchon knew that when she went to the *curé* the
priest would ask for written proof that Jacques Rolland's parents con-
sented to his marriage.

Neither the widow nor her prospective son-in-law wanted to
delay the marriage while a request went to Rolland's mother in far-
off Rennes. If winter came before the reply came back, a year could
be lost on this formality, and Rolland was impatient to settle and start
his business. Perhaps he feared the Mervins might lose their enthusiasm if given a year to consider his plans. The widow Cruchon was
equally determined. After four years of watching her social standing
fade and her economic difficulties grow, she wanted her family's circumstances changed with all possible speed.

If the marriage could be expedited by misleading the *curé*, the
widow was willing to do so. Raised in an educated urban atmosphere,
she was probably not greatly in awe of the priesthood. In any case, a
look at the clergy of Ile Royale suggests that they lacked the moral
authority which might have promoted a subservient attitude in their
parishioners.

The Récollet missionaries who provided spiritual care for the
people of Ile Royale had come there through a complex diplomatic
arrangement between the Crown, the Bishop of Québec, and the
Récollet order itself. In theory, the parishes of Ile Royale were the responsibility of the Diocese of Québec, whose territory stretched from
English-occupied Acadia to the westernmost fur-trade posts and down

to Louisiana on the Gulf of Mexico. This vast diocese, blessed neither with unlimited funds nor with unlimited priests, could only supply priests for communities large and prosperous enough to support a clergy. Since Bishop de Saint-Vallier assumed in 1713 that the scattered fishermen of Ile Royale would scarcely meet these criteria, the new colony became a missionary responsibility served by Récollet fathers from Brittany. Even as Louisbourg grew large and prosperous, the colony remained a mission field.

As missionaries, the Récollets could collect charitable donations from their flock, but they did not require their parishes to support them. Instead, their expenses were met by their order, which in turn received a compensating allowance from the King. This delicate arrangement, typical of church-state relations in the eighteenth century, was not entirely to the benefit of the Récollets. As missionaries, they owned no valuable lands in the colony and they lacked the normal clerical power to levy tithes on their parishioners. As a result they held no independent power. Subservient to a distant bishop, the missionaries were also wards of the state, as local officials regularly pointed out. On more than one occasion the order had been obliged to withdraw priests who had offended the civil power.

Dependent on official tolerance, cut off from temporal power, and serving brief tenures in the colony, the missionaries rarely planted deep roots in Ile Royale, and none of them could wield the kind of influence sometimes given the clergy in Catholic societies. Lacking tithes, the Récollets were unable even to build a parish church, and the prime quayfront lot reserved for that use remained empty, a symbol of the limited power of Louisbourg's clergy.

Knowledge of the Récollets' limited authority may have sustained the widow Cruchon when she resolved to mislead *curé* Athanase Guégot into believing that Jacques Rolland had parental permission to marry her daughter. She knew that parental permission was essentially a matter of civil law, and the missionaries clearly held no civil power. In any case, her determination to see the marriage take place overrode whatever scruples she retained. When she visited Père Athanase at the Récollet residence, she was sufficiently free from awe and fear to present the *curé* with a letter of consent to which she had forged the name of Jacques Rolland's mother.

Père Athanase was pleased to consent to the wedding. Though the bride was younger than most, she was a year past the canonical minimum age. The *curé* was familiar with the religious education she had received at the local convent, and he probably also understood the economic circumstances that pressed the Cruchon daughters toward early marriage. Though he knew less of the groom, parental consent had been given, and several Malouin associates of the young clerk could testify to his religious faith and freedom to marry. Père Athanase, whose predecessor had baptised Marie-Louise in the spring of 1729, prepared to marry her to Jacques Rolland in the summer of 1742.

All that remained was a contract of marriage. The religious ceremony would unite the couple in marriage, but both law and society understood that a marriage was always an alliance of families, each with its own lineage and property to safeguard. To set the terms of this worldly alliance, many families demanded a marriage contract.

In the civil law, the marriage of Jacques Rolland and Marie-Louise Cruchon would create a legal entity called the "community of goods," a joint partnership in the material assets possessed by the couple. Husband and wife would hold equal shares in this "community," but not because the sexes were considered equal – in fact the law firmly established the husband as manager and administrator of the jointly owned property of the community. Joint ownership merely reflected the fact that marriage was essentially an alliance between families, an alliance in which each family was investing a precious part of its slowly accumulated patrimony. By defining who brought what into the marriage, the regime of community of goods protected each family's investment, and within that general rule a written marriage contract set specific terms for the alliance. Once it was signed, the new couple would not even require a will to direct the eventual disposition of its property. When a spouse came to die, community of goods ensured that half the family assets would pass to the survivor, the other half to the children or, in a childless marriage, back to the family of the deceased. Inherited patrimony, however small, was a family's only material security in a hazardous world; the community of goods was another attempt to prevent its squandering.

Community-of-goods law was extremely detailed, and a written contract of marriage was really only essential when two families were so unequal in wealth or status that both recognized the need to modify the usually equal division of property; but the signing of a marriage contract was also a social event. Straightforward alliances that hardly required a written contract were often dignified by a formal agreement, in which the standard community of goods was embellished by flowery legal phrases and the exchange of gifts and promises among the parties, all witnessed by the notary, the families, and as many friends and patrons as could be persuaded to attend.

The Cruchon–Rolland contract signed on the ninth of August, 1742, was one of this type, for neither party had much to offer in material goods. To found the new community of goods, the frugal widow promised one thousand *livres'* worth of household furnishings, but the goods would come from the Cruchon home: in effect Marie-Louise received an early inheritance. In return, Rolland – for this occasion he was Jacques-François Rolland, Sieur Duverdé – gave his bride half-ownership in what he had just been given. The gifts described so generously in the contract involved little expense to anyone; the contract was chiefly a formal prelude to marriage, a replacement for the disappearing religious ceremony of *fiançailles*. It was a moment for celebration, enlivened by the notary's ritual demand for a kiss from the bride and dignified by the presence of all the couple's friends and all the Cruchons' patrons from more prosperous times.

With the contract signed, Marie-Louise's wedding plans moved quickly forward. Her fiancé moved from Tanguy Mervin's rented rooms to the Cruchon home, and Père Athanase published the banns of marriage at the Sunday mass. No one objected to the union, and the usual dispensation from the second and third banns was given. Three banns were rarely needed in the small community, and the donation accompanying the request for dispensation sustained the façade of both affluence and charity in the families involved.

Meanwhile Marie-Louise and her mother assembled the trousseau the bride would take into matrimony and adult life. Perhaps for the first time, the young woman became the proud owner of two *robes*, the full-length dresses that were the basis of women's formal wear.

One of these, an expensive satin creation, the skirt of which was split at the front to display a matching underskirt, would be her wedding dress. There were also several sets of skirts, blouses, and aprons, which were everyday garments, and the trousseau would have included other needed garments: practical stockings of wool and fancy ones of silk, hairpieces and bonnets, pairs of shoes and slippers, perhaps some imitation jewellery.

The groom, for his part, would be married in his best suit: short breeches over silk stockings, a sleeved or sleeveless *veste*, and a heavy, knee-length *justaucorps* coat, all in a matched fabric. If he could have afforded the expense, Rolland's shirt and collar would have been trimmed with lace, his coat shining with gold or silver buttons and swirls of expensive brocade. In his present condition, he probably had to be satisfied with a plainer suit, complemented only by a powdered wig and perhaps a brass-headed cane.

The wedding ceremony followed the daily mass on Tuesday, the twenty-first of August, and the sight of the guests at the Chapelle Saint-Louis in the citadel must have been gratifying to the widow Cruchon's thirst for a renewal of her family's social standing. Royal engineer Etienne Verrier, once a patron of the bride's father, was there, accompanied by his aide and the latter's wife. There were several military families, the men in Marine blue and white, their ladies in silks and cottons of every colour and style, everyone resplendent with lace and gold, powder, and the scent of perfume. Jacques Rolland's business friends from Saint-Malo and Louisbourg were present in strength, and the neighbours and friends of the Cruchon family crowded in to swell the regular attendance at mass.

At the altar Père Athanase offered the marriage service and received the vows of the bride and groom. A benediction was given, and before the wedding party paraded out, the *curé* opened the parish registers to record the marriage. Bride and groom signed their names, the bride in a noticeably shaky hand, and then prominent guests came forward to add their own signatures. The alliance had been made.

From the chapel the couple and their guests probably returned to a celebratory luncheon that would open daylong festivities at the Cruchon home. The couple had picked the date carefully, for the week that followed included the *fête Saint-Louis*, the feast day of France's patron saint. Wedding dinners and soirées given by friends of Rolland and the Cruchons probably extended their festivities until the general Saint-Louis celebration on August 25.

A holy day of obligation, the Saint-Louis festival was also a day of national and dynastic pride. It was marked by church services, artillery salutes, and military parades, and it climaxed after dusk with a festive procession to the eastern ramparts of the town, where the citizens lit a massive bonfire and cheered the eruption of fireworks. Amid drinking and dancing, young Marie-Louise and her fine new husband wound up their wedding celebration.

IV

When the *fête Saint-Louis* brought his honeymoon to a close, Jacques Rolland went to work, for the months between August and February would be crucial to his new career. Soon he was busy collecting the cod that Tanguy Mervin's clients had caught and dried that summer. As he settled accounts with the fishermen and supervised the loading of endless hundredweights of fish, Rolland also began to sell his new, independent status. He strove to persuade Mervin clients to give their business to him, and he searched for new contacts whom Mervin had never reached. The summer's wheat shortage had established a seller's market, but competition was brisk, and Rolland's judgment was constantly tested as he assessed each customer's creditworthiness.

The series of bad years the fishery had suffered complicated Rolland's efforts to build his trade. If another season of poor catches were to occur, the only successful merchants would be those with prosperous or particularly skilful fishermen as their debtors; but Rolland needed clients and so he had to be willing to gamble. To win a toehold in the market he probably spent the fall of 1742 travelling up and down the coasts of Ile Royale, staying with the fishermen of Baleine, Fourché, and the other stark little outports, tolerating complaints about the Malouin merchants' avarice as long as there were clients to take his merchandise who could show promise of eventual payment. So Rolland bargained and travelled and Marie-Louise remained in Louisbourg.

Jacques Rolland had not yet acquired a new home for his bride. Instead, the couple had moved into his apartment in the Cruchon home, and Marie-Louise stayed under her mother's eye. Younger than most brides, still at an age when young people expected adult guidance, Marie-Louise remained influenced more by her mother than by her young and preoccupied husband. She was being given little encouragement to transfer her loyalties and affections away from the Cruchon family toward her new spouse.

Still, Marie-Louise's continued dependence on her mother need not mean her marriage went unconsummated. At thirteen she was only a year or two younger than several other Louisbourg brides, and evidently old enough to be ready for sexual activity. In eighteenth-century Louisbourg, women became objects of sexual attention almost as soon as they reached puberty, though the habit of late marriage meant that most encounters with girls of Marie-Louise's age were illicit ones. In several cases angry parents had initiated court actions after barely pubescent daughters were seduced by older men or by boys close to their own age. Even Governor de Saint-Ovide had been forced as a young officer to acknowledge paternity of a child he had fathered on a fifteen-year-old. Though such cases took place in circumstances very different from the marriage of Marie-Louise Cruchon, they suggest she would not have been thought too young to enter into sexual relations with her husband. Sex would have been part of Marie-Louise's marriage from her wedding night. Had her marriage not been consummated, that fact would surely have been an issue in the stormy days that would soon come to the marriage.

Yet so long as Rolland was away at his business and Marie-Louise remained with her mother, even their sexual bond could hardly carry the marriage far beyond the economic alliance that had first linked the young couple. Such limited progress was probably quite acceptable to the one who had planned and guided the marriage from its inception. The widow Cruchon shared her culture's scepticism about youth, its ingrained caution in matters of family management. There might be a marriage – arranged by her – but that did not mean that a mature and self-reliant couple had been created. The widow was not yet ready to abandon her young protégés to fend for themselves. The new couple's residence under her roof reflected her assumption that she would continue to guide the family destinies.

Since Jean-René Cruchon's death, Thérèse Boudier had grown used to her burden of responsibility, and she did not intend to relinquish her authority just when the Cruchon fortunes might be about to turn. Marie-Louise was a child, Jacques Rolland little older. Rather than leave them to plot their own course, the widow had always intended to take her new son-in-law into her home and tutelage, slowly to guide him toward maturity as the family regained its place in society. So, limited as it was, the marriage seemed quite successful to the widow. Rolland had his business opportunity, the Cruchons had their financial support. Those had been the motives of the alliance, and there seemed no urgent need for further change.

The introduction of a busy and ambitious young merchant into the family had already restored the Cruchons' credit. Invoking Rolland's name to purchase clothes, furnishings, and all kinds of little luxuries, the widow and her daughter could begin to renew their sadly diminished place in Louisbourg society, and Rolland's frequent absences during the fall seem not to have inhibited their activities.

Now the widow hosted more of the dinners at which Rolland had first made the family's acquaintance, and she also made coffee parties part of her entertaining. No more appropriate beverage than coffee could have been chosen as the instrument of a campaign for readmittance into Louisbourg society. Coffee, known to Europeans via the Middle East for about a century, had been rare until Caribbean plantations developed coffee crops after 1715. From this new source the drink spread rapidly but unevenly through the European world. It quickly conquered the port cities and urban centres where trend-setting society clustered, but it only slowly gained acceptance in rural areas and more traditional communities. Even in Ile Royale, where Caribbean coffee was immediately successful, the social gap was seen: coffee drinking was soon adopted by the townspeople of Louisbourg, where every home had its coffee grinder and *cafetière*, but spruce beer and rum reigned unchallenged on fishing properties a few hundred yards beyond the town gates. Coffee parties were the perfect expression of the fashionable air sought by the reborn Cruchon family.

Despite the speed with which it took to coffee, Louisbourg society none the less preserved many traditional patterns of the culture from which it sprang. New ideas were more slowly diffused than new beverages. In its etiquette and intellectual tone, its talk and its music, the elite of the little colony looked back complacently to styles established in the previous century. Ideas and attitudes that would later be seen to epitomize the eighteenth century were quite foreign to Thérèse Boudier's Louisbourg of 1742.

When musicians entertained their cultured patrons at the soirées to which the widow Cruchon could once more expect invitation, Bach and Handel would rarely, if ever, have been heard. Each man was in his prime in 1742, having already given the world some of the great compositions of the century, yet their redefinition of musical styles was still innovative, possibly even radical – and besides, both men were foreigners and Protestants. Only late in the eighteenth century would great music break its national bonds to become a truly European culture. For its soirées and balls, Louisbourg probably preferred versions of the court music played at Versailles when the old king, Louis XIV, was defining the taste of his century.

A similar time lag governed intellectual fashion. The colony would show little interest in the nascent enlightenment, just then beginning its quest for characteristic eighteenth-century values of reason, scepticism, and scientific progress. The men of the French enlightenment were thinkers still on the fringe, their radical and anglophile opinions frequently subject to censure and censorship. Dubious about French colonization, they had no channels by which to spread their ideas among the colonies. Louisbourg's social leaders were practical servants of the Crown with a job to perform. They made unlikely converts to strange new notions and thought themselves well served by the previous century's faith in God, devotion to the king, and commitment to social hierarchy. Some had doubtless heard new opinions of government and society from their New England contacts, but most of Louisbourg's opinion-makers would have been conservative. Reflecting the placid mainstream of French culture at mid-century, their libraries – if they read at all – were filled with collections of sermons, Latin classics in translation, and practical volumes of travellers' accounts or commercial law. As if in retaliation, Diderot's iconoclastic *Encyclopédie* gave Ile Royale the briefest possible entry and got several of its facts wrong. New ideas were about to break, but little that was new or unsettling would be heard in the widow Cruchon's salon as she began to entice the best people of Louisbourg back to her home. That should have suited her. She wanted readmittance to the society she had always valued – that it seemed so changeless was part of its attraction.

Preoccupied with her social rebirth, the widow Cruchon probably evinced little interest in January 1743 when news began to circulate about the outcome of the winter fishing season. The fish had come late to the inshore banks, in smaller numbers than usual, and catches had been light – bad news for the fishing industry and its suppliers. From the widow's perspective, what seemed more important was the fact that Jacques Rolland was back in Louisbourg, eager to build the retail branch of his business, eager to assert his independence.

In mid-February the widow Cruchon saw her daughter and son-in-law take a small step away from her supervision. Jacques Rolland moved his bride to rented rooms on the Place d'Armes, a few blocks down Rue Saint-Louis from the Cruchon home. Their new quarters were small, just a single second-storey room with an adjoining dressing room. Filling one end of the room was the couple's curtained four-poster and an armoire of local spruce. At the other end, a table and chairs and the cupboards that held their dishes and utensils crowded close to the fireplace. The Rollands' lease gave them the use of the attic and part of the yard, but their motive for moving was the acquisition of the large ground-floor room that became Jacques Rolland's *boutique*.

If the widow was sorry to see her daughter leave home, she should have been consoled by her son-in-law's obvious industry on the family's behalf. *Boutiques* – retail shops – were the focal points of Louisbourg's daily marketing. Most of the colony's consumer goods were imported, and the streets of Louisbourg were dotted with the retail shops that distributed the cargo loads of merchandise to the consumers of the colony. For Rolland, now settled but hardly prosperous enough to support the large overheads of an entirely wholesale trade, retail trade would be the foundation of his business. He might continue to represent

Mervin *et fils* in their wholesale dealings, but the two thousand citizens of Louisbourg would be the steady clientele that he hoped to attract to the one-room shop on the Place d'Armes.

No sign or display window advertised the *boutique*'s presence when the widow went to visit, but she could have identified the premises by the stock heaped up to the small windows and by the cases and shelving that ringed the interior. Rather than handling the great quantities of flour, preserved foods, and fishing equipment on which wholesalers relied, Rolland and his retail competitors dealt in clothing, housewares, and all the small items where personal service and a varied stock gave the retailer an advantage over his wholesaling counterpart.

Cloth and clothing were foremost among the goods of Jacques Rolland's new *boutique*. Cloth was Europe's most important manufactured product, the economic mainstay of dozens of towns and regions and a prime consumer good. For the affluent and those striving to appear so, there were few better proofs of wealth and taste than a lavish wardrobe, and the well-to-do flocked to merchants like Rolland for all the items of fashion that would proclaim their eminence. Even the poor had constantly to replace torn or worn-out apparel, so the clothing market was always active. There were tailors in the community, but people made many of their own garments, so Rolland's most valuable items were bolts of fabric and sewing materials. All around his shop stood imported rolls of cloth. Most of these had been woven in the textile towns of France, but some came from Spain, Holland, Britain, and even the Far East. The range was great, for with Mervin's help Rolland had acquired as many colours and qualities as his shop could hold. Cottons predominated: there were heavy, striped cottons, a thick roll of cotton muslin, and bolts of red *camelot*, a woven imitation of camelhair. There were stacked rolls of the fine Dutch linen called *toile d'Hollande*, favoured for quality shirt-making, and a large amount of the Breton version of the same cloth. Rolland offered linen *batiste* for neckerchiefs and cap linings. For more expensive tastes, he offered a little silk and some silken plush and a substantial amount of lace for cuffs and trimmings. Along with the cloth, he displayed needles, pins, and thread, clasps and hooks and buttons of a dozen shapes and materials. He had yarn for those who knitted, ribbons, beads, and costume jewellery for decorating and embroidering.

Not every piece of apparel was homemade or tailor-made. Rolland offered ready-to-wear capes, breeches, neckerchiefs, and shirts in a variety of colours and styles, and his shop was particularly well-stocked with the accessories that completed an outfit. He could provide men's, women's, and children's shoes and slippers, gloves and mittens, garters and stockings of wool and silk. To men he offered black tricorne hats they might trim with a gold or silver band, and women could choose among a variety of bonnets and caps.

Rolland had no space to display furniture, but he could supply most household and personal items. He had tin and sandalwood boxes, pencils and bellows and yardsticks and corkscrews. For smokers he had tobacco graters and humidors, pouches, pipes, and tongs for tamping and cleaning. He offered knives and jackknives and combs with horn or wooden handles and scores of other practical odds and ends.

The shop could serve the mind and spirit as well. Seven crystal rosaries and fifteen wooden ones were on display, and Rolland was even a bookseller. His books were not the large, leatherbound volumes that were the rare and precious possessions brought from France by a few well-to-do householders. What Rolland sold were the publications of the *bibliothèque bleue*, cheap, ephemeral booklets in soft blue covers, aimed at the mass market. These collections of folk tales, Mother Goose rhymes, and fantastical histories catered to the popular taste for myth, legend, and heroic fantasy. Jacques Rolland had representative samples in his shop. He also offered *pastorelles*, verse narratives on pastoral themes designed to be read aloud by the most literate to an audience that was ready to join in at the refrains. There were a few *Noëls*, telling the nativity story in endless variations, sometimes moralizing, sometimes topical or even satirical. But most of Rolland's books responded to the desire of Louisbourg parents to educate their young. Rolland stocked several score of *Alphabets*, simple spelling primers using memorization and repetition drills to teach letters and then words. Children's hymnals and hourbooks serving similar purposes were sold by other shopkeepers in the town, along with moral tracts and religious texts. Though most of Louisbourg's people were illiterate, the habit of reading or being read to must have been widespread, for both enter-tainment and self-improvement. That Rolland and his fellow merchants could provide Louisbourg with these inexpensive books is com-pelling evidence of how closely they had linked the colonial town to European markets and goods.

One minor item in Rolland's *boutique* suggests the contribution his in-laws made to his business. In his stock were twenty bouquets of artificial flowers. False-flower making was an art often taught in convent schools, and these fragile bouquets were probably the handi-work of Marie-Louise and her mother and sister. The embroidered shirts and the boxes of lace Rolland sold may also have been crafted by the Cruchon women and their circle, for even the most refined ladies sewed, knitted, and embroidered clothing for eventual retail sale. It was natural that the women of Rolland's family would produce such work, but their contribution went beyond handicrafts. As the widow Cruchon polished her faded social connections, she could help the fledgling enterprise by encouraging her friends to patronize Rolland's little shop. At dinners and soirées she might mention his achievements to established businessmen, and always she was behind the scenes, ready to give the young man the benefit of her experi-ence. Rolland's career was a family enterprise, just as the widow had expected it would be.

While the widow Cruchon did what she could to promote his cause, Jacques Rolland probably spent his working days in or close to his new shop. He employed neither a servant nor a clerk, so his wife may have minded the store in his absence, but there should have been enough routine activity to keep the merchant busy. His major work was now simply selling: rolling and unrolling bolts of cloth, impress-ing clients with an encyclopaedic knowledge of styles and qualities, haggling over prices. The retail merchant sought above all to develop a bond that would bring customers back to his shop. To keep one client loyal, Rolland would occasionally rush out to another mer-chant if he himself lacked what the customer demanded.

Credit arrangements preoccupied him. Even the poorest people of Louisbourg could often jingle a few copper or alloy coins – the small change called *patar* – in their money-pouches. Some could even boast a few silver *écus*, but credit transactions were common. The amount of cash in the town rose and fell, growing when the colonial Treasury received a coin shipment to redeem the year's debts, shrinking when a poor cod catch and large import purchases drained money from the colony. Credit and barter were frequently more convenient, if not essential, so careful bookkeeping and regular collection of debts were crucial shopkeeping activities.

Boutiques like Rolland's became centres of business activity. The man who dropped in to change the silver *écu* he had just acquired might stay to look through the merchandise. Another client might seek a small cash loan against future earnings. Gradually larger deals would emerge: the visitor haggling over a cane or a pair of stockings might interest the proprietor in a venture involving a shipment of rum or even a share in the purchase of a trading schooner. Everyone dropped into the *boutiques*, which could rival the taverns as information markets, and even Rolland's small shop beneath the rented apartment helped push the young merchant toward the centre of the colony's trade. If it kept him busy in the early months of 1743, it was time well spent. He probably had more names in his ledger than coins in his strongbox, but he could hope that would change in the summer.

Watching Jacques Rolland at his business, the widow Cruchon could be well pleased with his achievement – which was also hers. After holding her family precariously together through several difficult years, she had scored a brilliant triumph by securing this industrious son-in-law to re-establish the family fortunes, and now her social rebirth was enabling her to expand their income by directing business toward the young man's shop. Perhaps the bride was young enough to set tongues wagging, and it was true that parental consent for the groom had been fudged, but the marriage had saved her family, secured her daughter a promising husband, and proven her a shrewd, bold manager of the Cruchon family affairs in bad times or in good. These should have been glory days for the little family: Rolland rushing about the colony and the town on his business, clearly a merchant on the rise, his wife blossoming into adulthood and society, the widow herself returning to social circles that had been slipping away from her. As Carnaval approached, the widow could feel she had much to celebrate.

Carnaval was the annual prelude to Lent. Lenten observance was less than total in Ile Royale – marriages, dances, and other festive occasions were not renounced – yet everyone seized on Carnaval to enliven the bleakest part of winter. For the governor's retinue and others able to afford it, a constant succession of dinners and balls from New Year to Ash Wednesday relieved the mid-winter tedium. For most people, Carnaval was the few days climaxed by Mardi Gras, a scene of masquerades, parties, and ribald drinking sessions in the taverns and inns. For the widow Cruchon, the holiday seemed perfectly timed to mark the achievement of her fondest ambitions, and as the festivities approached, she prepared to guide her daughter and son-in-law into her society's observance of the holiday.

Instead, Carnaval proved a mighty shock to the widow and a shattering blow to her carefully pursued vision of the Cruchon family reborn through Rolland's labours and shaped by her guiding hand.

Jacques Rolland, she discovered, was also finding Carnaval well timed for celebrating the achievement of his own ambitions. Since his wedding he had devoted himself wholeheartedly to work, leaving his wife to her mother's care as he sought to banish forever the insecurity and dependence he had known since the collapse of his own family. Now that the foundations of a career seemed well laid, Rolland wanted to celebrate in his own way. Instead of attending coffee parties under his mother-in-law's wing, he spent Carnaval dining and drinking with the merchants, ship's officers, and junior military men who had become his friends and clients in the past months. His bill for gambling debts rose past eighty *livres*, but the burst of revelry confirmed new friendships that the gregarious young merchant had been forging since the summer.

Young Rolland's friendly ways and unrelenting work were bringing him a circle of friends independent of the widow Cruchon, and he saw himself becoming steadily less in need of her patronage. He had already removed his wife from the Cruchon home, and now he began to substitute his influence for the widow's, making his bride part of his own circles rather than an ornament of her mother's more refined entertainments. More than a style of entertainment was involved: Jacques Rolland, businessman and adult by virtue of his marriage, was staking a claim to be head of his own household.

Such a claim had to dismay the widow Cruchon profoundly. The terms of an alliance that had seemed so satisfactory were suddenly being turned inside out, and she discovered that relationships she had taken for granted could be defined very differently. She had seen in Jacques Rolland a promising youngster in need of a family, ready to defer to her age and experience and accept her tutelage as he matured. Yet now that she was ready to guide the young couple into the fruits of their success, Rolland was rebelling, not acting like the youth she took him to be but posing as an adult, ready to run his own affairs and choose his own company.

The deception at the heart of the arranged marriage now came back to haunt the widow. For the sake of her family's prosperity, she had connived to join an inappropriately young daughter to a youth who lacked parental permission. Now her careful manipulations had given Jacques Rolland the illusion of maturity and legal grounds to claim the privileges maturity could give.

Had she looked more closely at the prospective bridegroom when they first met, the widow might have seen what drove young Rolland, but her own need to restore her family's fortunes had blinded her to Rolland's intentions. After depending first on his own family and then on the Mervins, the young man was unwilling to see anyone else assume lasting authority over him. Instead, he was eager to claim the rights and responsibilities that he felt he had earned by his hard work. Moving his wife from her mother's home to the rooms over his shop had been Rolland's first hint that he would no longer defer to the widow Cruchon, and the Carnaval celebrations a few weeks later confirmed his independent stance.

It was no small matter. How the family's meagre assets were managed could be virtually a matter of life and death, and as the widow Cruchon's own arrangements were turned against her she responded with fear and frustration. The son-in-law she had taken under her wing now challenged her authority as head of the Cruchon–Rolland clan. He rejected her guidance. He drew her daughter away. Even her control over the income that had fuelled their social rebirth was placed in doubt. Judging by his Carnaval, Rolland had very different ideas as to how the family should live. Worst of all for the widow, she found herself helpless to oppose him. By reason of the marriage she had arranged,

Rolland was legally an adult. He was also the wage-earner, and she had set him free to choose how to spend his money.

The conflict of generations that the widow and her son-in-law opened at Carnaval would simmer throughout Louisbourg's long winter. It was a struggle for power, the issue who would hold the purse strings and make the decisions for the Cruchon–Rolland clan. Such a conflict could only have started in a marriage born of desperation. Normally men did not marry until an age at which their elders would willingly pass them the responsibility to manage and preserve a family's well-being. Thérèse Boudier and Jacques Rolland had broken with custom, and when they found themselves in disagreement, custom could offer no rules to guide their conduct.

Soon the widow's frustration was growing as she brooded on Rolland's impudent self-reliance, his influence over her daughter, and his choice of friends; but if she ceased to promote him to her friends and contribute to his trade, pride and caution still obliged her to keep the quarrel within the family. She had to recognize that Rolland did control the family income on which she lived, and pride held her back from a humiliating spectacle of public conflict.

Inevitably it was Marie-Louise who became the focus of competition. By her fourteenth birthday the girl must have been torn between the filial deference to which her upbringing conditioned her and the obedience to her husband which the church, the law, and the community seemed to expect. Marie-Louise's response to these conflicting demands is hidden by the walls of her reticence, but she seems, consciously or not, to have muted the conflict. By refusing to abandon either her mother or her husband, the girl ensured that they would keep the struggle within the family, at least until one or the other could seize some new advantage.

No such advantage presented itself to the widow that winter. Cut off from the outside world and the summertime flow of imports, Louisbourg ate away at the stockpiles built up in the fall. The quality of the colony's flour, dried fish, and salted meat declined as people began to scrape the bottom of barrels filled months before. The pace of business dwindled, and shortages reinforced the Lenten austerity. The excitements of Carnaval faded. Like the rest of the townspeople, Thérèse Boudier settled in to wait for spring, praying that the new season might bring some solution by which she could wrest control of her family back from her wilful, immature son-in-law.

V
___

I n the first week of April 1743 a small fishing vessel named *Cheval Marin* broke through the last of the drifting ice pans that had been keeping Louisbourg cut off from the world. For the crew the arrival ended a cold crossing that had begun on Ash Wednesday in the Basque fishing port of Saint-Jean-de-Luz, but for Louisbourg it marked the launching of a new season. By the end of April a dozen more vessels had arrived, and though cold, foggy weather would last into June, the opening of the sea lanes meant the restocking of larders and the revival of fishing and trade. As the surge of activity swept through the town, Jacques Rolland set aside family quarrels to concentrate on his commerce.

In truth, Jacques Rolland was not much concerned by his mother-in-law's resentment. Forced into self-reliance since childhood, Rolland may have been puzzled by the woman's refusal to recognize his independence and her attempts to control his wife, but there is no hint that she caused him much doubt about his status as a mature adult free to run his own affairs. Though she might no longer guide her prominent friends to his shop, Rolland thought he was building his own network of contacts and clients, and beyond her dubious patronage she seemed without the means to help or harm him. In time she would have to accept his authority. In the meantime he had more practical concerns pressing on him.

One of the newly arrived merchant ships had delivered a new consignment of merchandise for Rolland's *boutique*, and as the town began to fill with sailors and traders, his shop became busy again. Though Tanguy Mervin would soon be back to take over most of Rolland's work in the fishermen's wholesale trade, Rolland remained interested in the progress of the industry. Indeed, its success was vital to him. In September his debts to his own suppliers, notably Tanguy Mervin, would fall due, and to pay them Rolland would have to collect from the fishermen to whom he had extended credit in the past fall. The fishermen would only be able to pay if they caught enough fish. Rolland redoubled his efforts in the retail trade of his shop, his uneasiness about the potential credit squeeze just beginning to mount.

Unfortunately for Jacques Rolland, the summer of 1743 became one of the worst ever experienced by the fishermen of Ile Royale. As catches sank to unprecedented lows, proprietors considered beaching their shallops and giving up the losing struggle. As the summer wore on, effects of the crisis spread throughout the colony, and soon the implications were clear for Jacques Rolland. The fishermen were not going to be able to pay him, and he in turn would be hard pressed to meet the commitments he had made to his own creditors. Suddenly his precious reputation, perhaps even his business, was in jeopardy.

As reports of the failing catch came in from the fishing stations, Rolland tried to limit the damage to his business. Exhorting his debtors not to abandon their efforts, he could hint at stronger measures: if the fishermen were unable to pay, he would be entitled to have the courts seize their property and equipment. The fishermen were largely unmoved, for it was obvious that young Rolland, lacking the financial resources to operate the fisheries, had no real desire to own them himself. His urgings and threats were intended only to keep his clients from ignoring him to pay off more powerful creditors. Even as he pressed the fishermen, Rolland began to plan how he would face his own creditors. It seemed likely that he would have to persuade Tanguy Mervin to be patient and to defer his repayment beyond the September deadline.

Rolland's hope that Mervin would not demand his money at once was based on the workings of business credit. Because suspicion lingered that to charge interest on loans was usury, a sin in the eyes of many Christian theologians, a short-term debt like Rolland's bore no regular interest. To convert such a debt into a long-term, interest-bearing loan required a routine court appearance at which the debtor professed his inability to pay and was sentenced to repay principal plus interest over an extended period. Rolland hoped to have Tanguy Mervin change his debts into a profitable long-term loan of this sort, to be repaid with interest over a number of years. Once Mervin granted Rolland this extended credit, the minor creditors could be appeased. To remain solvent, Rolland needed only to retain the confidence of Tanguy Mervin.

Rolland spent that summer tending his shop and striving to shore up his credit in the business community, until finally his bills came due on September 29, *la fête Saint-Michel*. The feast day of the archangel Michael bore no liturgical connection either to the fishing industry or to merchant banking, but its celebration coincided with the end of the summer fishing season along the maritime coast, and tradition enshrined it as the weighing day when cod stocks were measured and compared to the fishermen's debts. In Louisbourg "la Saint-Michel" had become the deadline for all kinds of accounts, from labourers' contracts to leases on property. When Mervin had left Rolland a stock of wholesale and retail merchandise in the fall of 1742, they had agreed to settle their accounts at the Saint-Michel. In turn, the fishermen to whom Rolland had supplied goods had assured him they would pay at the Saint-Michel, when their catches were complete.

Two days before the Saint-Michel of 1743, Jacques Rolland met Tanguy Mervin in the study of *notaire* Laborde, where both men had signed Rolland's marriage contract thirteen months before. Despite his efforts, Rolland was unable to pay his debts, and now he made his case for a delay in repayment. The sum at issue was 1,200 *livres*, roughly twice what Rolland's annual wage may have been when he worked for the Mervins, and much more than he had seen in cash all winter. Rolland must have argued that it was only the fishermen's failures that had put him in difficulty, and he probably insisted it was riskier for Mervin to foreclose than to give him credit. Stressing the expenses he had incurred to establish his business, Rolland implied that an attempt to seize his assets would bring down a horde of creditors to dispute Mervin's right to the proceeds.

Ultimately Rolland's case lay in the confidence he inspired. Appealing for Mervin's trust, Rolland displayed his well-kept accounts, the long lists of debts he could not yet collect, and the evidence of the vigorous business he had started in the past year. It was an impressive beginning in difficult times, and Rolland used it as proof that he was a responsible merchant, worthy of respect. Like any merchant of his time, he would stand or fall on his reputation.

Tanguy Mervin considered the proposal. He knew that the align-ment of forces in Europe's struggle over the Austrian succession made war with Britain imminent, and he had no desire to see his family's assets tied up across the Atlantic if naval conflict was about to close the sea lanes. The decline of the Ile Royale fishing industry was also troublesome. Yet Rolland's arguments had been effective. A wave of creditors rushing in for a share of Rolland's assets could cause a panic. Mervin might even be denied full repayment. The Malouin tempo-rized. Instead of holding Rolland to the Saint-Michel deadline, he gave his debtor one week's relief. During that time Mervin would make inquiries in the business community about young Rolland's standing and creditworthiness.

If Mervin retained some affection for his former clerk, his dis-coveries in the week after the Saint-Michel must have shocked him. He did not expect Rolland to collect his debts in a week, for too many colonists were equally hard pressed that summer, but he probably assumed that Jacques Rolland would have built up a fund of good-will among the merchants and townspeople, out of which would come offers of assistance. Instead, Mervin's quiet inquiries revealed disturbing rumours about the young merchant.

Many of Mervin's informants would have doubted Rolland's sol-vency, but Mervin evidently heard of problems that went beyond a temporary shortage of cash. Stories were circulating about Rolland's dissipated behaviour during Carnaval. Suspicions had been raised about his use of credit and his overall commercial aptitude. What was worse, most of the rumours were originating in Rolland's own family. His own mother-in-law was orchestrating the campaign of criticism.

Now Mervin could not dismiss Rolland's difficulties as a tempo-rary shortage of cash. True or not, the existence of rumours spread by Rolland's relatives struck to the heart of his business reputation, for a skilful merchant never alienated his own clan, the foundation of his enterprise.

Rolland would have been more shocked than Mervin. Since Carnaval, his mother-in-law had resisted his authority within the Cruchon–Rolland family, but that had not seemed serious. The difficulties he had been struggling against all summer had given her new opportunities to criticize his management and ridicule his claims to maturity, but Rolland had expected her to rally to his aid for the sake of the family. Now, instead of keeping their struggle private, she had taken it into the community just when he was most dependent on public support. Though his own friends might stand by him, few of them were wealthier than he was. The judges of his commercial standing would be the older, settled colonial businessmen, yet it was among these that the widow Cruchon was most influential. If Mervin gave credence to the tales the widow was spreading, he might force the collapse of the family business. Abruptly obliged to acknowledge that he still depended on his mother-in-law's intercession, Rolland now realized she could destroy him, though only at the price of destroying her own source of income.

Rolland's deadline expired, and Tanguy Mervin went to court, but not to levy an interest charge on Rolland's debts. No longer sure that Rolland's business had a future, Mervin reckoned the merchant's possessions were valuable enough to cover his debts, and he wanted the courts to seize them for sale by judicial auction. It was strictly a business decision: Mervin was cutting his losses. He may even have theorized that the court-ordered sale would settle accounts and clear the air, perhaps even permitting Rolland to rebuild his reputation and his business on a new footing.

Judicial auctions were familiar procedures in the courts of Louisbourg. The day after Mervin's complaint, bailiff Joseph-Félix Chesnay came with two soldiers to Jacques Rolland's rented rooms. Rolland answered the early-morning summons, and Chesnay handed him copies of the judgment given against him, explaining that Rolland had one last chance to pay his debt. When Rolland admitted his inability to pay, his statement was automatically taken as a formal refusal that made his goods forfeit.

The widow Cruchon had not turned everyone against Jacques Rolland, as Chesnay the bailiff learned when he sought witnesses to his seizure. Sympathetic to the plight of the harassed young merchant, the neighbours refused to participate even by giving their names, and Chesnay was obliged to have his soldiers sign as his witnesses. Moving through the little apartment, the bailiff made a careful inventory of what the soldiers were hauling out to the wagon in the street. Everything went: dishes, furniture, clothes, the bed, a cord of firewood from the yard, and of course the entire stock of the once-lively little shop – even Marie-Louise's artificial flowers.

With everything outside, Chesnay looked for someone to store the goods, preferably someone informed about the case but not a close friend of Rolland. Once again the neighbours refused to participate in the young merchant's downfall, but now Chesnay, like Mervin, discovered the source of Rolland's troubles. The widow Cruchon bluntly proclaimed her alienation from her son-in-law by agreeing to serve as the court's custodian. Soon Rolland's goods were on their way up Rue Saint-Louis to the Cruchon home. With them went Marie-Louise, for Rolland was losing not only his goods but also his wife. Like a prize in the family struggle, Marie-Louise was being returned to her mother.

In a few weeks the bailiff was out again, this time joined by a military drummer to rouse a crowd for the judicial auction. After the drummer attracted public attention with a long, rolling tattoo that echoed down the streets, Chesnay announced the imminent auction of Rolland's goods, inviting bargain-hunters to converge on the home of the widow Cruchon.

Few enough accepted the invitation. The Cruchon home was far from the usual auction site on the busy quayside, and the widow had made no effort to promote the sale. Only a small crowd stood in front of her house when the auctioneer presented the first item, a thick roll of cotton cloth. Few bids came in, and eventually a friend of the widow snapped it up for half what she might have paid in Rolland's store. As the sale proceeded, the widow herself began to pick up bargains, and the creditors grew alarmed to see such discounts given on the merchandise from which they hoped to regain their money.

The first auction session lasted three hours, and Mervin and the other creditors found themselves entering bids just to push prices toward a reasonable level. Mervin saw what was happening. To be sure of ruining Rolland, the widow wanted to see the lowest possible prices being paid. If she could prevent the creditors from getting full repayment from the sale, they would continue to hound Jacques Rolland, and his career would be finished.

Tanguy Mervin made another appeal to the courts and persuaded the judge that the creditors' interests were threatened by the paucity of bidders at the auction. To attract a larger crowd, the sale was taken out of the widow Cruchon's control and away from its inconvenient location in her home.

Once removed from the widow's influence, the auction began to gain momentum. Larger crowds were attracted to every session, and successful bidders came from every level of the society: Louis DuPont Duchambon, second-in-command and future commandant of Ile Royale, took part, as did several members of the wealthy Delort family, a visiting missionary priest, a sergeant of the garrison, and several seamen and merchants. Jacques Rolland seems to have avoided the bitter experience of watching his goods hawked in the street, but Tanguy Mervin, who attended regularly, may have felt that a successful conclusion to the auction would be the quickest and least painful way to end the young merchant's ordeal.

The widow Cruchon had other ideas. If Tanguy Mervin saw the seizure of Jacques Rolland's goods as an unemotional business procedure, Thérèse Boudier found in it confirmation of all her complaints about her son-in-law. Since mid-winter, the young man who had once seemed so appropriate an addition to the family had come to threaten all her plans. Instead of accepting the rightful authority of the family head, Rolland seemed to imagine that his legal status as an adult had given him an instant maturity that authorized him to flout all her guidance. In the widow's eyes, he had squandered family income on doubtful friendships and uncouth celebrations. She believed he had subverted his wife's natural devotion to her mother and blocked all of the widow's preparations for the renaissance of the Cruchon family. Convinced that her son-in-law was immature and headstrong and would drag her family to ruin, she interpreted his business difficulties as the inevitable consequence of youthful ineptitude. In his inability to pay his debts she saw evidence that further justified her public criticism of his management. When his creditors fell on him after the Saint-Michel, Rolland's incompetence became public knowledge. Henceforth the widow's only concern was to save her daughter from the wreck.

When Tanguy Mervin revitalized the auction by moving it to the busy quayside, new fears assailed the widow. She sensed that if the auction raised enough money to repay all Rolland's clamouring creditors, he might yet escape the consequences of his youthful extravagance. If he were persuasive enough to regain the confidence, or even the tolerance, of the business community, he could reassemble the shreds of his career, resume his former ways, and continue his defiance of her.

At the same time, financial worries that the widow had thrust aside in the heat of her assault on Rolland must also have reasserted themselves. Having decided it was better to break Rolland's authority and face her old difficulties than to suffer his mismanagement, she would need once more to husband every resource. Yet it was not only Rolland's merchandise that stood on the auction block. The bailiff naturally had seized the assets of the community of goods created by the marriage, and Marie-Louise's share of their joint estate was under the hammer along with her husband's. Whatever became of Rolland, the widow hated to see the goods she had given her daughter being sacrificed by her son-in-law's business reverses. As the quayside auction grew livelier, the widow hunted for a way to ensure Rolland's ruin and still preserve something for the Cruchons. Before the auction ended she found one.

Two days after accepting Mervin's request that the site of the sale be changed, the courts received another petition. This one, offered by the widow Cruchon on her daughter's behalf, asked the judge to order a separation of goods between Marie-Louise Cruchon and Jacques Rolland.

Separation of goods, the dismantling of the community of goods that marriage created, was the closest thing to divorce in the eighteenth century's law codes. Divorce itself was impossible – only death could separate a couple joined in matrimony – but the law could remedy some of the civil consequences of a bad marriage by dissolving the marriage contract. The community of property created by the contract could be broken, returning to each partner one-half of the extinct community.

Such separations were not lightly granted. Courts were profoundly sceptical of women who sought to be separated from their husbands, for the law was intended to uphold family bonds, not to assist in the breaking of them. But the old obsession with the preservation of patrimonies yielded one justification for women to leave their husbands. Since the law made the husband sole manager of the property he and his wife shared, the goods brought into marriage by the woman had to be granted some safeguard against spendthrift or incompetent husbands. If proof could be given that a husband had irresponsibly squandered his wife's inheritance, she might ask the courts to remove her remaining property from his control.

Here lay the widow's opportunity. Having married Jacques Rolland in 1742 (she wrote in her plea to the court) her daughter had suffered the heartache of seeing him waste and dissipate most of their goods by his misconduct and mismanagement, until finally his creditors had given public proof of his incompetence by seizing his goods and hers. Now their joint debts were so great that Marie-Louise was obliged to renounce their partnership, abandoning the hard-pressed estate to Rolland and taking only the personal effects she had brought into the marriage.

A drastic and rarely invoked section of the civil law, separation of goods suited the widow's purposes exactly. Legal separation would make a total break between the Cruchons and Rolland. Married only in name, Marie-Louise would bring home her possessions and live once again under her mother's care. She would be unable to remarry in Rolland's lifetime, but his authority over her would be gone, and the Cruchon patrimony would be beyond his influence.

Of course, the effect on Rolland in his difficulties would be devastating. Once Marie-Louise removed her goods from the community property awaiting auction, too little would remain to satisfy the creditors' claims. To compound his troubles, the widow had just added herself to the list of claimants, even demanding rent for the months the couple had lived in her home. If the plea for separation succeeded, Rolland would surely be bankrupted. He would be publicly exposed as a man unable to meet his obligations and unfit to support a wife, and that disgrace would be far worse than a mere conviction for unpaid debt. If the widow won her court case, Rolland would be shamed from Louisbourg, a ruined and humiliated failure.

Jacques Rolland fought, of course. To have his possessions seized and sold was painful, but to be faced with a separation petition was vastly more serious. Should it succeed, it would destroy the security of family, household, and position he had sought for so long. He would be left more vulnerable than ever.

So Rolland contested the widow's court petition, but his defence became another in the series of self-fulfilling prophecies that dogged his marriage. It had been the widow's conviction that her son-in-law was incompetent that provoked her to begin the whispering campaign that ruined his credit and brought down his business. And now that her legal challenge threatened the marriage that made him legally adult, Rolland gave weight to her claims by losing his maturity and self-confidence. Reasoned defence against the separation was left to Tanguy Mervin, who argued that it made a loophole by which creditors like himself would be denied their rightful repayment. Rolland's own series of counter-petitions against the widow's suit had little law in them. Instead, he offered an emotional retrospective on his career in Louisbourg, a half defiant, half self-pitying account of the ambitions he had nurtured and the opposition he had encountered, as if he hoped some fairy godmother from one of his books of tales would wave away his troubles.

Mostly Rolland offered a diatribe against his mother-in-law, "who seeks only my ruin." She had tricked him into marriage. She had lied to the *curé*. She had spent his money on coffee parties and sweets in his absence and turned his own wife against him. By misleading his creditors she had brought him down, and now she sought a final triumph. Rolland offered no defence against the charge that he had failed to safeguard his wife's goods, but he acknowledged he could no longer live in Ile Royale, "scorned as I am." If the court would permit him to take his wife to France, he would care and provide for her, "for I did not take a wife in order to abandon her." But if she yielded to the persuasion of her mother, "the cause of all the dissension between us," then Rolland was able neither to support her nor to stay with her.

In the nightmare weeks of October and November, while the judge considered his verdict, Rolland had moved his few remaining possessions to a rented room in Joseph Lachaume's inn, leaving the remnants of his business to Mervin. As much as possible, he would have avoided the gossip, mockery, and pity his situation had attracted, but even in his rooms he was not left undisturbed. When it became unlikely that the auction sale would ever raise enough to satisfy his creditors, the bailiff again pounded on his door. This time Chesnay was under orders not only to seize whatever Rolland still possessed but also to escort the convicted debtor to a jail cell.

Rolland was spared no humiliation. As he was led in custody from the inn, Lachaume's angry wife confronted the court officials, demanding to know who would pay the prisoner's rent. Again sympathy for the beaten, bankrupt young merchant emerged. A sea captain staying at the inn promised to see the bill paid, and the landlady permitted Rolland to be led off to his cell.

The jailing of Jacques Rolland at the end of October seems to have marked the end of his struggles. He was still in the cell two weeks later when the judge accepted the Cruchons' plea for the separation of goods. He remained there, his bread and water billed to the revenues of the auction, until the last sale item, a length of ribbon, was sold late in November. He stayed a prisoner while the court clerk totalled the proceeds of the auction. Once court costs and other expenses had been deducted, there remained about half the amount of all Rolland's debts. To each creditor the clerk doled out a share of what he was owed, and only then was Jacques Rolland released and permitted to slip away from Ile Royale. He went alone. For Louisbourg and for the Cruchons *l'affaire Rolland* was over.

For the town the family battle may have enlivened a largely unrewarding season, little more. Gossiping, the people could choose sides as they wished, but few would have doubted that every family needed the firm hand of an undisputed head. Perhaps many disapproved, titillated by the exposure of a usually discreet family like the Cruchons but disdaining the way both sides had tainted themselves in public feuding. The merchant community could pass off the affair: the failure of an untested merchant of no great standing in a time of hardship and fierce competition was something to be expected. Tanguy Mervin and a few others had to write off some bad debts – those too were inevitable in the complicated, risky ventures by which they lived. Mervin would continue to visit Louisbourg periodically until he succeeded his father and settled down, wealthy and comfortable, in Saint-Malo's merchant community. Like most of the colonists, he could afford to forget the incident as the details of the scandal faded.

But the lives of the three protagonists had been shattered. Hopes and obsessions about which they would normally have been reticent had been laid open to view, and none of them would ever recover from the experience.

Thérèse Boudier's attack on Jacques Rolland had given her a costly victory – even a foolish one – for it ended all hope for her family's resurrection. To preserve her domestic authority, the widow had cut the family off from its source of income, while the scandal of the feud and the undercurrent of sympathy for Rolland had sullied the reputation she prized. From 1743 the Cruchons lapsed again into the straitened circumstances from which Marie-Louise's marriage might have saved them.

The realization that she had condemned herself to hardship and diminished her social standing should have tempered what satisfaction the widow took from her triumph, but perhaps she also felt an expiation of guilt. She had arranged the Rolland marriage for her family's sake, but in the process she had flouted written and unwritten rules intended to ensure the smooth transition from one generation to the next. She had connived at a marriage that endangered family security by failing to define who made the crucial decisions of family management. If poverty and shame resulted when she re-established proper authority, perhaps she judged her punishment appropriate: family preservation always overrode individual convenience. Thérèse Boudier remained quietly in Louisbourg until 1745, and seems to have died in France not long afterwards.

His mother-in-law may have accepted her fate, but Jacques Rolland could not have been so philosophic. In the humiliating débâcle he had lost his wife, though perhaps he had never really had her. He had also lost his career, and that was surely permanent. Though he may have found clerk's work in some other French port, his chances of rising to wealth and security had probably been damaged beyond repair in Ile Royale. A merchant's reputation was his capital, and without it Rolland would have had a hard time starting over. At heart he must have known he had lost in the attempt to cope on his own in a hard world. He had tried to get by on skill and effort, with manufactured connections and hollow independence, and it was not to be done. Other men were rising from nothing in Ile Royale, where the social and economic hierarchies seemed so much more tolerant of ambition than they did in the Old World. But it needed luck, and when his ran out the New World proved even harsher than the one he had left. Misled into seeing himself as his own master the moment he was legally free, Jacques Rolland paid a heavy price for failing to maintain that mastery in a society wary of inexperience and committed to upholding parental authority over the young. With his flight from Louisbourg near the end of the unhappy year 1743, Jacques Rolland disappears from view a beaten man.

Maturity had been the issue in question in Marie-Louise Cruchon's tumultuous marriage, and ironically the fourteen-year-old showed more of it than either of her would-be guardians. Like a spoiled child, her mother had torn apart the marriage and the family's security rather than let someone else control it. In the crisis her husband's defence against legal challenge had been self-pitying and hysterical, showing none of the maturity he had claimed by his marriage. By comparison, Marie-Louise had been demure and reticent throughout the uproar, and these qualities seem to typify the rest of her career – so far as it can be traced.

She remained in Louisbourg. When the British briefly occupied the colony she went in exile to France, but she returned to Louisbourg and the house on Rue Saint-Louis as soon as French possession was renewed. By then her mother was dead, but her younger sister Marguerite returned with her, and the two women, then still in their teens, lived there ten more years alone, quite likely in poverty and very quietly.

Louisbourg continued to refer to her as "la dame Rolland" and not "la veuve"; evidently Rolland was known to be alive through the 1750s. She left no record of her thoughts about him, but there may be a hint in Rolland's court petitions, which in reference to her strike notes of genuine affection that must have elicited a response from the child-bride. Memories of the exciting year when she stepped forward as the wife of an enthusiastic, gregarious young merchant probably stood in lively counterpoint to the bleak decades of quasi-widowhood that followed, but in misfortune she was stoic and silent. In 1758 she and her sister were once more exiled from the recaptured colony, and then Marie-Louise Cruchon disappears from view in a swirl of refugees.

Charles Renaut's Letter

harles Renaut's letter crossed the Atlantic in the spring of 1731, a single sheet of heavy parchment paper folded twice and sealed with a blob of wax. Across one side an address was inked in large and laboured characters: "to be given to Charles Renaut at the abitation of ian filepot at Scaterie on Cape Breton." It was another letter from his wife.

Writing late in April in their Norman fishing-village home, Marie-Joanne Renaut had sent off the letter as the annual migration of the fishermen was reaching its springtime peak, leaving towns like hers populated by women, children, and the old as the New World cod catch drew their men westward in thousands. From Basque seaports in southwestern France, from Brittany and the Channel ports of Normandy, flotillas of tiny fishing boats and larger merchantmen were sailing west, crammed with supplies for a season's work, crammed also with fishermen and shore labourers. Some would catch the cod of the open waters of the Grand Banks. Others would go to deserted shore-stations in Newfoundland or Labrador or on the Gaspé coast. Others sailed for Ile Royale, seeking shore space in one of the outport harbours or steering for Louisbourg, where the captain could trade his cargo while his passengers sought employment.

Charles Renaut's letter probably travelled on one of the Louisbourg-bound vessels, to come ashore amid a heap of other mail carried by the informal postal service of the transatlantic trading ships. Most of this far-flung correspondence was written by and for the businessmen of towns like Louisbourg, but whoever agreed to deliver Charles Renaut's letter would soon have headed out the Dauphin Gate in search of a fisherman's wharf and a shallop sailing up the coast to Scatary. Charles Renaut was rarely to be found in the bustling town. The fisherman's domain lay beyond the walls of Louisbourg.

Raised in a fisherman's town, Charles Renaut had found his career more by inheritance than by choice. The cod fishery that occupied his village was France's great economic interest in North America, more valuable than the fur trade, source of an important foodstuff, great employer of ships and men. It gave the nation an esteemed product to export and consume at home, and every naval strategist stressed its contribution to the training of seamen. In fishing ports like the one that raised Charles Renaut, the cod trade was the vital livelihood that sustained a way of life. For two hundred years – since time immemorial, Renaut would have said – his Norman forefathers had been sailing to the harbours and headlands of North American shores they lumped together as Terre-Neuve, the New World. The elders of the community could boast of forty or fifty voyages to Terre-Neuve, six to eight months of each year devoted to the catching and shipping of precious cod. Tradition was strong: addressing her letter in 1731, Renaut's wife disdained "Ile Royale" in favour of the centuries-old "Cap Breton," and she might easily have added "Terre-Neuve" as well.

A fisherman by his ancestry and heir to the tradition of his people, Charles Renaut took up his community's seagoing vocation in his teens. Though he probably began in menial shore jobs, Renaut soon left these to inlanders. He graduated to small-boat fishing, the heart of the industry, where, by the mid-1720s, prowess proven in several seasons of work gave him a place among the veterans.

Thus established, Charles Renaut married and began a family – one he would leave behind to go with the fishing fleet each spring. Some years he sailed as early as February, for to be first on the fishing grounds was both a professional triumph and a commercial advantage. The fishing grounds kept him until September, and then the transatlantic migration began to reverse itself, to carry the summer's catch to market and take the migrant fishermen back to their families. Spring to fall at work in the New World, fall to spring at home in the old – like generations before him, Renaut was settling into the rhythms of the migratory fisherman, enduring half a year of privation to earn half a year in the security of his ancestral home.

In the fall of 1730 Renaut broke the pattern. Instead of sailing home after a summer in Ile Royale, he stayed on to take winter work. In the coldest months of the year, the fishermen who were settled in the colony extended their catches and revenues by sending boats out from November through January, pausing only when the ice drifting down from the north drove them ashore. One of those committed to this harsh winter fishery was Jean Phelipeaux, settler and fishery proprietor at the island outpost called Scatary, a few leagues east of Louisbourg. Catches had been good in the summer of 1730, and Phelipeaux wanted workers to expand his winter campaign. That fall he persuaded Charles Renaut and his brother Mathurin to winter in Ile Royale and work the second season with him. When the letter from France reached Jean Phelipeaux's fishing station at Scatary in the spring of 1731, the Renaut brothers' families had not seen them for a full year.

II

Close by the easternmost tip of Ile Royale the triangular island of Scatary lies cruelly exposed to the wild Atlantic, but the ecology that seemed so unwelcoming to human habitation drew schools of cod to the surrounding waters. Drawn in their turn by this rich resource, Renaut's forebears had noted the island's wood, fresh water, and snug harbours, and it was one of the first places settled when the colony took root. Seen from a shallop pitching in the Atlantic rollers, Scatary harbour in 1731 was little more than a series of wharves projecting from the rocky shore of a sheltering cove, with clusters of sheds and houses behind each wharf and the spruce woods closing the rear. Scatary existed only for the fishing, and only a mission priest and a surgeon lived there by other trades. The wives and daughters of a dozen proprietors were the community's only women. Migrant workers like the Renauts made up most of the population of about two hundred and fifty, and sea links to Louisbourg provided most of their scant needs in exchange for fish. At Scatary Renaut and his fellows lived the plain life of hired fishermen through weeks and months dominated by the demands of their work.

For all the brevity of the fishing seasons, fishing businesses needed large catches to ensure their profits. The fishermen worked every day they could, and the church even spared them the obligation of observing holy days in the summer season. Every morning that weather permitted, in fog or rain or just in morning chill, Charles Renaut sailed from Phelipeaux's wharf with two companions. Their craft was an open boat called a shallop, a broad-beamed vessel perhaps thirty feet long and equipped with sails and oars. Before the dawn departure, someone had gone out to tend bait nets near the harbour. Now the shallop's bait barrels were packed with fresh herring or mackerel. Stashed near by were long, multi-hooked lines, a heap of weights, and a grapnel. A chart and compass, spare clothing, bread, a keg of spruce beer or watered wine – all the sundry supplies of a day's work – were stowed beneath the bows.

Each morning Renaut's shallop might run several miles under sail to a favoured fishing ground, and every trip tested the seamanship, skill, and endurance of the three-man crew. A misjudgment of weather or a trivial piloting error could be a death sentence to the men who faced the ocean in these heavy-laden open boats, so the shallopmaster needed sailing ability as well as the knack of finding where the cod would swarm. A crew reputed for finding cod would rarely be left alone on the sea, for Scatary outfitted dozens of shallops ready to follow the lead of a successful fisherman.

Come safely to their chosen spot, their shallop anchored or drifting over their prey in twenty fathoms or less, Renaut and his fellows baited and dropped as many multi-hooked lines as they could tend. If their choice of site was good, they would be busy all day, hauling in the heavy lines, dropping the fish into compartments in the floor of the shallop, then baiting and casting out their lines once more. The long day of labour and risk was an unremitting test of the boatmen's endurance. They might pause to eat or drink, to hail their fellows or a passing ship, or even to hunt seals and seabirds, but pay as well as pride held them to their work, for hired fishermen were paid by what they caught.

The fisherman's work was gruelling even when warm sunshine lit an almost gentle ocean. More often weather exacted a further test of their hardiness, as squall lines and fast-moving fogs swept down upon the shallops. Even in high summer the intersection of warm land and cool ocean brought winds and damp fogs to chill them. The array of capes, caps, and gloves that every boat carried could never completely shelter the fishermen. In winter storm, frigid salt spray and ice-rimed gear were chronic hardships. It was a harsh career and a risky one. Each year storms and ice claimed a few shallops; each year collisions and accidents exacted their toll of lives and vessels.

If all went well, mid-afternoon of the fishing day saw Renaut and his crew hauling in their lines to hoist sail and find their way back to Scatary, their shallop now laden down with several hundredweight of fish. At Jean Phelipeaux's wharf, a rustic structure of poles, planks, and heavy wharfing spikes, Renaut helped pitch his catch to the shore crews, who began to prepare the fresh fish for preservation. Catching the cod was only half the job; now a careful curing would ready it for transport and marketing.

The shoreworkers split, cleaned, and boned each newly landed fish, tossing livers to the oil press and dropping wastes between the wharf planks into the tide. The fresh, wet sides of fish went promptly into an immersion of salt or brine until they were salt-caked, and then they were carried from the wharf to the drying "flakes" behind.

There was an art to drying cod, slowly transforming perishable fillets of fresh fish into firm, dry slabs perfectly preserved for long storage and international export. Heat was not the vital agent here – too much sunshine would cook the outer layer of the drying fish, breaking down its proteins and spoiling its appearance. Instead, salt and the open air slowly drew the moisture out of the fish. Every boat from France brought a salt cargo from the tidal flats around La Rochelle, and a skilled shore crew would use just enough to draw out the fish's water content in the open air. To assist this work, the fishing property that stretched back from Phelipeaux's wharf and cleaning sheds was a broad expanse of "flakes," table-like platforms of raised branches and boughs where the slabs of fish dried for a month while free circulation of air produced a steady and even cure.

As Renaut and the boatmen continued their daily voyages to add to the supply of cod, the shore crews tended the drying catch, keeping pilferers and animals away, turning the exposed sides regularly, covering the flakes against rain, and monitoring the progress of the cure. All awaited the time when clients and creditors would come to haggle over the quality and price of the finished product. Premium cod, perfectly dried, would be rushed away to take top prices from choosy European buyers. Carefully assessed by experienced traders, the undersized, sunburnt, or oversalted fish would be marked down, cutting the income of both the proprietor and his men. Badly spoiled fish might only be fit for the West Indian market, where plantation slaves lacked the luxury of choice and masters appreciated a bargain.

The labour of men like Charles Renaut in the catching, curing, and selling of cod was the engine that drove the economy of Ile Royale. In Renaut's years there, his boat was only one among four hundred shallops gathering in the cod that teemed over the inshore banks, and the ports of Ile Royale also fitted out sixty or seventy ocean-going schooners to pursue the fish to banks as distant as Saint-Pierre and Sable Island. Several thousand fishermen and shoreworkers worked at the catch. Toward the end of summer there might be 150,000 hundredweights of dry cod ready for shipment along with 1,600 barrels of valuable cod-liver oil – enough to pay the wages of thousands of men, enough to meet all the debts incurred for mountains of supplies, enough to fill the holds of all the trading vessels crowding Louisbourg's broad harbour.

It was not just fishermen who cared about the catches of the little fishing ports up and down the coast of Ile Royale. Almost all the trades of Louisbourg and its colony fasted or grew fat according to the progress of the fishing industry. Cod paid for the goods that occupied merchants and shopkeepers and their clerks and employees. It hired the transport that employed boatmen and builders. It drew the trading vessels of distant seaports, and the ships made work for the sailors and warehousemen and brokers whose wages supported the inns, taverns, and shops of Louisbourg. Ultimately it was cod that generated the colonial revenues that justified the King's growing investment in the rising fortifications of Louisbourg. Though they might touch a perfumed handkerchief to their noses as the breeze carried the reek of the fishing stations across the town, even the most refined of Louisbourg's elite could not be too disdainful of the trade that sustained their community.

Indeed, Charles Renaut's humble product could claim global influence. He would return to Normandy with his pay, but his catch might be sold in the Caribbean, around the Mediterranean, or almost anywhere in northern Europe. Though Ile Royale's production was only part of France's cod catches, which competed in international markets against abundant British and American supplies of the same commodity, the little colony's cod still formed a significant portion of the world's cod supply, in turn an important contribution to the food resources of a burgeoning European population. A global economy that the nations often found worth warring over, the cod trade and the wealth it produced had fired the imagination of New World explorers, colony-builders, and naval theorists. It still depended on the daily labour of obscure fishermen like Charles Renaut.

Like nearly everyone in Ile Royale, Charles Renaut shouldered a working day that filled most of his waking hours. After spending the day in his shallop and part of the evening helping to clean the catch, he might still have boat-caulking or net-making duties to attend to. Even when such chores were not pressing, a man there only for the work lived austerely, his horizons circumscribed by Jean Phelipeaux's fishing station. Renaut lived close by the worksite, rarely escaping the sound and smell of the fishermen's labour. He slung a straw-filled *pail-lasse* and stowed a padlocked sea-chest in a bunkhouse provided by his employer, a simple structure adjacent to the work-sheds and flakes and perhaps roofed only with sailcloth.

Like most migrant workers, Renaut had brought few possessions with him beyond his changes of clothing. Besides his wearing apparel, Renaut possessed only a comb, some religious medallions, and a port-folio of papers and letters. Some of his fellows owned a knife or a gun, a sewing kit or some tools, but few owned more than would stow easily in a small trunk. Some must have been athletic, some able to play a flute or a fiddle, but on the whole the migrants left their valuables in France and carried only the most meagre assortment of essentials to their temporary homes on the fishing stations. There for the work, working most of the day, the hired man needed little for non-working hours.

Still, the fishermen did not work without cease. Merchant Bertrand Imbert of Louisbourg tells of walking out of the town to inspect a stock of cod in the middle of an August afternoon. The summer work should have been at its peak, yet after closing his deal, Imbert joined several unhurried fishermen for a drink at their quarters. Employers could tolerate occasional interruptions of this sort, for they were merchants to their men. Most employers sold liquor and other merchandise to their fishermen, deducting the price of all they sold from the employee's wages. In seasons when catches were small and profits smaller, some proprietors earned more from rum sales than from their fish. There were lurid tales of hired men tempted to drink away their earnings at their employers' gain, and the owners countered with diatribes against taverns that stole their workers' time and money. Renaut was more careful or abstemious than that, but eating and drinking were probably the major diversions with which he passed his scarce hours of leisure.

The hired men of the fishing industry lived communally, sharing quarters and possessions as they shared the risks and hardships of their profession. Together they ate the evening meal, either preparing their own bread, fish, and dried vegetables at the bunkhouse or being served by the employer's wife and servant in the big kitchen. After their meal, the hired men of a fishing station were likely to remain together, sociably drinking away what time remained before an early curfew. Their drink was often *sapinette*, brewed from an infusion of spruce boughs in water, molasses, and a little brandy. Served with the rations, spruce beer was potable a day after brewing, and its alcoholic content must have been negligible. Needing stronger drink, the men could mortgage their earnings to buy rum, brandy, or wine, sometimes mixing their liquor with *sapinette* in a hot beverage they called *ponche*.

Music and dance, contests and gambling could add to the group's entertainment, but simple talk was probably the major diversion of hard-labouring men completing long days of work. In the isolation of the worksite, common origins and outlooks sustained the bonds between the workers. There was nothing unusual in the partnership of brothers like Charles and Mathurin Renaut, and since Jean Phelipeaux's roots were Norman like theirs, many of his employees had probably travelled out together from the brothers' homeland. Renaut likely had friends and cousins near by, and such comradeship helped knit the fishing stations together.

In the fishermen's sociable conversation, the difficulties and embarrassments of employers would have been a common topic. Many of the small proprietors of Ile Royale had raised themselves from the status of hired hands; their successes and failures directly affected the men they employed. One year fishermen would have talked of Georges Desroches, who at twenty-eight had risen to master of a fishing business by an expedient marriage to his employer, a twice-widowed woman of sixty-nine. If it were the cynical marriage it seemed to be, it proved not much of a bargain for Desroches, for his aged wife lived another twenty years. Another year the butt of jokes would have been Henri Nadeau *dit* Lachapelle. Illiterate, indebted, and ambitious beyond his means, Nadeau had rented his small fishing station to a visitor while he worked to clear a second property that would bring additional revenue. Unfortunately his new wharves, flakes, and sheds were not ready in time, and without revenue poor Nadeau was faced with losing both his assets. A court hearing that permitted him to cancel the lease of his first property cruelly exposed his managerial shortcomings; the tavern talk of hired fishermen would have been no less cruel.

Stories of hired men circulated just as widely. There was Nicolas Equard of Petit-de-Grat, a hired fisherman of twelve years' experience, now fighting his employer over money and being portrayed as a master of the art of evading his work. If the employer could be believed, Equard had perfected techniques for neglecting his duty: he would abandon his lines to go hunting, steal wine from the station stores, lose boats and equipment by his recklessness, and carry on a regular private commerce on his employer's time. Or there was the sad career of Claude Amiot, who had drifted out to Ile Royale mostly from a desire to see other countries. His urge to travel was not matched by a commitment to work, and Amiot floated from one job to another, never establishing expertise in any of the specialized skills of the fishing industry. Slowly he became one of the marginal men doing odd jobs about the fishing stations, and after eight years he was no more than a brewery boy preparing the spruce beer at a large fishing station at Fourché. Finally he turned a worksite fight into an axe-wielding attempt at murder. For that Amiot went back to France with a life sentence in the galleys, leaving behind only a brief notoriety among the fishermen and a cursory notation in the court registers.

More encouraging to a fisherman's hopes was the good fortune of Basque fisherman Pierre Damestoye. The girl Damestoye had married in France was related to a prosperous Louisbourg merchant, and one year the hired fisherman arrived in Louisbourg to discover that the bachelor uncle had died, leaving Damestoye's wife most of his estate. On his wife's behalf Damestoye accepted a generous settlement from the late merchant's partners. When he returned to the fishing shore, it was as a proprietor rather than as a hired man.

Rivalries with other fishing crews helped bring the men in Phelipeaux's crew together, with each group competing for the best stocks of cod and the consequent rewards in pay and prestige. Among single, transient, hard-drinking labourers such rivalries easily grew intense. At Louisbourg the guard occasionally turned out to quell struggling groups of fishermen, but in the outports there were only the proprietors' authority and the men's group loyalties to keep the peace. At Scatary many of the fishermen seem to have been Normans. Kinship ties and regional loyalties may have helped to build and preserve a measure of cohesion, and this ethnic loyalty was easily reinforced by opposition to outsiders. Normans like Charles Renaut could define themselves against other populations of migrant fishermen – not just the distant British but the Gaelic-speaking Bretons at Ile Royale, and particularly the Basques.

The Basques were unique, a people whose homeland straddled the French–Spanish border yet who were neither French nor Spanish, with a language and ethnic heritage absolutely distinct from both. Separate by choice as well as ancestry, their aloofness basic to their cultural survival, the stocky, dark-complexioned Basques were egalitarian, devout, and tough. Toughness was demanded by their homeland on the mountainous Pyrenean slope, and the virtues called *indarra* and *sendoa* were touchstones among Basque values. *Indarra* meant the power, strength, and physical good health that the Basques loved to display in games of force and endurance. *Sendoa* was its spiritual equivalent, expressed in strength of character, stoicism, and dedication. Forced by their rugged homeland to be wanderers, the Basques practised these virtues wherever they migrated, and they valued their far-flung successes as proof of both physical prowess and strength of character.

Indarra and *sendoa* were fundamental to the Basques' seagoing exploits. They had taken to the western ocean very early, and many Basques were convinced that their sailors had taught Columbus about the existence of the New World. Basques certainly helped pioneer the cod fishery of Terre-Neuve, and no one questioned their leadership in ocean whaling. As proof of their primacy they could point to place-name evidence from Port-au-Choix in Newfoundland to Menadou in Ile Royale, and they considered all others latecomers to the fisheries. Even the name Cape Breton had been derived from a Basque coastal town and not from any tribute to Breton explorers.

Unable to turn to a fertile hinterland as their Norman and Breton competitors could, the Basques were wholeheartedly committed to the sea. Bayonne, Saint-Jean-de-Luz, and other Basque ports renowned for the skill of their pilots and sailors sent fleets of fishing boats to Ile Royale every spring, and Basques manned the shallops in every weather and season for Basque and non-Basque employers.

Emigrants for generations, the Basques gave many settlers to Ile Royale. Jean-Peritz Harneder, of a Basque family that had hosted Louis XIV when the King went to Saint-Jean-de-Luz to marry the Infanta of Spain, proudly referred to forty years of New World voyaging before he began a settlement in Ile Royale. Many of his younger compatriots, Daccarrettes, Detcheverrys, and Hiriarts, became successful colonists, assimilating into the French population as they submerged their accents, changed Miguel to Michel and Ioannis to Jean, and married among French colonist families. But more of the Basques kept apart. Concentrated on Louisbourg's north shore and in the outports, where they had their own chaplains and did business among themselves, many settled or migrant Basques maintained their distance. Even if he admired their toughness and skill, Charles Renaut would not have been very close to his Basque fellow labourers, most of whom spoke only their own impenetrable language.

III

Though Ile Royale generally kept its face turned to the sea, the thick spruce forests closing in behind the fishing stations made no impenetrable barrier to men like Renaut, who would occasionally venture through them to tap the inland resources of Ile Royale. During the winter, as the fishing activity slowed and snowshoes made the woods accessible, Charles Renaut probably had opportunities to put down his fishing lines and join the stream of colonists heading into the interior.

Woodcutting might have occupied a gang of Jean Phelipeaux's men if a seasonal dearth of fish or a spell of rough weather kept the shallops ashore. Each winter a supply of firewood had to be cut and sledged to the shore or riverbank, mostly for the fishing station's own needs, but perhaps also for sale to Louisbourg's townspeople. As a by-product of the cutting, spruce boughs could be gathered for the *sapinette*. Or Renaut might have occupied himself cutting timber for boatbuilding. Little shallops lasted only three or four seasons under the hard usage of the fishing industry; proprietors always needed to have a few under construction, and off-season fishermen regularly tried their hand at ship carpentry. Renaut's co-workers might have attempted larger craft, for islanders like Phelipeaux usually owned at least one schooner, often built over the winter in a makeshift shipyard in a sheltered cove or inlet.

Renaut might also have penetrated inland to hunt. The coast swarmed with seabirds, seals, and other prey, but in the interior foxes and small furbearers could be trapped for their pelts, and there were partridges and rabbits for the stewpot. The partridges were so much in demand that hunting seasons had to be imposed throughout the island. No such protection seemed necessary for the easily killed passenger pigeons – their numbers were so great as to blacken the sky as they passed overhead in vast flocks. In ice-covered ponds and shallows eels were speared and fish taken with hook and line. Both for the thrill of the chase and the sake of the stewpot, Renaut and others might have borrowed muskets and dogs from their masters and gone in search of deer or even bear.

Ranging into the interior, a transient like Renaut glimpsed more of the colony that employed him. Though none of Ile Royale's towns and settlements lay inland, the woods were rarely deserted. A network of roads provided interior communications for journeys by foot or by wagon. Cattle and horses grazed in open range much of the year, and many settled colonists went seasonally to the forests to cut wood, to hunt, and to fish. It was subsistence as well as sport – garrison soldiers sometimes received months of leave to hunt or cut firewood. A few colonists even farmed. Had Renaut's tramping taken him to the valley of the Miré, a fertile crescent curving into the island's interior, he would have found pastureland and farmers struggling to raise grain and livestock. But most of the people Renaut met if he went to the woods were like himself: men of the shoreline making brief forays inland. Anyone more committed to the land and its resources was alien and slightly suspect in a community that lived by the wealth of the surrounding ocean.

Among those who had chosen the woods over the shore were renegades from the industry that employed Charles Renaut. Profoundly committed to stern standards of authority, Ile Royale offered neither redress nor sympathy to employees at odds with their masters. Since disobedience was an offence against hierarchy – and so against society – employers held almost every advantage in disputes against individual fishermen. The skilled workers like Charles Renaut might escape from harsh masters merely by waiting a few months: one fisherman was soundly whipped for fighting with his employer, but another had the sense to await the end of his contract before striking his hated master, and he escaped lightly. Less fortunate were the unskilled, who were frequently obliged to commit themselves to three years of servitude in exchange for passage from France, room and board, and a token wage. Called *engagés*, or "thirty-six-months men," these workers had no opportunity to recover their freedom if they regretted their bargain, and they had little protection against a brutal employer or one who neglected his side of the contract. Desertion was a disgruntled *engagé*'s only escape.

Some bold deserters from the fishing stations would steal a shallop and flee toward the west coast of Newfoundland, where a colony of outsiders had established itself beyond the reach of French law. Other rebellious employees simply took to the woods.

Those to whom the woods offered refuge were known simply as the vagabonds. Most had been fishermen at some time in their careers, though not all had run afoul of the law before leaving that work. Voracious for labour, skilled or unskilled, the fishing industry recruited any man expressing a willingness to work, and many footloose young men were tempted to join the steadier professionals in the migration to the New World. If pressed, they would say they came with a desire to see the world, to earn a better living, to seek adventure, but the hard, routine labour of the fishing stations could not always oblige them.

In 1737 Jean Galon was one who had learned how little adventure the world offered men with neither talent nor protectors. The son of a Norman stonemason, Galon claimed no profession. He had been offered passage to Louisbourg in his teens, and in over two decades he had never gone home. After working off his three years of servitude, Galon hired out as a salter for one fisherman or another, but he grew to prefer the quiet seasons when hunting and odd jobs replaced the drudgery of tending the cod. Gradually he gave up on the fishing industry, subsisting with like-minded friends on whatever work came their way – hunting, haymaking, piecework labouring. Slowly they slipped out of organized society altogether. By 1736 Galon and his companions lived more or less permanently in a shack in the woods. Inevitably they fell into conflict with a hardworking community naturally suspicious of their apparently idle ways. When they ran short of food during the winter and began helping themselves to the sheep and cattle pastured in the natural prairies, hostilities became overt. Galon and his fellow vagabonds were soon arrested, convicted of cattle theft, and shipped out for punishment; but as they ceased to trouble society, some other disgruntled fishermen probably drifted away from the shores to take their place.

The other, more tolerated aliens of the interior woodlands were the nomadic Micmac bands. It is not very likely that Charles Renaut encountered these people during his ventures into the interior, but had he done, the meeting would not have put his scalp at risk, for the Indian nations of Atlantic Canada were old allies of the French. Christianized by French missionaries, the Micmacs had united with the French to resist the expansion of New England's settlements. In war they made common cause; in peace they lived separately, meeting for trade and diplomacy but rarely transgressing on each other's domains. Missionary influence on the tribes was strong, but the priests had to earn their authority. Father Gaulin so totally adopted the rough nomadic life of the Indians that his fellow Frenchmen distrusted him, and Abbé Mailliard would eventually change his fealty from France to Britain rather than leave the Micmac people.

On the whole, distance had helped to preserve the friendship of the Micmacs and the French over several centuries of contacts between them. Transient or settled, Ile Royale's colonists lived in European towns, eating imported food and wearing imported clothing, their careers and attitudes shaped by international exchanges and global military priorities. The Micmacs, for their part, still lived in their traditional houses, preferring their own dress and diet. They resisted French pressure to have them settle in permanent towns on Ile Royale. Instead, the nomads ranged from the island to the mainland and back, ignoring imperial boundaries to follow the cycles of the game, the fish, and the wild crops, feasting when the harvest was good, accepting deprivation when it was not. Within Catholic rituals they preserved traditional ceremonies, and they retained many cultural values alien to the newcomers. Like all the tribes of the eastern woodlands, the Micmacs had been shaped by the austere life of a hunting and gathering people – the accumulation of material possessions was not a Micmac priority. Though they were canny bargainers when they sought muskets, metals, and woollens from the French, the woodland nomads must have found the Europeans' striving for security behind the walls of Louisbourg barely comprehensible.

Hunting skill was greatly esteemed by the Micmac. Each year their hunting parties sought the moose, deer, and bear of Ile Royale's rugged northern peninsula, and a trade in skins was one of the few enticements that brought Micmac bands to the coastal towns of the French. Despite his occasional hunting forays, and the Micmacs' skills in small-boat sailing, Charles Renaut and the natives of Ile Royale were most likely to meet when both the fishermen and the Indians were visiting Louisbourg to trade.

For Renaut as for most of his contemporaries, the presence of Indians was largely an exotic tale he could take back to amaze his children in Normandy. The land was not really his element, and his usual perspective on Ile Royale was the view from the fishing boat that demanded most of his attention. Struggling with his fishing lines or making sail in his little vessel, he glanced up to see only a hazardous rocky shore, a stretch of wind-cleared moor, and the forested hills. By contrast, his sense of the ocean around and under him was three-dimensional: he knew the depths of water off every headland, the bottom samples that identified each fishing bank, and the warmer or colder currents that guided him to the cod. Tossing in the ocean rollers he was in his element – a ceaselessly hazardous one, but more real to him than the forest frontier around his outport mooring.

IV

The winter of 1730 may have marked the first time Charles Renaut and his brother stayed a full year in Ile Royale, but already the colony was familiar territory to them. In earlier seasons they had worked at several fishing outports up and down the coast. They would have sailed occasionally to Louisbourg and ranged inland to cut wood or to hunt. In the fishing industry they were veterans, and throughout the colony they had a network of friends, co-workers, and potential employers. Transient though they were, little in the colony was strange to them, and probably much was appealing. Was their decision to winter at Scatary a prelude to bringing out their families, making a permanent commitment to the New World?

The incentive for fishermen to settle was what had given outports like Scatary their small permanent populations, and Jean Phelipeaux offered the brothers a close-at-hand example of a man who had seized the opportunity. The Renauts' employer was a man of obscure background and limited means, who shared his crews' hard work, but where the Renauts were employees, labouring for a fixed and small share of their catch, Jean Phelipeaux was an independent entrepreneur with property, equipment, and employees at his service. Scatary offered few amenities to anyone, but Phelipeaux had at least a permanent house there, with his wife and family and a servant, and the pride of a householder and master of men. He knew that the small proprietors bore the greatest share of the risks of the fishing industry, but he could also look around and see men who had risen from fishing stations like his to wealth and prestige in Ile Royale.

Michel Daccarrette for instance. Daccarrette and his brothers had begun as fishermen, travelling annually to Terre-Neuve with the fleets of migrant Basques. They began to prosper soon after they settled in the New World, and their business expanded mightily once they made Ile Royale their home. Soon Daccarrette fishing stations at the outports of Baleine, Fourché, Saint-Esprit, and Niganiche were employing as many as 170 fishermen every summer. Few of their employees earned more than 300 *livres* a season, but the Daccarrettes' annual haul of cod was worth at least 100,000 *livres*. Small profit margins sufficed to make the brothers rich.

Michel, the youngest brother and apparently the best educated, led the firm from fishing into trade. Just forty in 1730, Daccarrette commanded a commercial empire: fishing properties, trading ships, and commercial warehouses raised the name of Daccarrette to eminence. Despite his humble origins and alien mother tongue, Daccarrette was becoming a power in the colony. His Louisbourg house was tended by servants and slaves; his daughters could look ahead to ennobling marriages, his sons to dignified mercantile careers far from the smell of drying fish.

Jean Phelipeaux may not have aspired to match the Daccarrette fortune, but he could read and write, which gave him an advantage over some proprietors, and in 1730 his catches were cause for optimism. The fundamental support for his aspirations was the property he owned. In France and Canada the law of *nulle terre sans seigneur*, no land without its lord, still reigned supreme, but the Crown preferred to grant freehold tenure in its fishing colonies, whether the property in question was a Louisbourg town lot, a Scatary fishing station, or an inland woodlot. Owners had only to clear and put to use their newly granted land to gain permanent title. With property in hand, a man like Phelipeaux acquired collateral for the supplies he borrowed each fishing season, and success beckoned so long as his crews produced more fish than he owed to his creditors – among whom merchant-fishermen like Michel Daccarrette would have been prominent. In 1730 bountiful catches were beginning to repay Jean Phelipeaux's gamble on settlement.

By comparison, the migratory life offered no springboard to a hired fisherman, who would take home only some small savings. And even a labourer should have been able to discern a slow decline in the migratory fishery that had supported Charles Renaut's people for generations. In his grandfather's day, scarcely anyone had wintered in Terre-Neuve, but the steady increase in colonial settlements from New England to Newfoundland proclaimed the advantages held by resident fishermen. Closer to their work, the permanent residents could fish longer and concentrate on fishing, leaving the annual cross-ings of the Atlantic to merchant ships specialized for trade. The rise of men like Daccarrette and Phelipeaux was the personal side of a trend that would one day reduce the westward flood of migrant fishermen to a trickle. Already resident proprietors like Phelipeaux, with their crews of migrant workers, took nearly three-quarters of the total catch around their island. Each time some hardship afflicted the industry, the transients suffered a little more than the colonists and the balance shifted further. The future seemed to lie in the colonies, where a fisherman of experience and standing could quickly acquire title to land, then outfit his own fishing station and pursue the opportunities of proprietorship.

But the rise of the resident fishery was a trend for the centuries; even the prospect of personal advancement need not have been a powerful lure for Charles Renaut. Jean Phelipeaux might have prop-erty, authority, and hopes of wealth to show for his decision to settle on the stormy shore of Scatary Island, but his title to land would mean little if the cod harvest failed for a few seasons, or if a raiding privateer landed to loot and burn. There were as many risks as opportunities in the New World.

Despite all incentives, the Renauts had ties to hold them back from settlement. Their ancestry, running through generations of migrant fishermen, had shaped men who served their clan and community at least as diligently as they pursued personal fortune. More than a livelihood, not just the economic support of the towns devoted to it, the migratory fishery went deep into the folkways of a traditional society, shaping men like Charles Renaut to accept long exiles and slim prospects of advancement. In exchange, Normandy assured them an established place in a reassuringly changeless home society, for home bonds remained strong in a community that had always sent its men to sea. Renaut travelled and worked with brothers and cousins and friends from his own community, and went home with them to Normandy to rejoin wives and families bound in a seamless web of neighbours and kin. When emigration meant the snapping of such ties and traditions, community seemed more important than some dubious chance at fortune. The raw newness of an outport fishing village in Ile Royale seemed little compensation for losing the settled stability of his Normandy home. Even when he agreed to winter in Ile Royale in 1730, Charles Renaut seems to have declined the chance to settle there, and in the spring of 1731 his wife was writing in expectation of seeing him back home soon.

Had he been able to see a decade or two ahead, Charles Renaut would have seen much to sustain his conservatism. Whatever the long trends, the 1730s and 1740s would be hard years for the owners of Ile Royale fishing stations. Already, when the fish catches were large, employers like Jean Phelipeaux were finding it hard to recruit enough labourers, and the workers used the shortage of men to extract a better share of the catch and better conditions. Phelipeaux could not push his prices up to meet the rising wage bill, for Europe would do without Ile Royale's cod if the price should creep too high. Though settled proprietors were beginning to bully the authorities to help them with wage restrictions, that would hardly ease the shortage of workers. The diminishing gap between costs and revenues was starting to pinch many small proprietors.

Power had already shifted toward the men who had come in early, men like Daccarrette who now dealt in supplies and transport as well as fish. Indebted to these men every season, Phelipeaux had to keep up his cod production or risk the loss of his property and his business; but soon even the cod would cease to oblige him. Abundant as it was, the cod resource was not limitless. Late in the 1730s the shallopmen's relentless attack on local fish populations would cross an invisible boundary between harvesting and overfishing. Catches would plunge. Soon afterwards war between Britain and France would bring privateers and naval vessels to harry the fishermen of the coast. By the 1740s the survival of his business and then even his physical survival were going to preoccupy Jean Phelipeaux. There would be no gentle rise to wealth and prominence. If he were prospering in 1730, still his future was not one to entice men to join him in the gamble of proprietorship.

Charles Renaut could not see into the future, of course, and he would not be there to experience it. But he had made his choices, and through the winter of 1730 he simply did his job. Day by day, out in the boat, around the fishing station, off in the woods, he tolerated the extended hardships and limited pleasures of a transient workman on an Ile Royale fishing station, sustained by the home ties so well expressed in the occasional letters arriving from his wife.

V

The badly spelled, awkwardly phrased, and none the less moving letter that Marie-Joanne Renaut sent her long-absent husband in the spring of 1731 represented a small triumph of literacy. Renaut and his wife made unlikely correspondents, for even in prosperous Normandy literacy remained largely the preserve of the church and the leisured aristocracy. Three-quarters of the people of France were illiterate, and many in authority were content to have it so. Why educate one's servants beyond their needs? Since Charles Renaut's training in seamanship had probably required no book-learning, there was nothing in his vocation to demand that he, let alone his wife, be able to read.

Yet their literacy is perhaps symptomatic of the way their community had shaped itself to an economy built upon the distant fishing grounds of Terre-Neuve. A village that sent most of its men away for half the year or more had either to become a matriarchal niche in a powerfully patriarchal society or else it had to find a way for its men to retain some contact with their homes and families. Undoubtedly the women had shouldered some traditionally male responsibilities, but the effort to unite far-flung families had given the fishing towns a special motive for valuing and encouraging literacy. Though most of his fellows seem to have been illiterate, Charles Renaut was not the only hired man to send and receive occasional letters.

That such letters actually reached Charles Renaut in his Scatary Island isolation makes his communication with his wife a double triumph, a victory over distance as well as ignorance. Floods of mail reached Louisbourg each year, but little of it was personal correspondence. The mail was dominated by official dispatches, and even more by commercial exchanges: stacks of bills and credit notes passing between businessmen, orders from merchants to their distant agents, price news, market reports, and political summaries to support a global commerce. An individual might write to order goods, to manage a legacy, or to seek royal preferment, but even the literate seem to have cut home ties and let family contacts slip once they settled in the New World. Renaut's correspondence went against the colonial grain. It was proof of the migrant's bond to home and to family. Among the meagre possessions stowed in his sea-chest, the key to Charles Renaut's loyalties was the portfolio stuffed with letters.

Like any family letter, Marie-Joanne Renaut's began with wishes of health. "I let pass no occasion to inquire about your health which I pray God with all my heart is perfect as mine is good, thank God, and also that of our little girl who is doing well and who sends you her best compliments. She has been walking since two months after you left." Then the reference to the months that had passed led to an expression of need and longing. "All I ask is that you come home this year, for such a long absence is truly wearisome to me. Nothing has gone along well since you have been out." The importance of the husband's administering hand to set the family affairs aright was still acknowledged, even if he did absent himself for much of the year.

The traveller's wife cast around for news of home. Finding little, she fell back on a report of the weather. Four months of drought and cold winds were threatening ruin that spring, she wrote, and prayerful processions were being held daily. Still, the family apple orchard was looking very well. Next Marie-Joanne Renaut turned to family news, running through the activities of long chains of cousins and in-laws from the neighbourhood. Her brother Jacques would soon be coming to Ile Royale. A family inheritance had recently been divided; the Renauts now shared ownership of a house and land. A cousin and two aunts held the rest of the estate. No mere financial windfall, such a legacy underpinned the network of family ties that bound Renaut to his home. Temporary custodians of the wealth of their lineage, the Renauts would one day in their turn bequeath these holdings to new generations of cousins, sons, and in-laws.

Marie-Joanne summarized other letters she had sent, ones that might have gone astray. By Monsieur de la Vigne's ship she was sending her husband some more clothes – boots, two leather aprons, and a pair of shoes. By Captain Voisin's ship she had sent a twelve-pound pot of butter, a cheese, and some herbs. Such rations were items the migrant men took along in their sea-chests in the spring voyage to the fishing grounds. Since Renaut's stay had been extended, his wife sent these foods to revive his rations after a winter of dried vegetables and fish. Another tribute to the reliability of the transatlantic post, the dispatch of these parcels also underlined the couple's interdependence across the ocean.

Having covered all the family correspondent's eternal topics – health, the weather, family news, and the contents of previous letters – Marie-Joanne Renaut found herself without more to add, and she closed her letter with a brief prayer for her distant husband's good health. "I wish you perfect health and I am always, dear husband, your affectionate spouse, Marie-Joanne."

Concern for her husband's health was an expression of well-grounded fear as well as affection. Charles Renaut practised a dangerous trade: his wife need only look around her town to count the fishing industry's widows and disabled men. A dismembering injury, a bout of arthritis, or some debilitating disease brought on by his arduous work might wreck Charles Renaut's ability to work and earn a living. Pneumonia or smallpox or any of a dozen ill-understood diseases might strike him down in his exile. Above all he might succumb at any time to the numberless perils of the sea.

By the end of an unlucky fishing season, Ile Royale could have lost fifty or sixty fishermen in great storms, in sudden accidents, in unexplained disappearances. Each day that Renaut took a shallop out of Scatary harbour, he risked sudden squalls that could come down to swamp his small and laden boat. On the fishing grounds he kept a wary eye open for fast-moving merchant ships. More than one of his fellows had been run down in the heavy traffic at the approaches to Louisbourg. Whenever a fog came down upon the boats, he redoubled his vigilance and checked his position against signal bells and shots, for in fog a piloting error could doom a crew to death by exposure before they found the land. When he crept back to harbour, no matter what the weather, he was duly cautious of the hazards ringing every small and surf-wracked anchorage. And despite his ingrained caution the risks remained, in every voyage, in every season, only increased by winter storm and ice. Renaut's wife had cause to worry for his safety. All too often an outport fishing proprietor found himself auctioning away the scant possessions of a drowned employee, totalling his debts and wages and sending off what remained to benefit the widow and heirs.

Such an end, oddly enough, was almost the only way for an obscure migrant fisherman to draw some kind of recognition to himself. For all his skill and his dedication, a transient like Renaut could come year after year to one outport or another, earning his wage and contributing his share of the precious catch, and never leave a record of his presence in the colony. Yet should he die in his bunk or drown with his shallopmates, a tiny but permanent dossier reporting the disposal of his paltry estate would be drawn up by the clerks of the admiralty service, who would often add some note about his career and his end.

Inevitably, it is from such a dossier that we chart the career and read the letters of Charles Renaut. The slim admiralty file does not inquire about Charles and Mathurin Renaut's motives for setting out from Scatary three days after Christmas of 1730. Perhaps they planned a duck-hunting expedition along the coast. Perhaps the brothers hoped to celebrate the Christmas feast days with a sociable visit to compatriots down the shore. Or it could have been a routine fishing trip like a hundred others they had undertaken for Jean Phelipeaux.

Whatever the plan, something went wrong. The veteran boatmen got into trouble, and suddenly the shallop was lost, the men quickly drowned in the frigid waters.

When Marie-Joanne wrote in April 1731, Charles Renaut was already four months dead. He would never eat the cheese and butter she was sending, never see his daughter walk. When some messenger faithfully delivered the letter to Scatary that summer, Jean Phelipeaux could only add it to the papers of the dead brothers and go on with the hard routines of his trade. Because he died without seeing it, Charles Renaut's useless letter still lies in the registers with a note on his belongings and how he died, as if the cold Ile Royale waters that closed over his head in December 1730 had conferred on this obscure transient visitor some small and unsought immortality.

The Sea and Jean Lelarge

elarge was the sailor's name, and the name suited the man. In one of its senses, the French noun large means "the wide ocean." *Gagner le large*: to put out from sheltered waters for the open sea; to shake off safe ties in search of wider destinies. As sailor, privateer, and naval officer, Jean-François Lelarge always lived the life *au large*. Forsaking the apparent security of the town and fortress of Louisbourg, he pursued instead sea routes and career opportunities as far as they led, ceaselessly exploring the widest horizons that the colony offered to its people. From the vigour of his privateering, through the buccaneering bravado of his marriage, to the proud admiral's pennant he bequeathed his son, all his life showed his taste for new frontiers and farther shores. A man who found his security in the trackless, changeless ocean, Jean Lelarge was one Louisbourg resident who chose not to shelter his life behind the town's walls.

I

Jean Lelarge's maritime destiny was hardly evident at his birth about 1712 in Plaisance, across the Cabot Strait from his future home in Ile Royale. Founded half a century before as France's foothold in Newfoundland, Plaisance was a fishing village and a small military base on the eastern shore of the Avalon Peninsula. Built around a generous harbour joined to the broad expanse of Placentia Bay by a narrow channel under protective hills, Plaisance sheltered the summer fleet of fishing boats and trading vessels from France and was itself the permanent home of a few hundred colonists. Fishing and war were its livelihoods. From the 1690s, the townspeople became inured to the ever-present risks of attack and blockade-induced famine. Despite its meagre defences and the threat posed by privateers during the nearly constant struggle with Britain, Plaisance survived. Its people continued to gather bountiful harvests of cod in summer. In winter they put aside their nets to launch effective raids across the Avalon Peninsula against St. John's and the other English outposts.

Though most of Plaisance's citizens lived from the sea, a few craftsmen found a living on the shore. One who joined these craftsmen about 1710 was a master carpenter in his late thirties, Pierre Lelarge. The son of a builder from the Ile-de-Ré near La Rochelle, Lelarge crossed the Atlantic only once, and exhibited little desire to do so again. Instead, he settled at Plaisance with his wife and sister and found work as carpenter to the garrison. Settled, the Lelarges set about raising a family, and they had a son and a daughter by the spring of 1713, when peace was made between Britain and France and word came that Plaisance and all French Newfoundland, though unconquered, would have to be ceded to the enemy. The garrison and the fishermen prepared to found a new colony in Ile Royale. Lelarge gathered up his family and went with them, enduring a short sea voyage to reach his permanent home.

Pierre Lelarge arrived in Louisbourg in the summer of 1714 with a substantial household. He and his wife Catherine had only the two infant children, but their party included Lelarge's sister Geneviève, a servant, two carpenters, a mason and his wife, two apprentice fishermen, and a merchant tenant. It was the beginning of a clan that Lelarge had brought to the nascent colony, and soon both family and colony were prospering. There was a city to be built at the edge of Louisbourg harbour and Pierre Lelarge quickly busied himself erecting shelters and permanent dwellings for the soldiers, workmen, and officials newly descended on the town.

For some years, Lelarge worked in the service of the Crown, putting up the first public buildings of the new colony, but he became troubled by the determination of some senior officials to move the capital of the colony north and east across the island to Port Dauphin. Like most of the civilians, Lelarge preferred the growing town of Louisbourg, and so he resigned his official position to stay where he had first arrived. Since the swelling population's need for housing was at least as great as the garrison's, Lelarge continued to prosper. Even after Louisbourg was confirmed as the seat of government in 1718, Lelarge remained a self-employed craftsman.

Pierre Lelarge's skill was the working of wood, and it was wooden houses that the people of Louisbourg wanted. At first, made cautious by the insecurities of a new colony and the likelihood of having more changes forced upon them, property-owners chose the simplest and least expensive construction: the *piquet* house. In these houses the walls were simply formed from rows of poles about six inches in diameter and eight or nine feet tall. The poles stood upright in a line, their bases sunk in a trench a foot or two deep and their tops secured to a single crosspiece. Gaps between the vertical *piquets* were laboriously chinked with mortar, or even with mud and straw. Above such simple walls rose a roof of boards or strips of bark, and a *piquet* house might be completed with plaster, sometimes even with whitewash.

As Louisbourg became established, these rudimentary constructions were superseded. A well-built *piquet* house could be long-lived and comfortable – the early buildings were neither demolished nor abandoned – but over time that technique of building became limited to warehouses, storage sheds, and outbuildings. For their homes, the people of Louisbourg turned to the timber-framed house, the *maison de charpente*.

The framed house was something worthy of the art of master carpenter Lelarge. The house took its shape not from a row of stripped poles, but from good squared timbers up to a foot in diameter. Carefully measured and dovetailed together, the timbers formed a sturdy framework of horizontal and vertical members, solidly jointed so that only a few wooden pegs were needed to secure them. This carefully wrought frame did not rest on the soft, muddy ground to rot like a *piquet* post. A foundation of mortared stone supported the house timbers. Often a stone floor underlay the framework of the floor, providing, if not a full basement, at least a space for drains and storage underneath the floorboards.

With their sturdy frames and foundations, *charpente* houses were likely to have crafted wooden floors and solid shingled roofs, and the owner could choose how best to enclose his frame. Some *charpente* frames were infilled with masonry. Some used a modified *piquet* construction between the beams, with the chinked poles laid either horizontally or upright, and others were enclosed by boards nailed across the framing members. Gradually, these *charpente* houses became the typical residences of Louisbourg. Though some people accepted the expense of homes built entirely of stone masonry, most found wooden buildings attractive and comfortable. As one of Louisbourg's pioneer carpenters, Pierre Lelarge made a fundamental contribution to the appearance of the town.

Whether it was a quickly erected *piquet* shelter or a *charpente* home, the wooden house had a pre-ordained shape. Interior load-bearing walls were rarely used. With the four exterior walls bearing the full weight of the roof, buildings tended to be narrow and (since a lengthy interior was hard to heat) not too long. Many homes in Louisbourg measured about forty feet long and twenty wide. Inside, a chimney and a partition might split this rectangle into two rooms of equal size, each with a fireplace in the single chimney. One of these rooms became the kitchen and domestic working space. The other, subdivided into a main room and several sleeping alcoves called *cabinets*, provided living and sleeping space. Few homes had two full storeys, but a narrow staircase or ladder often led up to an attic used for storage and additional sleeping space. Such quarters were the customary accommodation of large Louisbourg families, where several children, a servant, an employee or tenant, and often a sister, brother, or parent of the household head lived together in crowded intimacy, using a backyard outhouse and adjacent well, eating, sleeping, and socializing in a few small rooms warmed only by the double fireplace.

Pierre Lelarge built many such homes for the people of his town. Though he could write – or at least sign his name – Lelarge rarely met his clients at the notary's for a formal contract-making. Instead he made his arrangements privately, perhaps settling the details in a tavern and sealing the bargain with a bottle of wine or rum. He needed no blueprints and architect's specifications, for his buildings conformed to a standard known to both client and craftsman. His clients wanted shelter, quickly raised at reasonable price. They might ask Lelarge to build only the heavy timber frame, or they might prefer to receive their new home "keys in hand," completed right down to the doorknobs. Occasionally, if the client were building a masonry structure or had begun the house himself, Lelarge might be asked only to lay a floor, to install windows and doors, and to build in partitions, railings, and cupboards. These subcontracts could keep the carpenter's workshop busy all winter prefabricating doors, windows, and surrounds. The windows were usually several small panes of glass cut from imported roundels and set in a simple pine frame hinged to swing inward. Rather than hanging curtains, Louisbourg householders sealed out the cold and dark with interior and exterior shutters – another product that kept the Lelarge *atelier* busy when winter stopped outdoor construction.

If the client did not provide the lumber, Lelarge might send men out to the woods to cut timber and sledge it back to his sawpits for squaring and trimming. But as the community grew and diversified, trade in building supplies expanded. Lelarge probably bought most of his materials commercially. When Lelarge left government service to remain in Louisbourg as a private contractor, an old partner of his, Pierre Chouteau, had accepted transfer to Port Dauphin, where the surrounding hills offered some of the island's best stands of timber. After Chouteau died there in 1717, his widow married a man named Goubert, another carpenter who was also a coastal shipper. Goubert found a good living hauling lumber that he cut at Port Dauphin down the coast to Louisbourg, where builders like Lelarge were among his best clients.

Lelarge's other materials were also provided by Louisbourg's bustling trade. Ships from France brought tools, window glass, nails, and other hardware. Pine boards, shingles, and brick poured off the schooners that had loaded at New England's mills and brickyards. And

Louisbourg had its own contingent of ironmongers, locksmiths, roofers, and furniture-makers to provide the fittings and details needed to complete Lelarge's work in wood. When the supply trade ran smoothly and Lelarge planned his work well, he could frame and finish a solid *charpente* house between the last snow of May and the first hard storms of November.

An independent craftsman, Pierre Lelarge was also a master of men. A permanent crew of workers assisted him in his craft, and in busy times he could hire day labourers out of the town garrison. Still, he was hardly an industrial employer, nor were his workers simply salaried labour. Mostly they were his apprentices, younger men who shared his home and table and served under him while they acquired his knowledge in anticipation of forming their own businesses and households. Such employees were part of the master carpenter's clan while they worked for him. Though the standards of the household might be firm – the Lelarges once instantly dismissed a servant girl who became pregnant – something like a familial tie compounded the economic ties that bound man to master and master to man.

When a house was in progress, Lelarge and his apprentices came to the worksite early. Soon after dawn, Lelarge would be co-ordinating several tasks. A carter might be bringing lumber and supplies from the sawpits or up from the quayside. There could be foundations to lay or frames to raise with the help of a block and tackle and some casual labourers. Always there were small pieces to assemble, measurements to make, errors to correct. Lelarge had to be an exacting supervisor, but there were limits to the pitch of efficiency on the worksite. Though the workday ran eleven or twelve hours, and the week stretched from Monday through Saturday, there would have been no time clocks to punch, and religious holidays – as many as forty a year – cut into the schedule. Also, discreet volumes of alcohol flowed into the long but flexible day. The temperance movement, seeking either to banish alcohol or to limit it to hours of leisure, was as yet unknown. Work might be started with a shot of brandy and interrupted periodically while the crew repaired to the tavern for a midday snack, to escape a rain shower, or in celebration of an awkward task handily accomplished. Supervisors of the government's large construction projects might lament their labourers' incorrigible propensity to drop their tools and drink themselves insensible, but on a smaller, more intimate worksite such as one of Pierre Lelarge's house contracts, it was probably the client rather than the master who was likely to complain of the casual mixing of work and alcohol. Lelarge and his men worked together much as they socialized together. It would take the industrial revolution of the following century to divorce the two activities.

As the streetscape of Louisbourg took shape and the lots laid out on the royal surveyor's chart were given definition by homes, storehouses, sheds, and fencerows, Pierre Lelarge achieved the comfort and security which seem to have been his goals in life. By the mid-1720s, a decade of hard work had given him a good livelihood and an established place in local society. As he reached his fifties, perhaps beginning to feel the rugged outdoor work affecting his physique, his interests shifted from the pursuit of more business toward plans for winding down his own activities and providing as best he could a secure future for his old age and his growing family.

Wherever he lived and whatever his success, Lelarge's craft had always been the framework for his life. An artisan earning his bread by his manual labour, he was indisputably part of the working masses, his outlook shaped by the popular culture of his time. Some few artisans moved from craftwork into trade and went in pursuit of wealth and prestige, but Pierre Lelarge had achieved his ambitions when he won respect and financial security as a master craftsmen. His friends were men like himself, other independent artisans, the smiths, roofers, and masons whose trades buttressed his own. His entertainments were taken in the company of these peers and their apprentices. As a master, he had a position of leadership in the workingmen's society, and his home became one of their gathering places. As he aged, Pierre Lelarge took advantage of this leadership. He made part of his home a tavern, a meeting place for his friends and protégés and a source of supplementary income to sustain his family as his active carpentry came to an end. The tavern was principally his wife's concern, but it was Lelarge's stature among his fellow workingmen that made the new business a success – one that could continue to thrive when Lelarge ceased to practise his craft.

If carpentry was the sturdy frame of Pierre Lelarge's existence, his family provided the roof and walls built around that frame. The clan he had led to Louisbourg in 1714 had constantly changed its members, but it had rarely shrunk. His sister Geneviève had soon left them to marry François Baudry, one of a group of brothers with a small fishing operation on the north shore of Louisbourg harbour. The apprentices of 1714 had also moved on, to be replaced by a succession of others. The family itself continued to grow. The son and daughter who came from Plaisance soon had brothers and sisters. By 1722 there were six young Lelarges – three boys and three girls – in the carpenter's crowded house and tavern on Rue de l'Etang.

The Lelarges' social circle, begun among the carpenter's fellow artisans, now included the godparents of these children and the families to which Lelarge and his wife were themselves godparents. It stretched across the harbour to encompass his sister's in-laws among the fishing community, and of course it included the apprentices who had gone forth from his shop. As his children approached adulthood, Lelarge looked to this broad network for their husbands, wives, and careers. His own society measured the extent of his ambitions – he would not expect his sons to become military officers or his daughters to marry wealthy merchants – but he had done well in his craft, and he intended his offspring to receive what benefits he could bring them.

By about 1730 Pierre Lelarge had ceased his active carpentry and was preparing to yield primacy to the succeeding generation. His busy tavern had grown into a small inn, providing room and board as well as drink, so an income was still assured. And, unlike carpentry, which needed his skill and experience behind it, the inn was a business that could survive him. His earnings and his stature had ensured the security of the clan. That year, his children's social prospects were symbolized by the marriage of his eldest daughter, Jeanne, to Pierre Chouteau, the son of Lelarge's former partner and stepson of the lumber shipper who had long been a supplier of the Lelarge carpentry. Chouteau was not rich, but his prospects were good, and the Lelarges were pleased to offer the couple a substantial dowry and two years of room and board in their home. The social networks were holding.

II

In the harmonious succession Pierre Lelarge had prepared, the most dependable element of all should have been his eldest son. Pierre Lelarge's society was not one in which such questions as "What do you want to be when you grow up?" were frequently asked. Even had a wide range of careers been available, such a discussion would have presupposed a world that provided safety nets for those whose career choices proved unrealistic or unattainable. The world of the working people of Ile Royale gave no such guarantees. Men deprived of their livelihoods or families left without a provider could suddenly find themselves on a sickening plunge from modest security into indigence, their shelter and their daily bread in jeopardy, their place in society gone, their children likely to be sent away as servants to more fortunate homes. These very real dangers, against which Pierre Lelarge had sought to insure his family, made career choices far too important to be settled by youthful desires alone. Had his son presented no clear and plausible career preference by his twelfth or thirteenth year, Pierre Lelarge would naturally have exercised parental authority to guide his son toward a secure livelihood in an appropriate profession. His choice for the boy would surely have been carpentry. Considering the success that had attended Pierre Lelarge's efforts in his craft, he could have had cause to foresee his eldest son becoming his apprentice, then his partner, and eventually his successor.

Yet such a destiny was not inevitably preordained for Jean Lelarge as the boy brought to Ile Royale as an infant came to adolescence in the Louisbourg of the 1720s. He had not been raised in some rural farming community where every young man went out to follow the plough as his father had done. Louisbourg's urban environment nurtured a certain range of skills and trades, and custom did not demand that every son follow his father's career. There were opportunities for change if a young man promoted an alternative career, and if his father or guardian could be persuaded that the choice was practical.

This seems to have been Jean Lelarge's story. If the boy was introduced to Pierre Lelarge's woodworking shop and building site, it must soon have been clear that he had little aptitude and no inclination for the carpenter's trade. Apparently he preferred to spend his spare hours at the harbour, demonstrating an interest in *bâtiments de mer* – ships – that far outweighed his scant enthusiasm for the *bâtiments* built by his father. With enough tenacity to win parental consent, Jean Lelarge embarked on the pursuit of a destiny more fluid and far-reaching than the solid, carefully crafted life preferred by his father.

Even so landlocked a resident as Pierre Lelarge could not escape the influence of the broad harbour beside which the town of Louisbourg spread. And though he might take for granted the shipping that brought in the materials of his trade, the harbour could be exotic as well as essential. A boy jaded by familiarity with sawdust-strewn building sites, or even with the blue-coated soldiers and the powerful walls around his town, could usually find something new and unfamiliar along the Louisbourg quay. In summer and fall the quay was the busiest part of the town, a forest of tall masts where ships, brigantines, schooners, and sloops changed rank endlessly. As long as the ships remained, the quay was alive with horse- and ox-drawn carts rumbling up for another load, with merchants' clerks and sea captains haggling over trade terms, with surges of newly arrived sailors celebrating shore liberty.

The sailors in particular should have been an endless fascination. The thousands who arrived each summer brought a Babel of languages. Boston-accented English echoed from the New England schooners exchanging their timber, livestock, and farm produce for sugar and rum. Basque, Breton, Spanish, and Portuguese could be heard from the transatlantic traders and fishing boats. Men raised under the endless sun of Martinique mingled with seamen more familiar with the frozen St. Lawrence. God-fearing Protestants from the puritan seaports of Massachusetts dealt with worldly captains from sophisticated French cities, and rustic Acadians from Fundy Bay encountered slaves newly imported from Africa by way of the Caribbean.

Equally alluring were the cargoes and souvenirs displayed by this array of ships and sailors. Jean Lelarge had been raised in a town used to consuming Canadian flour, New England meat, Caribbean coffee, and French wine along with its local cod. The clothes he wore, the furnishings of his home, almost the whole material culture in which he lived, came in on the ships, but there would always be surprises. A monkey or parrot brought along as ship's mascot might amuse the crowd, or a handful of strange gold coins from Spain or Peru, or just a piece of months-old news to be flashed about the town. The quay in summer made a world of endless diversity for a young local boy for whom the sea voyage that had brought him to Louisbourg could have been an earliest memory. The quay in autumn, with its ships and sailors gliding away before winter could close the shipping lanes again, might well have been the site of Jean Lelarge's decision to follow the departing sailors and discover the sources of their diversity.

Young Lelarge soon passed from quayside gawking to the exploration of the harbour itself, for Louisbourg abounded in small boats. Geography and economics combined to make water transport the commonest and most convenient way to get around. Perhaps Jean Lelarge first explored the water in a ship's dinghy rowed by his father. He probably wallowed in one of the flat-bottomed *gabares* the sailors used to move cargo between the quay and the deep-draughted trading ships anchored in mid-harbour. But before long, every would-be sailor in Ile Royale moved on to the colony's ubiquitous, all-purpose small boat, the shallop.

Fishermen brought the shallop to Ile Royale. In Newfoundland, where the cod swarmed close to shore, the shallop had been small – just large enough for three men and their day's catch. Powered only by oars, the shallop of Plaisance was scarcely large enough to survive a night at sea or a journey out of sight of land. But in Ile Royale the best fishing lay further offshore, and the shallop evolved as the fishermen's voyage grew longer. It sprouted a foredeck and a mast and stretched out toward thirty feet in length. Soon the larger shallops resembled small schooners, useful not only for fishing voyages, but also for transportation among Ile Royale's scattered settlements. Louisbourg had hundreds of shallops of all sizes. The harbour was alive with them, rowed or sailed, whenever it was not swept by storm or choked with ice.

Jean Lelarge probably acquired an introduction to shallop-sailing through his uncle François Baudry. By visiting his cousins at the other end of Louisbourg harbour, the boy could have enjoyed regular access to the small boats of the Baudry fishing station. Judging by the speed of his later progress, he must have used this opportunity to gain a fundamental and practical familiarity with small-boat sailing. Initially Jean, his cousins, and other companions would have remained within the spacious reaches of Louisbourg harbour, making brief jaunts under adult tutelage. In view of many vessels and protected from the ocean's full force, they were none the less tested by the harbour's range of winds and currents. Prompt handling was essential to keep a fast-moving boat off one shore or the other, and small boats had to be quick to evade the big merchantmen and naval vessels constantly moving about the water. Harbour sailing became no small adventure when an afternoon fog swept across the bay, blotting out visibility and provoking a chorus of bells, small-arms fire, and shouts, as vessels large and small signalled their movements.

Sailing may have been adventure to young Lelarge and his cousins, but their avocation was quickly turned to practical use. There were no pleasure craft in Ile Royale. If he sailed his uncle's shallops, Jean Lelarge contributed to the fishing business, going out before dawn to net herring for the fishermen's bait barrels, or delivering supplies from town warehouses to his uncle's pole-framed wharf. As they grew up and began to venture beyond the harbour, he and his cousins found opportunities to contribute to their families' larders, taking firearms and dogs along to hunt seabirds, or nest-raiding for seabird eggs on rocky headlands and islets along the coast.

In 1725, when thirteen-year-old Jean Lelarge should already have been an experienced small-boat sailor, he and every resident of Ile Royale received grim notice of the dangers a prospective sailor faced. Late in August, in a gale that had driven every ship to shelter, the naval transport *Chameau* struck on the Portenove rocks, a chain of reefs and shoals near the eastern tip of Ile Royale where young sailors like Lelarge must often have gathered birds' eggs. Off course, running before the wind in the wild night and unaware of the coast's proximity, *Chameau* drove onto the rocks with its sails still set. Torn to pieces so completely that only shattered fragments of the ship came ashore to be salvaged, *Chameau* left no survivors. The Intendant of Canada, the son of Montréal's Governor de Ramezay, and the elderly Louisbourg engineer Jacques L'Hermitte were among the three hundred and ten victims of the disaster, a wreck so violent that "even the strong swimming pigs were washed ashore drowned." Despite the efforts of divers, neither *Chameau*'s cannon nor the small fortune in gold coins it carried for the Treasury of New France were recovered. The worst disaster to strike the naval transports in a century of service between France and the Canadian colonies, the *Chameau* wreck reminded men of the risks they took when they ventured along the iron coast of Ile Royale.

The next year, embarrassment rather than disaster struck another royal transport. Slowly approaching Louisbourg harbour in a light breeze, *Néréide* gently grounded on an uncharted rock within sight of Louisbourg. The big ship would have broken itself apart as the tide fell had not a flotilla of schooners and shallops swarmed out from the town to take off the artillery and some of the cargo. Young Jean Lelarge could have been among the spectators when *Néréide* finally floated free on the returning tide to limp into harbour with thirty-six feet of its hull ripped away and twenty inches of water entering the hold every hour.

Royal vessels were scarcely the only ones at risk. Three fishing boats had been lost in 1725, though their crews escaped death in each case. Collisions with ice wrecked several ships in the spring of 1726, and that fall a great windstorm flung five ships and twenty-two fishing boats ashore inside Louisbourg harbour. Three men died that summer when a trading schooner ran down their shallop a few hours' sail from Louisbourg. In 1730 a New England captain put his schooner ashore in broad daylight and calm weather when he mishandled his entry to the harbour. On a foggy night that same year, a big Basque trader tried to pass south rather than north of Battery Island. Smashed across the shallows, *Notre-Dame* was a total loss, though prompt assistance from the town saved its twenty-six crewmen and thirty-four passengers.

The dangers so vividly demonstrated every year did not deter Jean Lelarge. Something seems to have made the long separations, the constant travel, and the perils of the sea more attractive to him than his parents' stable life amid the social and occupational networks of the working people of Louisbourg. The tightly knit Lelarge family, until now shorebound and down-to-earth, may not have applauded his choice, and the boy's stubborn determination at this time probably helped to build the family tensions that would explode later in his career. Still, the Lelarges reached an accommodation with their wayward son. As a buyer of timber and imported hardwares, Pierre Lelarge was neither unaware of the shipping trade's potential nor without connections among the sailors and shipowners. In 1727 the carpenter, who knew something about how young men should be apprenticed into careers, took steps to ensure that if his son intended to go to sea, he would do so properly. No longer would Jean Lelarge embark on boyish jaunts to set herring nets or collect birds' eggs. Pierre Lelarge, the master craftsman, used his influence to see his son apprenticed to the trade of seamanship in much the way he brought young carpenters under his own tutelage.

The most likely masters for fifteen-year-old Jean Lelarge as he entered the working world of adult Louisbourg in 1727 were the timber dealers François Goubert and his stepson Pierre Chouteau. A long-time family acquaintance with more than a decade's experience of the coastal trade of Ile Royale, Goubert would have been a steadying influence on the boy. Chouteau on the other hand was only five years older than Jean Lelarge. This son of Pierre Lelarge's old building partner and future husband of the Lelarges' eldest daughter was quickly pushing forward in his stepfather's business. In 1730, the year of his marriage, Chouteau would win premature emancipation from minority status and acquire his own coastal vessel. Even before then he had probably been running cargoes along the coast on Goubert's behalf. If these two were his teachers of seamanship, Jean Lelarge seems to have apprenticed himself as much to Chouteau's ambition as to Goubert's experience and stability.

Jean Lelarge served the first stage of his apprenticeship in short schooner voyages between his home in Louisbourg and the outports south and north of it. Workhorse of the coastal fleet, the schooner was a new breed of sailing craft. The New England shipwrights who first produced it about 1700 gave it slim lines and tall, raking masts for speed and grace, and tall, triangular fore-and-aft sails for unmatched manoeuvrability. Never the best bulk carrier, the schooner was designed instead to run the obstacle courses of the North American coasts, to weave easily through treacherous inshore passages, and to speed over the distances between isolated coastal ports. Simple in design, easy to build, the schooner could be put through its paces by a small crew. Speed, simplicity, manoeuvrability: these qualities endeared the schooner to the sailors of Ile Royale. They adopted it within a few years of the colony's foundation, renamed it *goélette* for the wave-skimming sea swallow, and introduced it to the world of French maritime commerce. Welcomed into the fishing fleet, schooners also conquered the coastal trading fleet. Small schooners thirty to fifty feet long plied the routes between the settlements of Ile Royale, and larger ones were soon sailing for the Caribbean and even Europe. Many were imported vessels, purchased at a cut rate along with cargoes of New England merchandise, but local ship-wrights also launched schooners from makeshift construction slips up and down the coast of Ile Royale.

Sometimes the coasters in which young Jean Lelarge began his apprenticeship ran northeast from Louisbourg, passing the fishing settlements of the Lorembecs, Baleine, and Scatary Island before swinging north to round the headlands of Baie-de-Glace and tack westward past Baie-des-Espagnols and the twin entrances to the Bras d'Or Lakes. On this run the destination might be Niganiche, a village of several hundred on two spacious bays set into the highlands of Ile Royale's north cape. Fish was the only cargo here, and since Niganiche attracted many fishing vessels from France, the town depended on Louisbourg less than did most of the other outports. More promising for a Louisbourg schoonerman was Port Dauphin. Nestled in the shelter of St. Anne's Bay, Port Dauphin boasted a detachment of troops to bolster its small community of fishermen, but the great attraction for cargo haulers lay in the hills behind. They abounded in game and timber and provided useful limestone and plaster quarries as well.

Lelarge would also have sailed south from Louisbourg, seeing the shallops fanned out from Fourché and Saint-Esprit fall behind as his vessel drove on for Port Toulouse on the southern shore of Ile Royale. Commercially minded military officers competed for appointment here. Freed from supervision, they could prosper in trading with the adjacent New England outpost at Canso Island. Port Toulouse was also the only settlement of Ile Royale that had attracted a substantial number of Acadians from their Fundyside farmlands, for behind the port lay some of the best pasturage of Ile Royale. Making hay, raising cattle, and planting crops, the Acadians were also shipwrights and sailors. Port Toulouse launched many small craft for the colony's fleet and was the true centre of the coastal shipping industry of Ile Royale. If Lelarge did not complete his apprenticeship under Goubert and Chouteau, he may have gravitated to Port Toulouse in search of seamanship training.

In the summers he spent sailing the waters of Ile Royale, Jean Lelarge experienced the daily life of the ordinary seaman. Rank meant little aboard a schooner crewed by only three or four men, and no one could claim privileges when six-foot holds packed with cargo offered little space for anyone's privacy. The navigation was not complex, for the schooners were rarely far from familiar shores, but keeping the ship on an optimum course, heading along rugged, foul-weather coasts in changing winds, tides, and currents, demanded long hours of vigilance. The men turned out at all hours to change sails or bring their ship to an anchorage. It was hard work, appropriate training for a prospective shipmaster.

Shipmaster was Jean Lelarge's goal. A few seasons on the coastal boats would teach him shiphandling, navigation by eye and compass, and the rules for managing cargoes and crews, but Jean Lelarge was destined for further horizons. His father, the master artisan, did not intend the boy to grow up a barely literate coastal boatman, lost beyond sight of Ile Royale's surf-washed shore. Both the boy and his father saw Lelarge as a qualified master mariner, a blue-water sailor. To gain the formidable education such a career presumed, the young apprentice seaman spent his winters at the school for sailors newly established by hydrographer Jean-René Cruchon of Saint-Malo.

The curriculum Lelarge followed in Cruchon's hydrography school began with arithmetic review. Cruchon assumed new students could read and write and figure a little: Jean Lelarge must have been taught in childhood by his parents or a tutor. Under Cruchon he now learned to calculate tide tables from the moon's phases and discovered the use of angles, dividers, and compasses in plotting and charting. The class then passed from geometry to astronomy, fixing latitude by the sun in daylight, pinpointing Polaris and the other guiding stars by night. Gathering on the ramparts on a moonless night, the class could have determined that from Louisbourg the pole star stood just a fraction short of forty-six degrees above the horizon. Wherever they travelled, they would never again have much difficulty determining how far north they stood. Then Cruchon led his students into geography and hydrography, teaching them the use of maps and charts and familiarizing them with the position of the major coasts and islands they would visit.

The students who mastered these subjects – young townspeople like Lelarge, officer cadets of the colonial troops, junior ship's officers wintering in the colony – moved on to practise their skills: position plotting; mapping; methods to measure distance travelled; the use of the magnetic compass, the sextant, and other navigational tools; ways to record soundings, keep sea logs, and compile maps. Jean Lelarge's subsequent career suggests he was the apt pupil of a gifted teacher, for navigational challenges seem never to have inhibited the career of this Louisbourg-trained sailor.

Then, some time around 1730, perhaps a little earlier, Jean Lelarge left behind both Cruchon's school and Goubert's coastal schooner to venture beyond Ile Royale's familiar shores. Junior officer aboard some ocean-going ship, the teenaged sailor began his personal discovery of the Atlantic Ocean.

III

The sailor came home in 1734. His ships had called at Ile Royale a few times in the intervening years, and it was the coast he knew best. Coming back, he would have recognized home waters far east of the island. Out where the deep ocean yielded to the Continental Shelf, a hundred-fathom sounding line would bring up pebbly bottom samples from the Grand Banks, and a few baited hooks would keep the ship's table supplied with cod. More seabirds overhead, whales and porpoises active in the water, mighty icebergs in spring and early summer. Also fogs "thick as buttermilk" to test a sailor's skills, and the coasts of Newfoundland and Ile Royale ready to doom an erring vessel. Before landfall, several leagues out from the coast, soundings would find bottom in fifty fathoms: the characteristic black sand and coal-studded gravel that told of proximity to Ile Royale. Finally a sight of land – probably an easy identification of Scatary Island, one of his old bird-egging haunts. Then a careful southwest run down the coast to bring the prodigal past Louisbourg's new light-house into the sheltered waters of his home port.

Jean Lelarge returned to Louisbourg an adult. For several years, sea experience in all weathers and climates had been toughening the brash youth, inuring him to the life of the ocean seaman, drawing him away from his father's settled ways. He had probably done an obligatory stint of naval service, but most of his time at sea had been in square-rigged merchantmen, the ships and brigantines of the North Atlantic fleet. Ocean-going craft, these vessels were not much larger than the coastal schooners of Ile Royale. A ship a hundred feet long and twenty wide would be thought large, and vessels half that size often crossed the ocean. But these were square-riggers, and they needed larger crews to climb the rigging for every change of sail. So there might be thirty sailors under the command of three or four officers – a polyglot band of Basques and Bretons, Frenchmen, colonists, and foreigners crowded together. The officers shared tiny cabins aft, the men slept in crew quarters at the bow. Hands of every rank shared the rhythms of four hours on watch and four hours off, the constant dampness of wooden ships, the endless meals of hard-tack and cold meat when bad weather put out the cooking fires. If storm or calm or contrary winds dragged out the voyage beyond six weeks, everyone began to look for the first symptoms of scurvy. As a junior officer, Lelarge faced most of the hazards of the men, climbing ice-rimed rigging in the face of freezing spray, pumping and praying below deck, risking lonely death overboard when waves swept the bridge. He mended sail, helped the carpenter, made rope. He shared the crew's leisure pursuits: singing and dancing and hearing stories – port exploits that no one believed, reports of sea monsters accepted by most. But he was also learning command: assigning duties more than carrying them out, and occasionally meting out the harsh punishments that sustained the officers' authority over rough and sometimes violent men.

Used to seaboard life, Lelarge had also mastered the arts of seamanship. By now he knew in his fingertips when to cram on sail and when to furl, when to run before the wind and when to come up into it. And he could transmit knowledge to action, sending his crews up mainmast or mizzenmast with a few commands to reef this sail and let this one fly. Sensitivity to currents and coastlines, garnered on the shores of Ile Royale, served him well, and now he also knew the ways of the open ocean, the prevailing winds and currents of the North Atlantic.

Lelarge's fundamental professional gain from these wandering years was experience in navigation. He now nurtured a calm assurance of his ability to take a tiny wooden ship, powered only by the wind, and go boldly beyond sight of land toward a chosen destination thousands of sea miles away. Dead-reckoning navigation, his duty and his pride, no longer held many terrors for him. With astrolabe or quadrant he could quickly determine latitude by sun or star. A compass showed him the angle of his course across the chart, and careful observation reported his ship's speed through the water. The calculations from these data were not simple, but they enabled him to estimate his longitude and determine how far distant and on what heading lay his destination. These calculations were never perfect, for the scientists of Lelarge's day still knew no way for a shipboard navigator to check his estimates against an observation of longitude. Measurement of east-west travel depended on the cumulative accuracy of the navigator's calculations of speed and course. As a voyage continued, tiny errors crept in to compound each other, as unnoted currents carried the ship sideways from its apparent heading and small changes of speed went unobserved. It was a mariner's pride to overcome these hazards, to bring his ship close to a chosen headland after weeks or months at sea. In Lelarge's day the state of the art permitted vessels navigating to the East Indies to make routine landfalls at mid-Atlantic pinpoints like St. Helena and Ascension. Yet even if a navigator predicted every sighting, a shipmaster's concern still mounted as he approached coastlines whose location had been foretold only by a long series of fallible calculations. To lessen that anxiety, every ship carried published descriptions of headlands, some sketched for firm identification at the earliest moment. Every officer also kept his own logbooks, charting his own estimates, drawing his own maps, and storing up his own accumulated knowledge.

When he came home in 1734, Jean Lelarge's logbooks were fat with the record of positions charted and coastlines observed. In these notebooks Lelarge's world revealed itself, a circle of shores bounding the broad Atlantic. It was a world-view appropriate to the child of Ile Royale, itself only a string of seaward-facing coastal towns, but it also expressed many people's experience in that era. Lelarge's voyaging taught him that Europe, Africa, and America, like Ile Royale, could be summed up as headlands to identify, shores to coast, ports to visit for trade. He might never have seen Paris, but already he knew the Gironde estuary that led to Bordeaux, the narrow entrance to La Rochelle, the Loire river mouth of Nantes, the Channel approaches to Saint-Malo, and perhaps even the shallows around Amsterdam. He never saw the Alps, but he had memorized the rocky tip of Brittany and the passage between Calais and England's white cliffs. Jean Lelarge never needed to go ten miles from salt water in his life; the only Europe he knew was the sailor's Europe. The other Europe, rural, agricultural, continental, was another world – people like Lelarge knew it only by its exports.

The sailor's Africa – the Guinea coast was what he called it – was the only Africa that existed for Europeans, just a long shore fronting impenetrable hinterlands. Lelarge made at least one voyage here, sailing to a port or river mouth that could have been anywhere between Dakar and Angola. Here his ship loaded two or three hundred slaves and made sail north and west with its human cargo, back across the Atlantic into the Caribbean archipelago.

Mastering the tricky passages of the reefs and islets of Hispaniola and the Windwards probably concerned Lelarge more than the fate of his passengers, but he could scarcely miss the avidity with which the planters of Martinique and Saint-Domingue bid for the slave cargo, a commodity as precious to them as fish or wine or sugar elsewhere. In his enormous circuit from the coast of North America to the coast of Europe, south to the African shore and across to the western islands, Jean Lelarge had touched base at each of France's major interests around the Atlantic. The boy who used to watch the ships from mysterious distant lands coming into Louisbourg had now seen for himself the French empire's stake in the trade of the world. He must already have known his career would be shaped by the great rivalries of the sea-trading nations.

A century before, the Dutch had dominated the shipping trade of the European nations, while England and France lay entangled in debilitating civil wars. Only after 1660 did Frenchmen and Britons begin to regain the trade they had lost to Dutch sailors, but with internal peace restored, their overseas expansion was rapid. Peace, growth, and colonial expansion doubled the shipping of the cross-channel rivals in thirty years. Long wars at the turn of the century disrupted trade, but naval and colonial competition continued apace as Britain and France surged to the forefront of world trade. From the Far East out to the Americas, the two nations entered a truly global competition, vying for the trade of all the coasts of the world.

Britain, long a maritime nation and a vigorous trader, was assured a lively ocean commerce by the growth of its American colonies, the success of its plantations in Barbados and Jamaica, and the busy trade of its outposts in India. Britain prospered, but the island nation's entry into the enormous market of continental Europe met fierce competition from France.

France's great strength lay in its population and its farms. With twenty million people, France far outnumbered every other European nation, yet it fed and clothed itself and had surpluses to sell abroad. As Dutch shipping declined, French exporters pushed into Spanish and Mediterranean markets. As its colonies took root in the West Indies, France locked up the continental market for sugar and coffee. Sales of French fur and fish also thrived. Ships of the French East India Company plied the enormous route from Lorient in Brittany to French outposts in India. Slavers from Nantes scoured West Africa. The ports of Italy and Spain filled with Marseilles's traders, and busy merchant fleets linked the French Atlantic ports to the New World.

With all these opportunities, France's shipping trade grew faster than Britain's in the years of Jean Lelarge's apprenticeship. "Britannia Rule the Waves" was only a pious hope in England when the famous song was written in 1740, but a clash was coming, and Britain's drive to fulfil that hope would profoundly alter the later years of Jean Lelarge's life. In the meantime, French merchants and seamen thrived. When Jean Lelarge completed his apprenticeship and returned to Ile Royale in 1734, prospects for a master manner in the French merchant marine had never looked better.

If the years had transformed young Jean Lelarge from a wilful youth to a seasoned navigator, they had also worked changes in the family he had left behind. Lelarge had missed his sister Jeanne's marriage to his shipmate Pierre Chouteau. Now he learned that the birth of their child, his niece Charlotte Chouteau, in the spring of 1733 had been closely followed by Jeanne's death. Later that year the unlucky Chouteau had left his infant daughter in the Lelarges' care while he set out on a coastal voyage, one from which he never returned. The fate of Chouteau, his ship, and his crew remained unknown, but by the time Jean Lelarge returned, proceedings were under way to place the fifteen-month-old orphan under her grandmother's guardianship.

During his travels Jean Lelarge had also escaped the smallpox epidemic that had ravaged Louisbourg. His family had been less fortunate. Among the first victims had been his fifteen-year-old sister Geneviève, who died in the fall of 1732. The next to sicken had been Pierre Lelarge.

When the aging carpenter fell ill at the beginning of 1733, his family must have sought all the medical aid Louisbourg could offer. The five friars of the Order of Hospitallers of Saint-Jean-de-Dieu were already overworked, trying to ease the suffering of the poor townspeople and the soldiers crowded into their hospital, so the Lelarges probably called in one of the surgeons. As well as being bone-setters, surgeons like the Lelarges' neighbour Louis Lagrange could prescribe medicine and potions to relieve at least the symptoms of disease. They administered enemas and bleedings to remedy vaguely understood internal disorders. But over smallpox they were powerless. Inoculation, the injection of a mild, resistible dose of smallpox to save patients from a harsher fate, had been introduced in Europe in 1718, but it had been vigorously resisted and does not seem to have reached the French colonies at all. Vaccination, rendering patients immune to smallpox by the injection of harmless cowpox, would not be discovered for decades. Medical science could do little for Pierre Lelarge, though broths, infusions, and sleeping draughts may have eased his passing. As hope of prevention turned to acceptance of fate, Pierre Lelarge strove mostly for the attainment of that eighteenth-century ideal, the good death.

At sixty, Pierre Lelarge was among the older men of his community: he had prepared for the inevitable end long before the onset of the smallpox epidemic. Carefully withdrawing from carpentry over several years, he had established the inn that would support his widow and his younger children after his passing. To have achieved this amid all the upheavals of a new community should have been a comfort to him, for preparing the earthly security of one's dependants was a major precondition for the good death. Even more crucial was spiritual security: Lelarge would have planned memorial masses for the repose of his soul and offered donations to the Récollets or the sisters of Notre-Dame. All preparations made, Pierre Lelarge could play out the last scene of the good death, which was marred only by the absence of his eldest son. After receiving the last sacraments of his religion from one of the Récollet pastors, the carpenter died at his home in January 1733, attended by most of his family.

Well supported through her husband's foresight, the widow Lelarge kept her household going. The epidemic ran out its course a few months after Pierre Lelarge's death and the family regained its equilibrium. The tavern flourished. When her younger son showed interest in following Jean's seagoing career, she was prosperous enough to begin investing in small coastal craft. In 1734 the busy home and inn on Rue de l'Etang housed her three children, her orphaned granddaughter, a pair of servants, and eight sailors, tenants whom she probably kept busy hauling supplies for sale to her late husband's friends in the building trades.

Characteristically, Jean Lelarge preferred not to join this comfortable, unambitious family enterprise. In November 1734 he took the decisive step that completed his apprenticeship, asking the Admiralty to certify him a qualified master mariner. Doubtless proud of the achievements of a local boy, a pupil of hydrographer Cruchon, the Admiralty officers winked at Lelarge's dubious claim to be of age and ordered that his skills be examined. Sweeping through the tests posed by Cruchon and two qualified sea captains, the candidate quickly won his certificate as "Captain Lelarge, high seas pilot and ship master, entitled to pilot and command any merchant vessel entrusted to his care in every kind of high seas voyage." The apprenticeship was over.

Jean Lelarge was not the only Louisbourg boy to have risen to master mariner, nor even the youngest, but he had been unusually fortunate. Most of his fellow captains from Louisbourg were sons of merchant shipowners who had assisted and supervised their children's progress by giving them work. Youths of Lelarge's age and background rarely passed through navigational school, even during the decade that one existed in Louisbourg. Like the unfortunate Chouteau, most stayed in the coastal trade, where no master's papers were needed and where a young man with a helpful family could aspire to command a schooner at an early age. By qualifying as a master mariner, Lelarge had definitively broken the bonds of his background. He no longer needed to go abroad to evade parental authority, and in Ile Royale his chances of command were excellent. The merchants and shipowners knew him well, and local pride probably encouraged them as they put the house-builder's son in command of the cod-laden schooners they regularly dispatched to the Caribbean.

So opened a decade of voyages between Louisbourg and the French West Indies, Lelarge always in command, always improving his seamanship, honing his commercial skills. In 1739 his command was *Concorde*, a trim schooner owned by a local entrepreneur who must often have dealt with Lelarge's father. *Concorde* loaded codfish at Louisbourg and the nearby outports, perhaps adding some bricks or lumber for diversity, then left Ile Royale below the northern horizon to run almost due south until the Southern Cross began to rise over the night bow. Near the Tropic of Cancer, three weeks out from Louisbourg, Captain Lelarge swung his course westward, perhaps making landfall among the tiny, arid Caicos Islands before closing with the lush north coast of Saint-Domingue.

This big island, named Hispaniola since the time of Christopher Columbus, had known European settlement since 1492, French control since 1697. Spanish conquistadors had subjugated and then wiped out the native nations of the island. They began the process of adapting the island to European needs, clearing the jungle to introduce new species of trees and plants, bringing cattle and goats that wandered off to join the local fauna, but they never fully mastered the rugged island. Distracted by the golden prospects of the mainland, they allowed other nations to complete the transformation of Hispaniola. It was under French auspices that the western third of the island, renamed Saint-Domingue, began its rise to world attention as a source of sugar and coffee.

Jean Lelarge's port of call in Saint-Domingue was Cap François, the colonial capital. Slightly larger than Louisbourg, though scarcely any older, Cap François was framed by green hills rather than fortress walls. Going ashore in the ship's boat, the visitor from Ile Royale might have noted some familiar aspects in the town: a quay crowded with the products of French trade, a network of merchants and clerks and customs men bargaining over them. But to see Cap François's *raison d'être*, Lelarge should have gone inland, for the few thousand city folk were only a tiny share of Saint-Domingue's quarter-million people.

Saint-Domingue was a sugar-grower's paradise; just beyond the town the landscape was dominated by fields of sugarcane dotted with their beehive-shaped stone windmills. There were hundreds of *sucreries* in Saint-Domingue, and each one was a large and valuable estate with expensive crushing mills and masses of labourers. The owners were often absentee landlords, living comfortably in Bordeaux or on a French country estate. The labourers were slaves, thousands of them brought from Africa every year until they outnumbered the white population by ten or fifteen to one. More numerous every year, they would consume all the dried cod that men like Lelarge could haul down from the north. In the lush climate and broad expanses of Saint-Domingue, their labour enabled the French planters to increase sugar production at an explosive rate, cutting costs and prices until cheap French sugar commanded the European market. Planters born in the islands were known as *créoles*, and their prosperity in these years made "rich as a creole" a byword for new-found wealth and opulence.

Travelling through the countryside to visit a client at his plantation, Lelarge would have spotted small holdings of coffee, cocoa, indigo, and cotton adding variety to a vista dominated by pale green acres of waving sugarcane. Some of these small holdings belonged to blacks, for wealthy masters occasionally freed a favoured slave, and

French law gave freedmen all the rights of citizenship. Freedmen and mixed bloods were to be found throughout the colony, even serving in its militia, but few slaves could expect such fortune. Some sought freedom more directly. The mountainous interior of Saint-Domingue sheltered groups of escaped slaves whom the French called *marrons* and accused of unspeakable crimes. The *marrons* nursed a spirit of rebellion among the slave majority of Saint-Domingue. In the 1790s, when half a million slaves rose to create the first black republic in the Americas, some Louisbourg families who had settled in Saint-Domingue witnessed the beginning of this bloody and destructive liberation before escaping to yet another refuge. But Jean Lelarge was not one of these. He knew Saint-Domingue between 1730 and 1745, and usually limited his visits to the ports of Cap François and Léogane, where he exchanged cod for sugar and rum, probably without much concern for the complex, tragic society the sugar island was building.

Saint-Domingue was not the only French island Lelarge would visit in his Caribbean voyages. Island-hopping down the long chain of the Leeward and Windward islands, Lelarge could touch at Guadeloupe and Martinique and perhaps also at Grenada, far down by the South American coast. Frenchmen had been the original European conquerors of these islands, dislodging the fierce Caribs in a series of wars begun in 1635. By Lelarge's day, none was as valuable as huge young Saint-Domingue, but they remained important producers of sugar and spice. Martinique in particular thought itself superior to the brash new colony of Saint-Domingue. It had a long-established, wealthy, and cultured white population of fifteen thousand, twice as many as Guadeloupe. About eighty thousand slaves laboured at the *sucreries* that covered almost all the arable land of the two islands, but, even here, hilltop refuges harboured a few desperate *marrons*.

By the 1740s Jean Lelarge was a veteran of the West Indian trade, as familiar with blue Caribbean waters as with the stormy coasts of his home. In the small, heavy-laden schooners with their crews of eight or ten, the southward voyage took about a month. Another month or two could be consumed in inter-island voyages and in bargaining, as the captain or travelling merchant sought the best exchange of cod for sugar. Delays at this stage could mean a dangerous race against both the autumn hurricanes of the Caribbean and the winter ice of Ile Royale, so Lelarge sometimes sold his vessel and discharged his crew in the islands, waiting out the winter to find a new ship and another crew for the northward voyage. On one occasion, finding the new ship gave him an unsought opportunity to see the ultimate destination of much of the sugar he hauled north from the Caribbean: Boston.

In Lelarge's day the British colonies of New England were off-limits to French sailors, but not to the goods they transported. Like most maritime nations of that century, France discouraged its colonies from foreign trade, hoping to keep trade within the empire and mono-polized by French ships and seamen. But when two vigorous and complementary colonial economies lay close together under different flags, some compromise had to be devised, if only to keep the customs services of both empires from a wearisome war against smugglers.

Trade between Ile Royale and New England had precisely this irresistible logic. Ile Royale needed the livestock, fresh produce, and building materials of the Thirteen Colonies, and thirsty New England sought the cheap rum and molasses Ile Royale acquired from the French sugar islands. So practical an exchange won grudging tolerance from the French authorities, but the principle of imperial prefer-ence was maintained. Only specified commodities would be traded with the foreigners, and the exchanges had to take place at Louisbourg, under supervision. No French ship or captain was permitted to sail from Louisbourg to trade in New England. That route was left to American ships, whose captains would have to flout or evade the British customs regulations. Though everyone knew the sugar prod-ucts Jean Lelarge brought north travelled quite licitly on toward Boston, Newport, or Salem, Lelarge himself could only have made that voyage at risk of forfeiting his career to a charge of smuggling. He stuck to the Caribbean sailings.

Then in 1743 bizarre circumstances diverted him from his regular course. He had wintered in Saint-Domingue that year and sailed north from Léogane in June in a brigantine manned by eleven of the usual multinational assortment of footloose mariners. Owned by a Léogane merchant named Berge, the brigantine carried molasses and a low-grade rum called tafia. Lelarge's northward voyage was entirely routine until roughly the latitude of Bermuda, when eight of his sailors abruptly took up arms and seized the ship. Announcing themselves to be New Englanders, the mutineers forced Lelarge and the three loyal men aboard to set a course for Boston. Effectively pirated, Lelarge could only comply. Within a few days he gained his first sight of the metropolis of British North America.

Though few of them had been there, Louisbourg's people knew Boston through the New England sailors and merchants who came regularly to trade at the French port. Despite language barriers and imperial rivalries, an affinity could be seen between the two cities. Like Louisbourg, Boston was a port city on an inhospitable shore, yet it had prospered from fishing and shipping, then made itself the trading heart of the northern British colonies. In 1743 it was a century-old city of 16,000 people, the largest city in the Thirteen Colonies, the centre of American overseas trade, and the home of a secure and prosperous merchant community. Could a few farseeing Louisbourg merchants have found in Boston an ideal to emulate? In Lelarge's day the difference in scale was tremendous. All of New France had barely 50,000 people in 1743, when the Thirteen Colonies boasted nearly one million. Yet Louisbourg's trades were Boston's in miniature, and in the long run Nova Scotian schoonermen would take up what Jean Lelarge was beginning. Carrying fish and timber all over the Atlantic and picking up whatever cargoes offered, the Bluenose fleet was to be a powerful force in the late days of sail, and Halifax merchants like Samuel Cunard would build fortunes their Boston counterparts had to respect.

When Jean Lelarge's hijackers permitted him to go ashore in Boston, he counted on the affinity that linked the shipowners of Boston and Louisbourg to help him take revenge on the mutineers. Seeking redress, he went straight to a leading Boston merchant house, that run by the heirs of the recently deceased businessman and civic benefactor Peter Faneuil. Like most New England merchant firms, the House of Faneuil often bought French sugar products, directly or by way of Louisbourg. The Faneuils, descended from French Huguenots, dealt frequently with Berge, the owner of the pirated vessel. Since they also traded at Louisbourg, Lelarge presumed they would have every reason to assist him in putting down piracy and preserving friendly relations between the French and American merchant communities.

Instead, he got a rude rebuff. When the Faneuils bluntly announced that Berge owed them money from previous dealings and that they intended to hold the brigantine until their accounts were settled, Lelarge discovered who had motivated the pirates in his crew. The Faneuils, thwarted in their attempts to pursue their foreign debtor by law, had sought redress on their own, engineering the seizure of one of Berge's vessels on the high seas. Lelarge, an innocent victim of the dispute, could now see why the pirates had so blithely brought the brigantine straight within reach of the law. Nonplussed for once in his career, he sought advice. Boston was full of merchants and captains familiar with Louisbourg and probably with Lelarge personally. As one man, they warned that if he approached the customs service the ship and cargo would probably have to be seized as foreign contraband, since French–Bostonian trade links were officially nonexistent. Better to gloss over the piracy and let Berge make his own arrangements with the Faneuils.

While he considered his options, Captain Lelarge might have taken the opportunity to see the landmarks of Boston. Notable among them was the newly completed market building and public forum, donated to the city by the man for whom it was named, Mr. Peter Faneuil.

After further unsuccessful representations to the parties involved, Lelarge finally sought passage aboard a Louisbourg-bound schooner, bringing home only such cargo as did not belong to the unfortunate Berge. It was an ignominious homecoming for a proud captain, but within a year Lelarge would be back in New England waters to wreak a personal revenge on New England ships and seamen. His years of peacetime sailing were drawing to a close.

Jean Lelarge had spent a decade sailing between Louisbourg and the French West Indian ports, and in those years he must have spent almost as much time in the Caribbean as in Ile Royale. Each time his ship battled its way through chilly northern waters and all-enveloping fogs toward the stern coast of Ile Royale, did he look back with regret to the sunny skies, warm waters, and luxurious breezes of the sugar islands? His own feelings were never recorded, but other sons and daughters of Ile Royale have left opinions surprising to our sun-worshipping century.

Jacques Iger was a contemporary of Jean Lelarge who married at Louisbourg in 1739 and raised a large family. Exiled by the capture of their home in 1758, the Igers lived on charity in France until 1765, when their eldest son, Pierre, found work in the colonial service and took his family with him to his posting in Guadeloupe. For years afterwards, members of the family bombarded successive colonial ministers with the tale of their woes there. First to write was Pierre's mother, wife of Jacques, the once-affluent Louisbourg merchant. "In 1765 this unhappy family travelled at royal expense to Guadeloupe," she wrote. "There the father and one of the sons succumbed immediately to the heat of the climate, so different from that of Ile Royale. Your petitioner and the two sons and two daughters left to her have continually been ill. . . . They can no longer withstand the climate of Guadeloupe . . . but are condemned to drag out in this island a languishing existence."

Later, back in Paris, Pierre Iger wrote in similar terms, and his pleas had some effect, for the colonial ministry offered him a promotion. But by then France had few colonies left in northern latitudes: this time the post was in Martinique. Iger finally put career over climatic preference and returned to the Caribbean, but his family's horror of the West Indian climate was widely shared and broadly based. The hot sun and tropical diseases of the Caribbean exacted a fearsome toll from the Europeans and Africans who laboured there in the centuries before medical technology, improved sanitation, and air conditioning made the tropical climate pleasant and comfortable. The health dangers of the Caribbean prevented many people from appreciating warm climates the way later centuries have. Europeans of the Igers' time went all over the world to build their empires, but the only climates they approved of were temperate ones. The Caribbean was not considered temperate, but Ile Royale was: after eighteen years in the tropics Pierre Iger was still nostalgic for his birthplace.

By 1745 Jean Lelarge's voyaging had taken him all over the Atlantic Ocean, but he probably shared Pierre Iger's opinion of the climates he had seen. Appropriately enough, for later service in tropical waters would ruin Lelarge's health and hasten him to an early grave. The sea captain probably expressed no sorrow when northward voyages brought his ships to a latitude where he could replace the light cottons and silks he wore in Saint-Domingue with the woollens and leathers sailors needed in the northwest Atlantic.

But Jean Lelarge had another reason to hurry home from distant ports. On every voyage, from the time he received his captain's papers, there had been a girl awaiting his return to Louisbourg.

IV

Louise Samson was an Acadian. Her father, Gabriel, raised in Québec and trained as a shipwright, had moved to Port Royal and married a local girl by 1704. Carried to Boston by raiding privateers in 1705, the Samsons saw their eldest child born in New England, but they managed to return to Acadia soon afterwards. There they raised a large family, staying on even after the English captured Port Royal in 1710. In 1713, when English possession of Acadia was confirmed, the Samsons chose to remain in the old town, now renamed Annapolis Royal. Louise Samson was born there in 1715. But her father must slowly have been nurturing the old grievance against the rulers who had once held him prisoner for a year: about 1720 the Samsons moved from the English domains to Port Toulouse in Ile Royale, where Gabriel joined the small community of Acadian carpenters and navigators who built and sailed many of Ile Royale's coastal craft.

Jean Lelarge may first have made the Samsons' acquaintance through his professional links to the mariners of Port Toulouse, but soon Louise Samson had moved to Louisbourg. Her older sister, Boston-born Madeleine, had married a Louisbourg man, Jean Richard, and when the girls' mother died, young Louise went to live with her sister and help out in her brother-in-law's inn, just a block from the Lelarge home on Rue de l'Etang. The friendship of the shipwright's daughter and the aspiring navigator seems to have blossomed in the lively, sociable atmosphere of the Richard inn. Each time

Lelarge returned to his home port, their mutual attraction grew stronger, and by the time he won his captain's papers, Lelarge was her recognized suitor. Early in 1735 the couple called a few friends to Richard's inn, where they solemnly exchanged written promises of marriage. It was a curious, romantic venture, for the private agreement apparently left aside all the hardheaded financial details that were the meat of most marriage contracts. The signing was witnessed only by their close friends, but both felt bound by it. Jean Lelarge paid court to the girl each time he returned to Louisbourg, and Louise Samson virtuously refused the other young men who sought her company.

The private engagement lasted two years. Then, waiting out the long layoff of the winter of 1736–37, Lelarge decided it was time he was married. There was no objection from Louise Samson, who already had the consent of both her father and the brother-in-law under whose care she lived. The problem lay on Lelarge's own side, as a visit to the *curé* soon confirmed. Captain Lelarge was barely twenty-five in 1737; since Plaisance's baptismal registers were lost he may have been uncertain of his exact age. Because men under thirty needed parental consent to marry, the *curé* felt duty-bound to consult the prospective bridegroom's parents. He did so, and found the widow Lelarge unwilling to consent to her son's marriage.

Why?

It seems unlikely that any simple matter of economics, or even a question of social prestige, formed an obstacle. A rising young navigator with business opportunities all around might have aspired to a match more illustrious than an Acadian girl who helped out in a tavern, yet Lelarge himself was of unashamedly plain origins and his mother's tavern enjoyed no greater cachet than Jean Richard's substantial inn. The match would have seemed perfectly appropriate to the town's marriage brokers; the proudest mother should have seen no disgrace in it.

Some personal antagonism between mother and bride-to-be could have surfaced during the couple's courtship, but had this been the only factor, the *curé* could probably have shamed the widow into consent. Inclined to prefer early marriage to the temptations that might attend enforced bachelorhood, any priest would have swept away so unchristian an obstacle. A likelier cause lay in more subtle conflicts between mother and son, deep-rooted ones that the *curé* would hesitate to oppose.

All his life Jean Lelarge seems to have done pretty much as he pleased. At every step he neglected filial duty as the widow Lelarge might have interpreted it: choosing a career at sea in preference to the family trade, ranging off on his own while his family suffered through the smallpox epidemic, seeking his own fortunes when he might have been contributing to the family estate. Perhaps it had galled his hardworking mother to see her son's capricious ways rewarded with the string of successes that had left him largely free from dependence on his family. Lelarge's private betrothal to Louise Samson seems to have been another step taken without care for his own family's interest or concern. When he decided quite on his own that it was time to marry, his mother may have held back her consent merely to make her wayward and youthful son observe the proprieties for once. If he would not humble himself to plead for her approval, then it might be good for the proud captain, the independent world traveller, to cool his heels until he was undeniably old enough to act for himself. If such was her motive, the widow must have been horrified by the precipitate action that her refusal provoked in her headstrong son.

One February Monday in 1737, Père Etienne Legoff, *curé* of Notre-Dame-des-Anges and a well-liked Récollet of long experience in Ile Royale, was offering morning mass at the barracks chapel for a congregation perhaps slightly larger than usual, including Jean Lelarge and Louise Samson, both of whom he knew well. The mass, a perfectly ordinary event of the town's day, proceeded unexceptionally until Père Etienne turned to offer the final benediction. As he began to bless the congregation, the priest was surprised to see a young couple stand and approach the balustrade fringing the altar. Surprise turned to amazement. When Jean Lelarge and Louise Samson began announcing in loud voices that they took each other for man and wife, Père Etienne seized the consecrated host from the altar and fled in horror to the sacristy, shocked and angered by this profanation of the divine service. In the chapel, pandemonium was erupting. Lelarge rushed from one spectator to another, demanding they be witnesses to his marriage. Some refused angrily, some accepted. One young man raised a laugh by observing that if they had just been married, they should hardly be standing around collecting signatures. "Off to bed with you" was his ribald advice.

It was not so simple. Père Etienne had gone straight from his sacristy to the civil authorities, protesting the scandalous behaviour of two people who sought to perform their own imitation of the marriage sacrament in defiance of ritual, custom, and good order. Such anarchic behaviour would not be ignored: the civil authorities acted with dispatch, lest the mock marriage lead to an all-too-real consummation. By mid-morning Louise Samson had been escorted firmly to the convent, where the nuns were advised to be sure she remained. As for Captain Lelarge, the would-be bridegroom had been flung unceremoniously into a guardhouse cell while priest, townspeople, and authorities tried to determine what was going on.

Jean Lelarge, unwilling to be thwarted by convention, had worked up a self-serving theological rationalization by which to circumvent his mother's opposition to his marriage. First he had consulted Père Etienne and the other Récollets at a dinner party. By skilful questioning, he had elicited from them confirmation that a marriage was in essence an exchange of vows between two people before God. The moment of marriage was the freely given vow, binding for life, made in God's sight by the bride and groom, and the priest who sanctified the marriage vows was really only God's witness. This was sound theology as far as it went. On the strength of it, Lelarge had decided to make the *curé* an inadvertent, or even a reluctant, witness, by rising to take the marriage vows with Louise Samson in the middle of mass.

In devising a theology that discounted both priests and parents, Lelarge and his bride were following a well-worn path of rebellion against society's constraints. At one time the church itself had held that a priest could not refuse to bless the marriage of any couple who met the religious requirements. But society demanded that the church tailor its stand to practical requirements. If marriage could be made by the couple alone, ran the argument, how could young heiresses be protected from unscrupulous fortune hunters? Youthful heirs might be inveigled into hasty marriage by any comely adventuress. There were, after all, civil consequences to the sacred contract that was a marriage. Estates could not be managed or lineages preserved without a close rein on the impetuous desires of one's heirs. Eventually the church yielded to this civil pressure. Parental permission became a requirement of the canon law, and in time clergymen became as conservative as the fathers of impressionable heiresses. But the romantic theory espoused by Lelarge had survived, a lovers' underground in resistance to the dreary practicality of church and family. The belief that theology supported those who stood up in church to exchange marriage vows in defiance of authority gave birth to the scandalous tradition of *mariage à la gaulmine*, named for a seventeenth-century courtier who had evaded parental opposition to his marriage with the help of a complaisant priest and fast horses.

By Lelarge's time, Gaulmin's custom was in decay. Throughout the French realm, the only men to attempt marriages *à la gaulmine* were military officers whose commanders had been slow to accord them permission to marry. Such men could often rely on aristocratic privilege to save them from the wrath of church and state. They needed such shelter. Conservative bishops and magistrates, now united in abhorrence of the custom, had suppressed the popular tradition of marriage *à la gaulmine*, and one had never been attempted in Ile Royale before 1737. The reckless couple faced grave consequences if the courts and the public were inclined to look harshly on their Monday-morning sensation.

Jean Lelarge's bravado was extinguished neither by the failure of his gambit nor by his incarceration. After a few days in the guardhouse cell, he sent his judges a cocksure petition. "I ask a grace from you, Messieurs," it began, "that you should define the matter in question. If it is a criminal matter then may the law take its course. But if it is not, I pray most humbly that you do not waste a young man's time."

After brazenly questioning whether the matter should even concern the civil courts, Lelarge expanded his defence. He had sought no fortune in this marriage beyond what was appropriate to him, he said. Happiness was all he sought, and he wished the thing were finished without offence to the church, to his mother, or to the public. He paraded injured virtue: should an inclination that might have come from God be blocked by force, ruining two reputations in the process? "If I had abused the trust of a member of the weaker sex," he cried, "is it not true that they would have obliged me to marry her that I had abused? Yet no one can claim anything against this girl's virtue." Noting that the King himself wanted to see marriages that would help the peopling of his colony, Lelarge closed with the same bold flourish of his opening. "I beg very humbly that you be so good as to allow me not to waste the time that I need for a career that I believe well begun."

Lelarge's petition became part of the dossier of a careful investigation by civil powers vigilant against breaches of public decorum in their community. The would-be bride and groom were each interrogated. Jean Lelarge claimed he had taken his theology from catechism phrases cited by Père Etienne himself. He denied that anyone had counselled him but admitted mentioning his plans to friends. Called in her turn before the powerful judge in his chambers, Louise Samson was as unawed as her fiancé and equally circumspect. Asked about their associates, she avoided criticism of Lelarge's mother and exposed no accomplices to their action. Though she admitted she had been following Lelarge's lead in going to the church that morning, she staunchly pointed out that the young man had been promising marriage for a long time and that for his sake she had refused all her other suitors. She was twenty-one, after all, and had younger friends already married and raising children. Unable to read or write, she declined the invitation to read and sign her deposition.

By this time, the worldly young *ordonnateur* supervising the case seems to have been finding it hard to maintain the appropriate air of shock and scandal. The matter hardly seemed sinister, and the behaviour of some witnesses suggested an undercurrent of public sympathy.

Among the witnesses called was Louis Loppinot, the man who had joked when asked to witness Lelarge's irregular marriage. Loppinot, the son of a royal official of Acadia, had been enrolled since childhood as a future officer of the colonial troops, but owing to the crowd of candidates he was, at the age of thirty, still a cadet awaiting an ensign's posting. His interrogation suggests some of the suspicions aroused by this affair. Military officers, privileged, protected, and left with time on their hands, tended to be leaders in most matters of illicit sexuality, and there may have been concern that Lelarge and Samson were following their bad example. Louis Loppinot himself kept a mistress, a widow who would cause a sensation in 1738 by presenting one of Loppinot's illegitimate daughters for baptism barely two weeks after the young officer married someone else. Less aristocratic than some of his brother officers, a neighbour to Jean Richard and future husband of an innkeeper's daughter, Loppinot enjoyed the easygoing society centred on taverns like Richard's. He had been a witness to the betrothal of Lelarge and Samson, and the judges suspected he had helped to plot their attempt at marriage. Under questioning, however, he disclaimed all knowledge of the defendants' plans, as did every other witness.

Such evidence helped to calm the judges, for every description suggested the young couple's behaviour had been inappropriate but not immoral. Nevertheless, another military officer's name mentioned in the investigation renewed memories of a scandalous affair several years old. In his testimony, Jean Lelarge claimed a priest told him that Captain de Gannes had successfully been married in the unorthodox fashion attempted by Lelarge and Samson.

Lelarge and the priest were mistaken in this notion, but the marriage in question had indeed been a public scandal. In 1730 Captain Michel de Gannes de Falaise of the local garrison had been prevented from marrying the daughter of a fellow officer. The priests had refused to perform the ceremony, citing the opposition of de Gannes's mistress, Marie-Anne Carrerot, who claimed he was still bound by a promise to marry her.

This débâcle was only one step in a contest between Michel de Gannes and Marie-Anne Carrerot that had opened in 1728. At that time, de Gannes was a twenty-six-year-old lieutenant newly arrived from Canada and very popular with the ladies of the local elite. Marie-Anne Carrerot, at least ten years older, was the widow of an officer and had at least one child. She later testified she had at first rejected de Gannes's courtship because of his faithless reputation. Won over by his promises of marriage, she eventually relented so far as to sleep with her persuasive young suitor, and in the summer of 1728 she became pregnant. She asked de Gannes to save her honour by a hasty marriage, but the lieutenant first temporized and then refused outright. Facing disgrace, she prosecuted her former lover for his breach of promise.

Marie-Anne Carrerot's plea to the court makes an enlightening discourse on love and sexuality. To justify sleeping with her lover before their marriage, she gave the same rationalization Lelarge would use for his irregular marriage a decade later. "In effect," asserted the abandoned woman, "the reciprocal consent of eligible parties produces the essential form of the sacrament of marriage." In Marie-Anne Carrerot's eyes, the exchange of promises – that for Lelarge constituted the essence of a wedding – was a justification for her affair with de Gannes. The *curé* to whom she explained this theory in 1728 was unconvinced, but he did support her contention that to marry before the birth of her child would save her honour and legitimize the infant.

De Gannes remained obdurate to legal pursuit, to clerical pleading, and to his mistress's tears. His word as an officer and a gentlemen was at risk, so he said as little as possible, but he would not marry Marie-Anne Carrerot. She and little Michelle-Ange had to be content with the child support he was obliged to pay, and de Gannes eventually succeeded in making the marriage he preferred.

In her misfortunes, Marie-Anne Carrerot shared her community's attitudes about the limits of acceptable behaviour. Many children of all social classes were born and proudly presented for baptism just weeks or months after their parents' marriages, and there was also tolerance for relationships out of marriage that were forced by circumstance: a deserted wife living with a sergeant she was unable to marry, a needy widow supported by a wealthy protector. But in general the people of Louisbourg were far more restrained in their sexuality than prestigious officers like Loppinot and de Gannes. More inclined to wife-beating than to adultery, the working people of Louisbourg feared illicit sexuality. Affairs involving married women were rare, and servants, slaves, or needy mothers whose consent could easily be coerced were the victims of seducers much more often than single women of Marie-Anne Carrerot's standing. But if adultery was repressed, talk of it was not: accusations of sexual misbehaviour were among the commonest of insults. A woman actually suspected of wantonness could rarely be forgiven. She was liable to the harshest abuse possible: the suggestion that she was hiding a previous career of prostitution. No one knew this better than the Bonnier sisters, Servanne and Perrine, a pair of busybodies who turned up as witnesses or antagonists in a remarkable number of petty street-squabbles. As a teenaged dressmaker's apprentice living in her uncle's home, Servanne had become pregnant by her cousin. The widow Lelarge had delivered the child. It was later established that the pair were not first cousins, and they eventually married with a dispensation, but the desperate vigour with which both Bonnier sisters thereafter gave and got accusations of disgraceful sexual careers suggests how dangerous it was to permit any licentious taint to attach to one's family name. Fear of public whispering restrained Marie-Anne Carrerot from misbehaviour until de Gannes's promise of marriage legitimized their relationship, for only the military aristocrats could safely transgress the community code. If their escapade in the chapel had been given sexual connotations, Jean Lelarge, Louise Samson, and both their families would have been extremely vulnerable to their community's disapproval. Therein lay the importance of the court hearing: a conviction would be a reflection of community censure and would expose them to further disgrace.

Lucky Lelarge got his way once more. Vigorously defending his fiancée's virtue, Lelarge successfully projected himself as an honourable suitor forced to unorthodox behaviour only by the obstacles cruel authority placed in the way of true love. The community was won over – indeed the bravado of their action seems to have enhanced their popularity. Even the courts yielded to the lovers. Lelarge the seasoned captain and Samson the fiancée who worried she was getting too old were called "boy" and "girl" by the judges, who chose to see their exploit as one of youthful impetuosity rather than of defiant immorality. They were admonished and given a token fine. Samson spent a fortnight in the convent, Lelarge the same time in the guardhouse; then both were sent to seek the *curé*'s forgiveness and discuss with him a more proper marriage.

These meetings must have gone well. Just six months after their scandalous mock wedding, Jean-François Lelarge married Marguerite-Louise Samson in the same chapel – this time in a formal ceremony with Lelarge's mother and their other relatives in attendance. Jean-Aimable Lelarge, the first of their four children, was born nine months and nine days afterwards.

Despite Captain Lelarge's frequent absences, his marriage was a long and successful one. Even his mother was reconciled to it and to her son. In 1743, when Lelarge limped home from his encounter with piracy in Boston, his mother advanced the money that bought a ship for one of his regular employers. He promptly hired Lelarge as its captain. The widow earned a tidy profit in the transaction, and Jean Lelarge was back in command.

V

Born near the close of a long war between Britain and France, Jean Lelarge grew up in decades of peace, and his career swept forward in the surging global commerce of those times. In peace Lelarge learned seamanship, explored the Atlantic, and mastered the intricacies of his business. In 1744 he was in his early thirties, prosperous, experienced, an established master mariner with a family in Louisbourg and regular work in the Caribbean trade.

That year war came, and his career turned inside out. Suddenly caught up in the struggle for control of the seas that would pit Britain against France in each succeeding decade until 1805, Lelarge would never again be a merchant sailor. Henceforth his vigour and his seamanship would be put to the service of the Crown. From 1744 to the end of his life, Lelarge was a privateer and naval officer, and the battles that dominated the history of his colony would transform his family's future.

The war that changed Jean Lelarge's life in 1744 began far away and four years earlier, with the death of a king of whom Lelarge would barely have heard. The demise in 1740 of Charles VI, the Hapsburg emperor of Austria, encouraged France to join Prussia in seeking aggrandizement at the expense of his successor, Maria Theresa. Great Britain, warring since 1739 with France's ally Spain, could not tolerate the prospect of a French victory that could leave Louis XV the master of continental Europe. The stage was set for conflict between Britain and France. This war, inevitably named the War of Austrian Succession, was destined to be an inconclusive struggle in which central Europe was the prime concern of all the belligerents, so the outbreak of Anglo-French conflict in March 1744 sent no fleets of warships speeding to Louisbourg. The French Marine strengthened its usual patrols in North American waters, but the small, duty-laden French navy kept to European waters, relying on privateers to carry the war to the English in America. The declaration of war went to Ile Royale along with an exhortation to outfit as many privateers as possible.

Privateering was a legitimate part of naval warfare throughout European history, and every seafaring nation offered letters of marque to its captains and shipowners at the outbreak of war. Privateering let maritime nations carry war wherever their merchant fleets sailed, and offered seamen and shipowners a livelihood when war made trade hazardous and expensive. The French Marine reasonably hoped that Ile Royale, the home of a substantial maritime population, would quickly become a centre for privateering exploits against New England's nearby shipping lanes.

At first the response was disappointing. After five years of slumping fish catches and struggling trade, many of Louisbourg's hard-pressed commercial leaders were cautious about flinging their small ships and smaller resources into risky privateering ventures. Many acquired letters of marque for their fishing boats, so that these vessels could make easy plunder when they met English fishermen unaware of war's outbreak, but most refrained from major investments in large, well-armed combat craft.

Only two keen privateers stepped forth that spring. Pierre Morpain and Joannis Dolabaratz, two of the colony's senior captains, sallied forth immediately in *Succès* and *Cantabre* to make several quick prizes. Their exploits encouraged more cautious men, and Louisbourg's war fleet began to grow. But the easy pickings quickly disappeared. Captain Dolabaratz soon discovered that New England was outfitting its own privateers and coast guards. On his second cruise into New England waters, he fell in with a larger Boston warship and was captured.

As more vessels joined the campaign, the privateering war of 1744 became a vicious, hazardous struggle which only the strong ships survived. A well-armed *corsaire* might make capture after capture with ease, meeting only lightly armed merchantmen or amateur privateers, but his fate was quickly sealed if he met a large privateer or a naval vessel. Territory meant nothing; neither power's privateers could sweep the other's from the sea. Even as Dolabaratz and his partner Beaubassin were ravaging the New England coast in *Cantabre* and *César*, American privateers were attacking fishing boats within sight of Louisbourg. Morpain went out in *Caribou* and seized one of them, but when he was recalled to port, other raiders returned to capture fishing schooners, shallops, and four French merchantmen along the coast of Ile Royale.

It was late fall before Jean Lelarge went privateering. Perhaps a winter voyage – making up for the humiliation of 1743 – had occupied him well into summer. Perhaps he had been in Louisbourg all the time, vainly seeking a *corsaire*'s command from the cautious shipowners of the town. It may even have been family responsibility that held him back. In May 1744 the Lelarges' third child was born, and in September they conceived a fourth. Perhaps the wayward son, growing into a dutiful family man, hesitated to answer the call of war.

Finally, late in the year, Lelarge joined a new privateer, a large one intended for a winter campaign against New England's trade with Europe. *Brasdor* was owned by a visiting businessman named Maillet and financed by a dozen prominent men of Louisbourg, including Lelarge's military neighbours the Loppinot brothers. Their detailed records tell how *Brasdor* prepared for war. Four six-pound cannon, eight three-pounders, and six swivel guns were mounted. A large stock of powder and ball came aboard, and the gunroom received sixty-six muskets, forty sabres, and six battle-axes. Bills poured in as carpenters, smiths, sailmakers, and draymen helped put the vessel into fighting trim. Maillet hired a drummer to rouse recruits and signed on 104 men, giving each a bonus of twenty *sols*. To feed his warriors, Maillet loaded nearly nine thousand pounds of bread into *Brasdor*'s holds, following that with twenty hundredweight of salt pork, and nearly as much in dried peas. There was a little butter, a little cod, four big barrels of rum, and eight of beer. Maillet did not neglect to load a few delicacies for his officers. *Brasdor* carried four penned sheep, a little coffee, and two big barrels of wine.

Jean Lelarge later claimed to have commanded the voyage of *Brasdor*, but the seniority of Maillet, who signed the bills as captain, seems beyond dispute. He owned the vessel and had invested heavily in its outfitting, while Lelarge had put up no money at all. Probably Maillet as owner wielded overall authority aboard the privateer, leaving Lelarge, the experienced sailor, to handle the ship. He would not be the only pilot aboard, for the privateer would need one for every ship it captured.

Whoever commanded, the expense of preparing this powerful commerce raider was soon justified. Cruising out in November 1744, *Brasdor* reported seventeen prizes without any opposition worth mention. Its large crew was now fully occupied, for men had to be detached to each prize ship. Spirits must have soared as men calculated their shares in the booty. The Admiralty would have its tenth, and the investors their eighty per cent, but there remained that vital tenth of the prize to be shared by the crew. Many had borrowed against their salaries when they signed on; prize money justified the risk. If *Brasdor* were run like Dolabaratz's unfortunate *Cantabre* and Beaubassin's *César*, the tenth would have been divided by man and cannon, with those who served the guns in combat taking an extra share.

Brasdor's run of luck ended when the big privateer fell in with a rival of equal force. Recounting his exploits much later, Lelarge merely referred to a "combat très vif," but one of his relatives was more eloquent. For once, there was no immediate surrender of one outclassed vessel to a larger foe. Instead began "a murderous battle, in which each mauled the other viciously." These were not heavy men-of-war trading broadsides from long ranks of cannon. The privateers were speedy schooners of a dozen guns. There were long stretches of manoeuvre and musketry as each sought to rip away the other's sails and topple its masts without itself receiving a crippling blast. Well-matched privateers could fight for days. "The advantage might have rested with Lelarge [wrote his relative] had he not been wounded, but a musket ball passed through his right arm and shattered his elbow, and he was put out of action." The setback discouraged the crew. Unable to conquer, *Brasdor* eventually broke off the engagement and limped back to Louisbourg under another captain. Lelarge's wound would trouble him for the rest of his life.

Service aboard the *Brasdor* brought official recognition to Jean Lelarge. For the spring of 1745, the colony was preparing a coast-guard schooner named *Tempête*; Lelarge was given the command. But *Tempête* never sailed. A New England invasion came to Louisbourg when *Tempête* and most of the colony's other vessels were locked in the ice-choked harbour. Jean Lelarge scuttled his new command where it lay and served in the militia throughout the siege. When Louisbourg capitulated, the Lelarges went into French exile with the rest of their neighbours.

Jean Lelarge's seagoing experience let him land on his feet in France, where he soon took command of a merchant vessel ready to sail from La Rochelle to the West Indies. But the war would not leave him alone. Just before he sailed, a royal order drafted him aboard the schooner *Sirène* and then on to *Northumberland*, the flagship of Admiral d'Anville. A great war fleet, sailing to avenge the loss of Ile Royale, required his knowledge of western Atlantic waters.

The d'Anville expedition of 1746 seemed a magnificent demonstration of the power and resilience of the French Marine. In every port of western France, great feats of logistics outfitted a fleet of twenty men-of-war, seventy transports, ten thousand soldiers and sailors. If Louisbourg were lightly held, this armada would recapture the colony, and if the enemy concentrated its forces to defend Ile Royale, the fleet would pluck Annapolis Royal or Plaisance. It might even sweep down the New England coast to smash the privateers and scour the defenceless ports. Jean Lelarge became one of many Louisbourg soldiers and sailors going back to fight for their homes.

But the huge expedition quickly grew out of control. Politics crept in, to give command to a shorebound admiral and officers advanced by tenure rather than achievement. The sailing date slipped back: not until late June did the fleet put France behind it.

The first hints of impending disaster surfaced in mid-July, when the great fleet simply ran out of wind. Expected to cross the Atlantic in six weeks, d'Anville was still at sea in mid-September. Cooped up aboard ship, thousands of his men began to suffer scurvy and fever. Worse, the delay brought the armada to the Nova Scotia coast as the season of autumnal gales approached.

D'Anville sighted land on September 13. The storm struck that evening. A classic September gale, the backwash of a great hurricane far to the south, it raged all the next day, and when it blew itself out the fleet was hopelessly scattered. Damaged, short of food and ravaged by illness, ships began to drop out and run for France.

D'Anville's *Northumberland* was among the first to reach the harbour of Chebucto Bay, where Halifax would rise just three years later. Only a dozen vessels anchored alongside, and it was early October before reconnaissances by Lelarge and other pilots had gathered forty ships at the Chebucto rendezvous. Here the full extent of their disaster unfolded. Scurvy and ship fever ran rampant: of seven thousand men at Chebucto, nearly six hundred died. Scarcely half of the living were fit for duty, and supply officers struggled to distribute short rations to the hungry crews. D'Anville died in an apoplectic fit, and his successor collapsed under the strain of command, disabling himself in a botched suicide.

Yet the fleet had not been reduced to impotence. Its new commander, La Jonquière, was an experienced sea officer, able to assess the strategical situation even as he struggled to restore order to his command. Mere rumours of the fleet's intentions had forced the British to abandon plans to attack Canada, and the overwhelming superiority that had enabled d'Anville's frigates to seize several privateers on the Nova Scotia coast still offered scope for a successful offensive. Before venturing forth, La Jonquière needed intelligence of British naval movements in the region. He dispatched Lelarge and several other officers on scouting missions.

Captain Lelarge made contact sooner than he might have wished. Intercepted by an eighteen-gun privateer, his tiny schooner was chased down the coast to Passepic harbour near Cape LaHave. Lelarge evaded capture by running into the harbour at low tide, and inside he had the good fortune to capture and burn four unarmed schooners.

"This action, conducted within view of the privateer, incited it to pursue him into the harbour and open a vigorous fire. Lelarge could not resist, for his schooner mounted only four cannon and a few swivels. Forced to beach his ship and manhandle his guns ashore, Lelarge set up a battery at the edge of the woods. With this battery he prevented the enemy from taking his schooner even though it was beached and useless. The privateer, firing constantly, was kept from close range by the shallows of the harbour, but it armed its boat to capture the beached schooner and its crew. Repelled with the loss of most of its crew, the boat retreated to the privateer. A second attempt was no more successful than the first: the boat returned to its ship worse mauled than ever. After this last attempt, the privateer made sail and departed. Lelarge was left in peace to repair his schooner as best he could, and he rejoined the fleet."

This escapade won Lelarge command of a larger ship, the recently captured corvette *Catherine*, of sixteen guns. Two days after Lelarge returned from his eventful scouting mission, *Catherine* sailed from Chebucto with the rest of the fleet. La Jonquière's scouts had told him the British were far away. With the remains of his command, he headed for Annapolis Royal, where three hundred troops, come overland from Canada, were pinning down the fort's small British garrison. Late as it was, La Jonquière's arrival at Annapolis Royal would have meant its immediate capture and a reversal of authority in Acadia, but the bad luck brought on by d'Anville's late arrival in North America still dogged his unfortunate fleet. The storm season was not over. Five days out from Chebucto the fleet met another tempest and was scattered again, forcing even La Jonquière to recognize the impossibility of further operations. In ones and twos, the surviving ships of d'Anville's armada struggled back to France. One of the largest naval expeditions of the war had been destroyed without a fight.

Meanwhile, a single ship of d'Anville's fleet reached Annapolis Royal. Jean Lelarge had been patrolling the flanks of La Jonquière's fleet when the second storm struck. *Catherine* barely came through afloat – Lelarge had to jettison four of his precious cannon – but when the storm abated, Lelarge pressed on alone for Annapolis Royal, hoping to rejoin the fleet.

Catherine's arrival at Annapolis Royal was too little and too late. By the time the corvette struggled into the basin on November 6, the Canadian besieging force led by Captain Jean-Baptiste de Ramezay had retreated to winter quarters on Minas Basin, leaving the British firmly in control of the town and harbour. Doubtless surprised to see a single small ship appear and then flee, the British sent a vessel in pursuit. Jean Lelarge was once more outgunned and overtaken, and once more he prepared to run his ship ashore. But this time there was no desperate shore fight. "The vessel, a faster sailer than his, gave a lively pursuit and had greatly gained on him when suddenly it struck a shoal and was flung over on its side a wreck. This happy event let Lelarge pursue his course in tranquillity."

Saved from the enemy, Lelarge did not turn for the open sea and France. Though the d'Anville fleet was no more, Lelarge's independent cruise was just beginning. Swinging his helm northeast, Lelarge took *Catherine* deeper into the Bay of Fundy, heading for the Minas Basin and Ramezay's three hundred Canadians. Lacking transport, food, and ammunition, Ramezay's men did not lack initiative. Seeing a large privateer nosing cautiously into Minas Basin, they prepared a cutting-out expedition, and had they not recognized his colours, Lelarge might have found himself attacked by the troops he had come to help.

In reaching Ramezay's small and beleaguered force, Lelarge performed the only specific military achievement of d'Anville's expedition. The dispersal of the fleet had ended the French thrust at Acadia, leaving Ramezay stuck at Minas, lacking supplies and facing annihilation from a New England force advancing from Annapolis under Colonel Arthur Noble. Lelarge's providential arrival saved the Canadians by transporting them around the rugged south shore of the Isthmus of Chignecto to safe quarters at Beaubassin. Revived with *Catherine*'s supplies and beyond reach of Noble's New Englanders, Ramezay planned a return to the offensive. In February he sent his men on a snowshoe journey back to Minas, where they destroyed Noble's outpost in a wild winter assault.

By then Lelarge had sailed for home. With Ramezay's men safe at Beaubassin, *Catherine* ran cautiously down Fundy Bay, only to meet a third enemy on Christmas Eve. This one, fortunately, posed little danger. The privateer lying at anchor in the lee of Partridge Island was so rimed with ice that its crew could not make sail. Instead, judging *Catherine* to be a hapless merchant craft, the privateer sent out a boat and sixteen men. Still well-armed, Lelarge had the satisfaction of making one tiny capture, taking the dozen survivors of the unfortunate boarding party back to Rochefort as prisoners of war.

The return of *Catherine*, long since posted missing, brought her captain the honour of a temporary commission in the navy. His seamanship and perseverance were needed, and the Louisbourg boy who had watched big naval transports arrive each year to lord over all the ships in Louisbourg harbour now found himself in command of one. In each of the next several years, Lelarge took the frigate *Parham* to Louisiana carrying supplies, troops, and funds for the Treasury. The New Orleans climate sapped his health, but he won praise on every voyage. When war's end gave Ile Royale back to France, the navy kept Lelarge on the active list, and so the Lelarges did not go back to Louisbourg with the rest of the exiles. They settled in the naval town of Rochefort with Lelarge's mother, his siblings, and his orphaned niece. The only one of the family to go home was Jean's younger sister Marie-Josephe, who had married a young military officer, artilleryman Louis-Félix Vallée. In 1749 Vallée took his family back to Louisbourg, committing their future to the strength of its walls and the power of his cannon.

Jean Lelarge no longer depended on walls. His trust had always been placed in the sea, and the sea continued to serve him well. A naval run to Louisiana in 1752, marred only by Lelarge's serious illness, won particular praise from the colonial officials, and soon the navy rewarded him with a permanent rank. Like most ex-merchant captains, he was kept to transport duties, for service in the combat fleet remained the privilege of career officers risen from the elite midshipmen's school. Lelarge would not have been dismayed: simply to win naval rank was a tremendous feat for the son of a colonial carpenter. Resplendent in the naval officer's red and blue uniform, he commanded big three-masted frigates, imposing even when stripped of their guns for transport duty. Huge compared with the schooners he had been proud to command a decade earlier, his naval commands offered cavernous cargo space on several decks. Personal servants tended spacious, well-appointed officers' quarters. He commanded fifty to eighty sailors, with a whole corps of junior officers for the routine duties of navigation. Jean Lelarge was now respected and well-to-do, a rising young officer on the fringes of the military elite. His family's prospects were assured, and with their father's assistance his growing sons' prospects for military careers were excellent.

In 1753, the year he took rank as a naval lieutenant on the permanent establishment, Jean Lelarge sailed to Louisbourg in a new command, the naval transport *Rhinocéros*. His assignment was the routine supply run between Rochefort and Ile Royale, but the crossing was a difficult two-month ordeal. Finally, groping down the coast of Ile Royale in fog, Lieutenant Lelarge spotted the lighthouse still standing sentinel over his home port. Perhaps remembering how the transport *Néréide* had grounded in 1726, Lelarge declined to take *Rhinocéros* nonchalantly into harbour like one of his old schooners. He prudently had a few guns fired and awaited pilotage. The port captain who responded to his signal was his old comrade in privateering Joannis Dolabaratz, who had also won naval rank for his service in d'Anville's ill-fated expedition.

Louisbourg was bigger than Lelarge had known it. The military establishment had tripled in size. The port was even more crowded with Caribbean cod schooners, local fishing boats, and French merchantmen. There were still many familiar faces along the quay to make a proud homecoming for the local boy returning in command of the biggest ship in the harbour. Lelarge and his officers dined with the same elite that had always dominated colonial society, but Lelarge now outranked many of its members. To discharge his cargo he dealt with the senior administrator, successor to the official who had judged his marital escapade in 1737. Though *Rhinocéros* stayed only a month, it should have been a satisfying time for Lelarge, and also for his son.

Jean-Aimable Lelarge had begun to serve under his father's eye at the age of eleven, and the voyage to his birthplace was another step in a naval career that would last fifty-two years. Rising slowly in sea service and port duties, Jean-Aimable was to win the cherished knighthood of the Order of Saint-Louis in 1777. He would be promoted *capitaine de vaisseau* – post captain – in 1785, and in 1793 the colonial boy would become an admiral. Retired from Napoleon's navy in 1801, Admiral Lelarge was to die in 1805, six months before the destruction of the French navy at Trafalgar culminated the sixty-year struggle to rule the waves that his father had seen beginning in 1744.

The voyage to Louisbourg was followed by another southward trip, this time to Martinique. Then 1755 brought the advent of another war – later to be called the Seven Years War. Lelarge was given command of *Rhinocéros* again, putting his experience to good use in two voyages to Ile Royale. With British fleets and American privateers scouring the western Atlantic, the lightly armed transports could no longer enjoy leisurely midsummer crossings. The 1755 visit was a late autumn one, followed very quickly with a second trip. Leaving Ile Royale just before Christmas, Lelarge reached Rochefort in mid January 1756, reloaded in five weeks, and sailed back to Ile Royale before the end of February. This crossing brought *Rhinocéros* to Ile Royale before the winter ice had drifted off the coast: entry seemed impossible. Lelarge damaged his hull trying to push through the ice floes; but then the wind changed and he had his ship towed in as the ice drifted out to sea. Sailing again before the end of April, the eight-gun *Rhinocéros* brushed through more ice to escape to France a month before the enemy blockade ships took up their station off Ile Royale. That summer Lelarge was promoted naval captain third class.

Late in 1757 Captain Lelarge drew another winter voyage for the provisioning of Ile Royale against another threat of siege. Lightly armed as ever, he sailed from Rochefort in *Chariot Royal* late in November, but the increasingly bitter struggle for North America was turning naval warfare into an all-seasons conflict. First light one morning revealed the tops of a British squadron. Lelarge veered northwest and lost them over the horizon. By mid-morning the lookout spotted another sail straight ahead. Lelarge threw out sea anchors and brought the frigate quickly about, hoping to escape to the northeast. But this enemy was more alert. Against a less-experienced foe, Lelarge might have managed an escape, but the captain of HMS *Tor Bay*, seventy-four guns, was one of the most distinguished sailors of his generation. Augustus Keppel had circled the globe with a British naval expedition while Jean Lelarge was running loads of cod to Saint-Domingue, and he would rise to be First Lord of the British Admiralty. *Tor Bay* steadily overhauled *Chariot Royal* in a day-long chase. Lelarge sent his men up the rigging to add on every possible square of sail, but there was no escape. He actually hazarded a few shots as his pursuer came into range, but *Tor Bay*'s firepower was overwhelming. Lelarge struck his colours and *Chariot Royal* surrendered.

Captain Lelarge soon returned to France in an exchange of captured officers. In 1758 he was dispatched to Louisiana. He was there when the Marine proposed him to succeed Dolabaratz as port captain of Louisbourg, a post he was to take up at war's end. It might have made an appropriate culmination for a career: leader among the sailing men of Ile Royale, instructor of seamanship to young lads who discovered the harbour in small boats. Though hardly a rank to compare with those his son would hold, Jean Lelarge's achievement in rising so far from his humble origins was far greater.

Jean Lelarge never became port captain of Ile Royale, for neither he nor Louisbourg saw the end of the Seven Years War. In 1758, as Louisbourg entered its death agony under Amherst's relentless siege, Jean Lelarge's health collapsed in New Orleans. Worn out in a harsh vocation at the age of forty-nine, still bearing the shattered elbow from a privateer's bullet in 1744, his health again assailed by the insidious tropical heat, he struggled back to Rochefort, fighting one last sea battle to reach there. He never sailed again. Ile Royale fell and then Canada, and Lelarge was taking the cure at the waters of Bagnères. After two years as an invalid, Jean Lelarge, bold lover and bold sailor, died quietly in his bed in Rochefort in 1761, the same ocean that pounded the shores of Ile Royale sending a faint salt tang to brush his fading senses.

Sergeant Koller in Peace and War

he armies that came to lay siege to Louisbourg posed an ultimate challenge to the efforts of its people to amass some small security there, for a besieged town is a community with its survival in question. Under such challenge, the value of a Louisbourg life stands out in the career of one soldier, a man professionally involved in the defence of the colony, yet equally concerned to preserve a community of which he had become part.

He had come as soldier rather than colonist, and Louisbourg might have expected him to take his pay and go the moment his enlistment expired, for he seemed little suited to Ile Royale. Was he not, after all, a mercenary, a stateless warrior hired out to fight wherever foreign masters sent him? His home lay in the mountain country where the eastern cantons of Switzerland bordered the Hapsburg empire of Austria, utterly remote from French colonial preoccupations and as far as a European could get from salt water and fishing fleets. His culture was foreign, his faith perhaps Protestant, his native tongue German. Even his name seemed impossible to the Frenchmen of Louisbourg, who embroidered endless variants on his favoured spelling. Yet even as it struggled with his name, Louisbourg was discovering that this Col, Colle, Kholler fellow had come to stay. Indeed, when he stood in powder smoke and saw enemy cannon pounding down the ramparts of his adopted home, the depth of his caring may have been a revelation to Jodocus Koller himself.

The town of Constance on the shores of the Alpine lake called the Bodensee, where Koller was born around 1700, seems no more likely as an inspiration for military vocations than as a source of settlers for Ile Royale. Switzerland across the lake was already far advanced in its history of military non-involvement, and the jigsaw principalities of southern Germany were rarely united or powerful enough to mount and maintain significant armies. As expensive and complicated firearms replaced hand weapons as the basis of infantry tactics, war had become increasingly the prerogative of nations able to maintain standing armies of professional soldiers. Smaller states, whatever their history of martial glory, were finding the new demands of war difficult to bear – unless, like Prussia, they devoted themselves almost totally to war.

But if these small states could not outfit standing armies, they could still produce young farmboys enamoured of military glamour, young city poor desperate for employment, and young aristocrats born to the profession of arms. This potential soldiery was not diverted by the pacifism of their own states. The young aristocrats gathered up their humbler neighbours in private regiments and led them away to serve in the armies of larger or more bellicose kingdoms. So Scots companies were found in the Dutch service, Hessians and Hanoverians in the British army, Hungarians in the employ of any power that valued the light cavalry they called Hussars. In the French army the largest foreign contingents were the regiments recruited in Switzerland and the friendlier German states. By the mid-eighteenth century, twenty thousand of the 140,000 men in the peacetime French army were soldiers of foreign regiments, mostly German or Swiss. Marshal de Saxe, Louis xv's finest general and himself a German Protestant, said, "A German serves us as three men. He spares one for France, he denies one to our enemies, and besides he fills his place in the ranks." Saxe's remark hinted at the diplomatic objectives that encouraged foreign recruiting: the presence of a large body of Germans and Swiss experienced in the

French service was thought to keep the eastern frontiers well disposed to France. Once young Jodocus Koller discovered in himself a military vocation (or simply ran out of other means to keep himself clothed and fed), a regiment destined for the service of Louis XV became his best prospect for employment. Obligingly, the Régiment de Karrer came looking for recruits.

Franz Adam Karrer, a Swiss veteran of the French army, began to raise a Swiss regiment in 1719. In return for an annual retainer from the French, Colonel Karrer had undertaken to recruit, train, and equip a regiment that would bear his name, to be raised outside France and to serve in naval depots and colonial garrisons. Soon Karrer's officers spread across Switzerland and Germany seeking recruits among the young men of their home districts. Jodocus Koller enlisted in one of the first companies raised. Leaving home almost at once, he marched with his company to regimental headquarters in Rochefort on the west coast of France. He would not return to Switzerland.

In his new surroundings Koller was spared immersion in a wholly foreign environment. Though he now served a French monarch on French soil, he was nevertheless in a Swiss regiment. The regimental language, on duty and off, was German. Many of the men were Protestants, their religious rights guaranteed in the midst of the Catholic nation as long as they remained in Karrer's corps. The regiment used Swiss uniforms and flags, Swiss military rituals, and Swiss courts martial. Even the women who followed the regiment were Swiss and German. Karrer's regiment was a small German–Swiss community in the heart of the French army, and young Koller could at first remain largely untouched by French influence. He probably expected to return to Switzerland at the end of his service.

What was new to the young man was army life. Not the forced obedience – authority in the army largely recreated the hierarchies of civilian life, and Koller's officers may have been the same young aristocrats he had been taught to obey at home – for Koller knew his place. But other aspects of army life would have been radically new. A musket must have been a strange, unwieldy object to a young man of humble birth who may never have held a firearm, let alone aimed or fired one, before some sergeant of Karrer's first thrust one into his unsure grasp. Military technology did not come easily to uneducated and generally illiterate recruits of the eighteenth-century army. The drill-sergeant's classic lament that his men didn't know their right foot from their left was sometimes literally true. That they knew nothing of military weaponry was even more certain.

The musket, as the principal infantry weapon, was the corner-stone of army organization: it would rule the next phase of Jodocus Koller's life. He had first to learn how to hold and load his piece – no simple task with a smoothbore, muzzle-loading flintlock like the Charleville musket. The Charleville was a smoothbore because its barrel was simply a smooth tube of metal, without rifled grooves to hold and spin the round, one-and-a-half-ounce ball it fired. "Muzzle-loading" meant that powder and ball for each shot had to be injected down the length of the barrel with a ramrod before the musket could be shouldered and aimed. "Flintlock" described the firing mecha-nism, a subtle arrangement of flint and steel. When Jodocus Koller obeyed the sergeant's shouted command, the trigger he squeezed sprang a flint forward to strike a polished steel plate. Sparks showered down on a tiny pan of black powder, freshly primed for each firing. Flaring in the pan, the powder carried flame through a pinhole in the barrel to the tightly wadded powder and ball inside, and the ensuing explosion drove the musket ball out of the barrel with power enough to kill at a hundred and fifty paces. The blast also shot a jet of grey-white smoke back through the pinhole, inches from the face of the man squinting down the barrel. Koller learned to fire this sensitive, deadly instrument – not at his leisure but over and over again in precise accord with a closely controlled series of commands from his officer or sergeant. His transformation from farmboy to killing machine had begun.

The musket's smooth bore limited its accuracy; it was not a sharp-shooter's weapon. Muzzle-loading restricted its rate of fire: even a skilled soldier could only load and fire two or three times a minute. No wonder that untrained soldiers put more faith in the bayonet they mounted on the musket barrel, or discarded their firearm to attack with sabre or sword. Only when fired in volleys by regimented masses

of men could the musket be an effective battlefield weapon. It was
useless unless the soldier acted in concert with his fellows. So even as
he mastered the loading sequence and learned to control and aim his
piece, Jodocus Koller was being tuned to act in effortless harmony
with twenty, fifty, or five hundred other men like himself. The set-
piece battles of his time were won by the volley or series of volleys
delivered at close range by thin lines of well-trained infantry. The
preparation for such volleys required endless drill, until, by company
or regiment, men would automatically – almost thoughtlessly –
march, wheel, turn, halt, load, and fire on command despite all the
tumult of battle and the hail of fire directed against them.

In Koller's day it took eighteen months to train a recruit in the
basics of infantry drill, just to see him accustomed to his musket and
comfortable in the widely spaced, slow-marching formations
demanded by the long-barrelled Charleville and its smoke-blasting
lock. But it took five years, reckoned the experts, to produce a real
soldier. Only time could instil the fear-numbing habits, the iron discipline, that commanders wanted on the battlefield. The musket
volleys that won battles were most effective within eighty paces. At
that range a few murderous volleys could leave the enemy shattered
and vulnerable, ready to be swept away by a culminating bayonet
assault. Before those decisive volleys went home, long, bright files of
soldiers would be required to march, manoeuvre, and finally stand
motionless and exposed to artillery fire, snipers, cavalry, or even the
enemy's musket volleys, seeking no cover and holding fire to await
their commander's order. Discipline, the tactics began and ended with
discipline; and discipline depended not on courage but on habit.
Soldiers were drilled until habits of mindless obedience outweighed
fear, hesitancy, and rational self-interest on the battlefield.

The rest of army life reflected and sustained the overriding need
for obedience. Since years of effort went into the shaping of a capable
infantryman, standing armies of professional soldiers were essential
even in peacetime. At the outbreak of war, the militia might be called
out and civilians hastily enlisted, but the battle-winning core of the
army would be the professionals who made careers in the service and
found their identity in their company or regiment rather than in the

civilian background they had left behind. Even if he enlisted with
friends and neighbours under the command of an officer from his
own region, the soldier who joined an eighteenth-century army
made an irreparable break from the local community that had raised
him. The army that could give him a new home in exchange for the
one he had left could hold his loyalty no matter what demands it made
on him. As a result, even a small regiment like the Karrer paid scrupu-
lous attention to regimental dress, military ritual, and martial music,
for matters as small as regimental songs and traditions reinforced the
soldier's sense of belonging. In the ideal military company men
identified themselves with their unit, looking up with respect
and affection to the sergeants and corporals who ran their lives, and
beyond with fear and awe to the distant officers who controlled their
destinies. The rigorous discipline that could hold the men firm on
the battlefield or form them into a firing squad for the execution of a
disobedient comrade was half the army-building system. The other
half was that sense of community achieved by a well-run regiment.
It was regimental loyalty that sustained the soldier's commitment,
even as discipline and drill built in him the habits of instant obedience that were the hallmarks of the professional infantryman.

Jodocus Koller probably never became the paragon of self-
sacrificing efficiency that military theorists imagined. With a regiment
of recruits to be made into soldiers, the Karrer regiment should have
spent its first several years of existence in training exercises. Instead,
the needs of the Marine Ministry to which Karrer was contracted
overrode all textbook specifications. Just three years after its creation
was first mooted, the regiment was ordered into the field. It could
not even remain a single unit. That year, 1722, Captain de Merveilleux
took fifty Karrer soldiers to Louisbourg. Fifty more joined them in
1724. Setting off across the Atlantic with one of these groups, Jodocus
Koller put behind him the arduous training that would have prepared
him for the line of battle in infantry warfare. Still new to the profession of arms, now also a newcomer to the New World, Jodocus Koller
was about to discover the art of building and defending a fortified
place – the fortress of Louisbourg. He was also about to find the community that would eventually supplant the army in his affections,

much as the army had replaced his birthplace in far-off Constance.
The mercenary was going to find a home.

II

The imposing fortress that rose on the shores of Louisbourg
harbour was the eighteenth century's best answer to the chronic
insecurity of colonial outposts on the maritime shores of Canada. On
the long coasts of the maritime region, scores of fine harbours offered
shelter to ships and men of any seafaring nation. With the sea lanes
open to all, and every port a potential base, no nation had managed
to secure the whole region under its authority. By Jodocus Koller's
day the British dominated in Newfoundland and exercised uncertain
sway over the French settlers of Acadia. France preserved the islands
of the Gulf of St. Lawrence, and fishing fleets and trading craft of
both nations cruised offshore. With competition for hegemony sure
to continue, France intended to assert its power throughout the
region from Louisbourg. Hence the need for troops, and more than
troops. As the centre of a colony, of an economy, and of a military
command, Louisbourg became too valuable to depend on the
outcome of musket volleys exchanged in the open field. It lay exposed
upon the coast; whatever troops were stationed there might suddenly
be assailed by larger numbers landing from the sea. To be secure, the
town of Louisbourg must be fortified; and so the hazards of military
posting that brought Jodocus Koller there early in the 1720s introduced the young soldier to the art and science of fortification. His
own labour would help this particular fortress to rise. In fact, it was
the Swiss companies' reputation as workers that had brought the
Karrer to Ile Royale when the fortress of Louisbourg was little more
than a geometry of salient angles and lines of defence in the minds of
the army engineers there. The senior engineer, Jean-François de
Verville, was just a year away from a transfer back to France, but
ingénieur du roi Etienne Verrier and the obscure Swiss soldier Jodocus
Koller were each destined for careers in Louisbourg, both of them
struggling on their own levels to bring the fortress into being. As they

worked, each would witness the gradual elaboration in stone of a precise and subtle concept of fortification, a concept as fundamental to siege warfare as Koller's neglected Charleville musket was to infantry tactics.

Fortification had been revolutionized some two centuries before Jodocus Koller's birth, with the advent in Europe of siege artillery. Cannon mobile and efficient enough for siege warfare doomed the lofty castles that once soared skyward in defiance of armoured cavalry and labouring footsoldiers. Tall and ancient battlements tumbled helplessly before the gunners, and in response fortification began a love affair with the earth that has never abated. Gradually, the siege trains of artillery that came to batter down every opposing wall found the tall, vertical ramparts of older fortresses growing thick and sinking low, hunkered down behind heaped earthworks and protected by cannon of their own. The defence had come to terms with artillery, and the new "artillery fortifications" both used and resisted artillery effectively enough to restore cheer to defenders' hearts. Besiegers were left scrambling for new techniques by which to batter their way past massive walls bristling with cannon. In the two centuries before the building of Louisbourg, this contest had revitalized the science of military engineering and generated new theories of fortification by the score.

The man who brought the new theories about the attack and defence of artillery fortifications to their classic formulation was a military engineer in the army of Louis XIV, Sebastien LePrestre de Vauban, history's greatest siegemaster and fortress-builder, a warrior who several times faced the curious challenge of besieging fortresses he himself had built. With a wealth of military experience from the Sun King's wars and a mind restless enough to have produced a calculation that Canada might have a population of twenty-five million by 1970, Vauban worked out the essential rules of fortress-making and fortress-breaking, and then demonstrated them in countless sieges and defences along France's borders. Though he died in 1707, when Koller was a child and Louisbourg unborn, Vauban left behind treatises on fortification that set the script from which Louisbourg's military history would be acted out.

Vauban's theory of defensive siegecraft began with the wall and its weaknesses. The wall, time-honoured obstacle behind which small forces resisted larger and stronger foes, could be battered down by artillery or scaled by desperate men with ladders. Against such threats, defenders of artillery fortifications went beyond their walls to heap up earthen mounds that would block artillery fire and to scoop out ditches that an attacker must struggle to cross. Yet, mere static obstacles would rarely keep out a determined and ingenious foe, so the defence had to prepare an active resistance with cannon and musketry. Long before Vauban, defenders seeking to weave around themselves a deadly network of interlocking fire had learned that straight walls wasted firepower and were soon outflanked. Instead, engineers designed their rampart around projecting bastions, strong-points that combined to sweep every inch of ground with unimpeded fire from several angles. Vauban's genius lay in the way he took the existing placement of bastions, worked out by trial and error in many earlier fortresses, and made it a system, Vauban's System. More successfully than his many rivals, Vauban set fortification to geometry.

Vauban's geometry opened with a measure called the *toise*, about twice the length of a yard or metre, and a postulate that every point outside the wall must be swept by the maximum of criss-crossing fire from cannon and muskets. The musket of his day was ineffective beyond about one hundred *toises*, so bastions designed to cover the intervening terrain had to be less than two hundred *toises* apart. Vauban took one hundred and eighty *toises* as his basic measurement, and the rest of his elaborate design appeared as if by theorem. In relentless geometrical specifications he measured the face and flank of each bastion, then joined the bastions to create a fortress, a town sealed behind ramparts. Geometry assured the walls the most efficient lines of fire over an outer perimeter carefully landscaped to yield no scrap of cover to an attacking foe. A hundred specifications prescribed the placement of ditch, *ravelin*, counterscarp, covered way, and *glacis* among the outer defences. An ingenious engineer could go on endlessly in search of additional obstacles before and behind the ramparted line of defence: citadels and *caveliers*, redoubts and advanced works, subterranean chambers, moats, sluices. All the esoteric paraphernalia of a Vauban fortress would not render it impregnable, for (as Vauban well knew) no such place has ever existed, but a fortress well built and actively defended by his precepts would concede an attacker the least possible advantage at the greatest price in toil and blood. Such was the goal pursued by the Verriers and the Kollers who built the fortress of Louisbourg.

Despite their origins in the geometry of the System, no two Vauban fortresses were identical. Vauban had been a master in the use of terrain, which always offered peculiarities to be used or neutralized. At Louisbourg a port as well as a town had to be defended. The harbour had to be secure from naval assault, the town from land-based siege. After surveying the ground and the likeliest lines of attack, engineer Verville chose to protect the town from land assault with a line of defence laid across the low triangular peninsula that forms the south shore of Louisbourg harbour. The length of this line dictated two bastions at the centre. These became the King's and Queen's bastions, supported where the line of defence met the shore by two half-bastions, the Dauphin and the Princess. Measuring bastion-to-bastion lines on his drawing board, Verville confirmed that the longest line, from the Dauphin to the King's, kept within Vauban's classic one hundred and eighty *toises*. Geometry ensured that the ditch and the outer defences were satisfactorily swept with interlocking fire.

Key to the landward front and nerve centre of the town's defence in Verville's concept was the King's Bastion, crowning the highest ridge of the peninsula. Here Verville planned the citadel of Louisbourg: the military barracks, the governor's quarters, and the townside earthworks that made a self-contained military command, the fort within the fortress.

To protect the harbour, Verville and Verrier had less need for their geometry. An eye for terrain showed how independent shore batteries would suffice. The threat here came from ships, and long experience confirmed that the rolling wooden gun platforms of even the stoutest men-of-war were no match for cannon mounted behind stone walls on solid ground. The engineers could seal the harbour with a compact thirty-six-gun battery on a rocky, surf-battered islet commanding the only channel into Louisbourg's spacious port. They supported the island battery with shore positions: the big Royal

Battery facing the central harbour and two more gun platforms framing the town quay. Before the shore defences were erected, the Governor of Ile Royale had feared that even a pirate ship might seize the harbour and hold his capital to ransom, but once they were standing and their guns mounted, no unwelcome ship ever forced passage under Louisbourg's formidable shore defences. The likeliest threat to the town, a seaborne raid, had been effectively countered.

Walling in the town of Louisbourg on the ground furthest from the hills that enclose most of the harbour, then adding a bristling array of shore defences, Verville had done his best to design fortifications that could respond to every threat. Nor had he ignored the town within the walls. Civic design was an important aspect of the military engineer's art, and Verville planned Louisbourg as a handsome, orderly town whose streets and squares would be surveyed by imposing public buildings as well as by the brute mass of the encircling ramparts. The officers of the Corps du Génie were architects and planners as well as military men. They turned without inhibition from fortification plans to the design of town wharves, official residences, and even garrison latrines. Louisbourg's major edifices, the citadel barracks and the town hospital, testify to the reliance on geometry that Vauban's System imbued in the engineers, but their lines also show how these men could bring aesthetic flair to the classicism of their century. Etienne Verrier would devote no small portion of his time to purely civic architecture. The lavishness of the engineer's residence he designed brought him the envy of his neighbours as well as an official rebuke, but generally his contemporaries shared his views on the importance of style. A city named for the kings of France would not fail to reflect Bourbon magnificence.

The engineers' thick portfolio of designs for the fortress of Louisbourg, checked, criticized, and revised by military men and cost clerks on both sides of the Atlantic, eventually won royal approval, with Verville's prestige as a member of Vauban's elite Corps du Génie helping to ensure a favourable verdict. The intricacies of design could now give way to the challenges of construction.

Had the fortress of Louisbourg been in France, its construction would have been a routine project for a fortress-building industry long experienced in the Vauban System. Powerful, bellicose France, poorly endowed with natural defences for its northern and eastern frontiers, had sought to remedy nature's defects with a maze of fortifications, many far larger and more elaborate than Louisbourg's. Vauban had personally built or rebuilt no fewer than sixty fortresses. They stood in rows two and three deep along vital frontiers, so that an invading army struggling to reduce one was liable to be taken in the rear by relief forces advancing from the others. No fortress could withstand permanent siege – Vauban thought forty days sufficient for reducing a well-defended fortress if it were cut off from all relief – but most fortresses could no more be ignored and bypassed than they could be surprised and taken by storm.

The decision to fortify Louisbourg introduced a new scale of military planning to northern America. Earlier maritime strongpoints, French and British, had consistently fallen to strike forces unprepared for formal siege yet strong enough to surprise and overwhelm the meagre defences they faced. By fortifying Louisbourg according to Vauban, France served notice that its new colony would not be left to so ignominious a fate, but the decision brought its own problems. How would the huge expenses be managed and the elegant designs executed so far from the centres of authority and population? Could Vauban's European designs withstand the ravages of the Canadian winter? Could the brick, stone, timber, and iron be provided in enormous quantities by an unexploited new frontier? Above all, who in a colony of fishermen and traders would build a fortress, labouring through the years to move tons of earth and rock by barrowload and to mortar endless stones into massive ramparts?

France faced these challenges with the confidence of a nation whose energies and resources were harnessed to an unprecedented degree under the long absolutisms of Louis XIV and his great grandson Louis XV. In the thirteen decades these two kings ruled, from the Sun King's childhood coronation in 1643 to Louis XV's death in 1774, Europe's largest population was taxed to an unprecedented degree, and a far-flung royal service ensured that those taxes furthered royal intentions.

War and defence consumed much of the royal revenue, making the ministers in charge of military spending important councillors of the King. The War Ministry bore the responsibility for building and paying for most of Vauban's mighty fortifications. Louisbourg, however, would be a project of the Ministry of Marine, which jealously retained control of naval and colonial affairs. From 1723 to 1749 the minister here was Jean-Frédéric Phélypeaux, Comte de Maurepas. Until dismissed in disgrace for satirizing the new royal favourite, Madame de Pompadour, Maurepas was the instrument of royal authority over all the fleets and colonies of France, and Ile Royale and its fortress were just a small part of his duties. Easily, routinely, Maurepas delegated management of construction at Louisbourg to his royal officials on the site. To fortify Louisbourg according to Vauban, thousands of pages of ministerial correspondence would cross the Atlantic, petty empires would rise with the fortress, vicious struggles would rage between them, and administrative careers would be made and broken. But the managerial capacity of the royal service would not be strained. Nor would its financial resources: one more military expenditure among thousands, the cost of Louisbourg seemed entirely justified by the thriving trade of the colony it defended.

If management of the fortification project was routine, the actual building became a thornier problem – one Maurepas delegated to professional fortress-builders. It was they who faced the technical challenge of constructing a Vauban fortress in the Canadian environment. The fortress-builders came to Ile Royale full of preconceived notions from European conditions, but their adaptation to colonial realities began abruptly and continued for a long time. Obstacles to European construction abounded.

The builders soon found how unwelcoming the climate could be. Ile Royale's long winters cut the building season to less than half the year, and the succession of frosts and thaws impeded the drying of mortar, so that freshly laid wall threatened to crumble in its first year. The fortress-builders had to surmount the Louisbourg weather just as they had overcome the European challenges of foggy coasts, snowy alpine passes, and swampy lowlands. The climate remained a technical challenge to the builders and a hardship to their labourers, but neither fog nor frost possessed magical powers to dissolve well-built masonry. To fight the freeze-thaw cycle the builders learned to swathe their work in planking that held the stonework in place as the mortar hardened around it. The short working season had to be accepted.

Supplies and labour frequently caused headaches for the builders. Ile Royale soon began to produce stone, plaster, limestone, and timber, and Louisbourg's lively import trade supplied the worksite with the output of far-off mills and brickyards, but the costs were high and the loss of a single mill or shipment could wreck a whole season's plans. Labour remained expensive and skilled tradesmen scarce, so the contractors had to run a permanent job-training program to turn unskilled recruits like Jodocus Koller into fortress-builders.

Every aspect of the job had its costs and problems, but the costs proved tolerable, and when the problems seemed intractable, the contractors found ways to badger their royal client into modifying designs and revising budgets. They made errors – some never cured, some that needed costly revision – but no builder resigned in despair. Each year the work crews raised up *toise* upon *toise* of stone and mortar. Slowly a fortress took shape.

It did so largely through the efforts of men like Jodocus Koller, for the contractors' manpower problems had been met by military postings. The Ministry took it for granted that the troops needed to man a Vauban fortress would busy themselves in peacetime by construction work. Still under military discipline, fed and housed by the general staff of Ile Royale, soldiers in fortification labour were serving military objectives even as they supplemented their meagre military pay. When companies of troops were being collected for service in Ile Royale, good workmen were more eagerly sought than good soldiers.

Jodocus Koller discovered the challenges of construction in the new colony as soon as he arrived to join the working garrison of Ile Royale in 1722 or 1724. The new troops had been assigned quarters in a massive barracks under construction in the citadel since 1720 but still far from complete. When the Swiss arrived, the defects of the building were becoming obvious. Verville's designs had produced a basement that flooded every year, a roof too gently pitched to shed driven snow and rain, and doors and passages that gave inadequate shelter in storms. Isabeau, the builder, had been unable to maintain quality control over his suppliers, so French quarries sent second-rate slates for the roof, and the products of the local brickyards crumbled in the salt air. Hurried, inexperienced workmen had built in errors: stone walls went out of plumb, beams joined badly, mortar cracked. The roof leaked and its timbers rotted even before the building was finished. Perhaps these were the inevitable teething problems of the huge building project (although the men in charge quarrelled bitterly over the blame), but it was Koller and his fellows who had to live in the damp and smoky rooms of this handsome failure. Barracks were new to the French soldiers. Used to billets in civilian lodgings, the men may not immediately have noted the lack of mess halls and workspaces, but the barracks' structural weaknesses were a constant trial.

While some of the workmen struggled to make their quarters liveable, growing numbers of labourers began to build the fortifications, delayed until then by the slow progress of the barracks. As an inexperienced newcomer, Jodocus Koller probably began in the most labour-intensive stage of rampart-raising, the preliminary digging and piling chores that Vauban called *déblai* and *remblai*. In that stage workmen with picks and mattocks swarmed over the site where the engineers had surveyed their lines of defence. The workers dug earth and rock from a deep, wide ditch circling the outer edge of the future rampart, piling up what they quarried to form a long, imposing mound that would be the base of the wall. At the other edge of the ditch, they piled more earth, but this had to be carefully sloped and shaped, for it was to become the *glacis*, the earthen barrier that would shield the stone rampart from enemy fire. *Déblai* and *remblai* were mostly hand labour, requiring few skills from the recruits and demanding intervention from the engineers and their black-powder charges only when the diggers hit bedrock too solid to be hand-quarried.

As the unskilled workers pursued this massive job, the contractor and his craftsmen prepared later stages of the work. Timber, iron, and hardware were stockpiled and crafted to shape. Limestone was quarried up and down the coast, and skilled limeburners fired the stone in kilns, seeking the precise temperature that would turn it to quicklime. Gathered from the cooling kilns, the quicklime could finally be mixed with water to form hydrated lime, the basis of mortar. It was no easy job, for the kilns released clouds of noxious smoke, and the slaking with water began a chemical reaction that emitted enormous heat, but mortar by the ton would be needed for the walls of Louisbourg.

As work progressed, stonemasons came steadily to the fore among the fortress labourers. The ramparts were rubblestone, not cut or squared to lie together like massive bricks, but laid down in their rough natural shapes in a cake of sand-and-lime mortar. The art of laying mortar and stone was usually practised by a master mason, who might be a civilian, with a crew of soldier apprentices. Over the years of work these *ateliers* of masters and pupils trained soldier-labourers to select good stone, to mix sound mortar, and to combine the elements in a thick and solid rampart. Other *ateliers* specialized in the auxiliary tasks – forging iron, erecting scaffolding, cutting shaped stones for corners and openings.

Jodocus Koller soon moved from the ranks of the unskilled diggers and haulers to one of these stonemasonry teams, probably the one led by Jean Laumonier. Working under Laumonier, a civilian recruited in France by the first contractor, Koller discovered there was more to the mason's job than laying great quantities of stone. The subtlety of the mason's art increased as each section of the wall moved slowly toward completion. Atop the wall, the masons shaped gun embrasures and firing platforms to give the defenders a clear field of fire without weakening the wall. Overhanging watchpoints had to be jigsawed into the rampart, and passageways were cut through the wall to permit communication between the town and the outerworks. Even the humble needs of drainage demanded close attention, for any mass of stonework is prone to the corrosive power of dripping water. Everywhere, the masons had to build little slopes and tunnels to dispose of casual water, even tunnelling drains out through the wall to the ditch below.

It was all hard physical labour. Work began in the cold, foggy weather of early spring when the pack ice still crowded the shore, and the men worked outdoors in all but the worst weather until winter returned. The day was long. The engineers liked to see the men at work from five in the morning until seven at night. With three breaks, this meant eleven working hours in a fourteen-hour day, the same long schedule of most industrial labourers of the time. The strength and health of the men were constantly tested. Men wore themselves out manhandling heavy stone, they crushed hands or feet, they broke limbs in falls from scaffolding, or they ruptured internal organs in landslips. It was little wonder that the military labourers, safe from the threat of dismissal or the loss of their food and pay, would shirk their jobs to go off in search of a few bottles of wine. Every engineer and contractor bemoaned the labourers' propensity for idleness and drink, and several attributed their own failures to this problem.

Still there were compensations for the men. Perhaps the greatest benefits accrued to those unskilled soldiers who acquired a marketable trade by working their way through one of the construction *ateliers*. Jodocus Koller, the apprentice stonemason, was one who later made such training the basis for a new life as a colonial settler.

A more tangible reward was money. Since the soldiers were the contractors' only source of labour, pay rates in Ile Royale had started high, and the worksites of the 1720s were enlivened by several disturbances as the men, often inspired by the uncompromising Swiss, used the labour scarcity to extort more money from their employers. An ambitious or abstemious soldier could accumulate substantial savings, to the annoyance of some of his officers, who considered a soldier with money too independent for the good of the service. As the contractors and the officer corps began to eye the soldiers' earnings with growing interest, the men would come to learn that the labour shortage gave them no real power. In the interim, however, Jodocus Koller seems to have succeeded in putting money aside, probably the first savings of his footloose life.

When Koller had gained both a marketable skill and some money from his fortification labour, was there perhaps also some private satisfaction if he paused at his piece of work to gaze along the length of the wall, from the mound being heaped up by the diggers at one end past the shapeless mass of scaffolding and stone to the smooth geometry of the finished rampart where cannon were being mounted? Vauban had believed a fortress could be a beautiful thing, and Etienne Verrier pursued an ideal of architectural harmony in every detail he designed. Contemplating the man-made cliffs and grass-green earthworks that were Louisbourg's fortress, Jodocus Koller might have shared their feeling, watching walls that loomed grey and dank when the sky was overcast turn to rich earth tones under a sunny sky.

Against the bulk of the rampart and the long line of defence yet to secure, his day's work seemed infinitesimal, but could he look upon the totality of Louisbourg's fortress, flaws and all, without admiring the achievement?

For a conscientious worker who was acquiring both savings and a skill from his labour, the challenges of fortress-building must have begun to compete with the military duty that was supposed to be a soldier's first and only allegiance. Jodocus Koller could not help being aware of the conflict, for after a few years accumulating his savings and developing his stonecutting skills, he was tossed back into the military routine.

The Karrer officers in Ile Royale had apparently seen promise in the young soldier. Within a few years of his arrival at Louisbourg, they made Koller a sergeant, promoting him past the lower rank of corporal. Corporals were the most experienced men, whose presence gave stability to a company, but sergeants were chosen for merit and leadership, often quite early in their military careers. Promotion was a significant step for Jodocus Koller. A sergeant was a master of men, and authority was always accorded social status. Sergeant Koller suddenly found he had some small standing in the community – surely another new experience for him. But the promotion inevitably drew him away from fortification labour. As a private soldier he could have devoted himself to the building trade, but as one of the Karrer's four sergeants, he was drawn back into the life of the Louisbourg garrison.

Colonial garrisons of France, like colonial defences, were the responsibility of the Ministry of Marine. Only in exceptional circumstances would regiments of the War Minister's regular army go off to fight France's colonial wars. The army fought the great European campaigns, and the Marine Ministry formed its own military force, the Troupes de la Marine, to garrison naval bases and the colonies. The men of this corps of Marine infantry, in their blue uniforms and white greatcoats, were the regular troops of New France. Commissions in the Marine companies became the monopoly of the Canadian colonial aristocracy, which grew into a military caste as sons followed fathers into a small officer corps. Recruits for the ranks still came from France, as did the arms and equipment, but the soldiers

were encouraged to put down roots in the colony. Since the mid-
seventeenth century, many soldiers of the Marine troops had settled
in Canada. The Canadian companies became a field force, skilled in
wilderness warfare, posted in small detachments to all the scattered
outposts of French North America. As a frontier force, often co-
operating with the warriors of allied Indian nations, the Marine
companies introduced their new recruits to North America, preparing
them for settlement there.

The original garrison companies of Ile Royale, the ones that
founded the colony in 1713, came from the Marine garrisons of
Québec, Acadia, and French Newfoundland, with the Ministry
making the same stipulation it would later give for the Swiss mercenary company: the troops for Louisbourg were to be good workmen.
After this initial infusion of troops, the Ile Royale garrison began to
diverge from its Canadian counterpart. Sons of local officers received
the commissions for new companies, and the soldiers recruited in
France were trained to the particular needs of Ile Royale. Where
Canadian troops learned frontier tactics in small detachments – not
even Québec was extensively fortified – the Louisbourg troops would
form a large urban garrison, trained and equipped for European war
in the style of Vauban.

In the Marine garrison, numbering 360 men by 1724, the Karrer's
100 Swiss were an anomaly. Since many of the Swiss spoke little
French, they tended to stick together, emphasizing their special status
as soldiers of a foreign regiment. The Marine officers, they must have
learned, were sceptical of the foreign detachment that suggested competition and disharmony to a Marine hierarchy used to a monopoly
of the colonial military service. Koller, however, would have been
unperturbed by what he might have heard of such feelings. The
Karrer detachment at Louisbourg held a high opinion of itself, particularly when it compared itself to the Marine companies.

The Marine companies never comprised an elite unit. To keep
numbers up and costs down, the Ministry of Marine enlisted younger,
smaller, sicklier recruits than a conscientious company commander
might have wished to accept. The mass of men in the Louisbourg
Marine troops were barely taller than the minimum five-foot-five,

and many joined as sixteen-year-olds. Prospective soldiers sharp enough to compare the enlistments available to them headed for the regular army or special forces like Karrer's mercenary corps, which had higher standards and an appropriately larger signing bonus. Probably the decisive factor that steered the best recruits away from the colonial service was the Marine's length of enlistment. Where the regular army and the mercenary units generally required six years' service from their recruits, the Marine enlistment had no fixed term whatsoever. Burdened by the cost of sending garrisons off to distant colonies, the Marine obliged its men to serve "at the King's pleasure," that is, until the Marine saw fit to release them. Such uncertain prospects must have daunted all but the most dedicated or the most desperate potential recruits.

Men willing to settle in the colonies usually won their discharge, but the Louisbourg troops even found limited appeal in the settlement discharge, for the colony offered soldiers scant prospects outside the service unless they had a skilled trade. The Marine soldiers of Ile Royale tended to arrive young and serve long terms, of necessity making the service a lifetime vocation – not aching to leave perhaps, more securely fed and lodged than they might have been in France, but still with very little choice about their destiny.

The Swiss soldiers at Louisbourg tended to be bigger, healthier men than the Marine troops. Jodocus Koller had joined for a higher pay rate and a larger enlistment bonus. Some had previous military experience, so their average ages and military skills were higher. None was obliged to see garrison duty at Louisbourg as a lifelong destiny, for passage home was guaranteed to those who declined to extend their term of enlistment. This sense of distant freedom, together with the *esprit de corps* fostered by their special identity as outsiders, seems to have given the Swiss detachment higher morale and a sense of greater good fortune than their Marine counterparts.

They let these feelings be known, reinforcing the doubts harboured about them by the Marine officers corps, who saw insolence in the Swiss company's independence and often recommended the mercenaries' recall to France. Marine and Swiss officers at Louisbourg clashed frequently over the privileges the Karrer regiment demanded as an independent unit. The men, despite their regimental loyalties, may have been friendlier, at least once language barriers were overcome. French and Swiss barracked together, worked as one group on the fortifications, and doubtless went off to drink in company, jointly confronting mere civilians with the proud camaraderie of military men. The differences between them would never be dissolved, but Jodocus Koller need not have been particularly alienated from the Marine soldiers once he had learned their language.

Turning to purely military duties with his new rank, Sergeant Koller immersed himself in the routines that were the common experience of all garrison troops. For fortress garrisons, as for field infantry, the fundamental need was well-trained, disciplined soldiers. This was familiar ground for Koller, but as a sergeant he bore direct responsibility for training men and building strong companies. Training was particularly necessary to the Karrer contingent, which lost many of its veterans as enlistments expired. He and the other sergeants were also expected to maintain morale and efficiency in the Swiss company, by the intangibles of leadership and also by routine military administration. As a sergeant, Koller shouldered new responsibility for keeping company rosters, assigning duties and postings, managing military stores, and dispensing justice. That he could handle all these tasks is almost our only evidence that Jodocus Koller could read and write, in German if not in French. He may have picked up these skills in Louisbourg, for some educated soldiers earned money as part-time tutors. However acquired, literacy further distinguished Koller from the men he led, less than half of whom would have been able to sign their names.

During the building season only a skeleton force could be spared for military duties. Serving with these men, Koller must often have been detailed to gunnery, for cannon were the life and death of fortresses in the Vauban style. At the heart of every siege lay an artillery duel: attackers trying to batter a gap in the walls through which their troops would pour, defenders seeking to dismount the enemy guns with fire from the ramparts. An unbreached rampart with its guns firing was virtually immune to assault, but a town with its walls pierced and its artillery silenced was on the verge of destruction.

To defend the rampart and the town, the landward front and the shore defences alike bristled with heavy artillery, and every garrison soldier had to be introduced to their service.

King of the rampart was the thirty-six-pound gun. Thirty-six pounds* was the weight of the projectile it launched, a round ball a foot in diameter. Propelled by the explosive force of fourteen pounds of black powder, this chunk of iron would fly with killing force for half a mile, or much further in a long, arching trajectory. The cannon that launched the thirty-six-pound ball was a gigantic cousin to the smoothbore musket barrel: a hollow metal barrel straight enough to impart a reasonably accurate line of travel to the ball. The difference was a matter of scale. Since the thirty-six-pound ball was 384 times heavier than the musket ball, the cannon barrel had to be strong enough to withstand the explosions of the mighty powder charges packed inside. Cast iron, the thirty-six-pound gun barrel weighed more than three tons, and though the wheels of its blocky wooden carriage let it roll back a foot or two under the recoil of firing, the thirty-six-pounder required a crew of sweating artillerymen with block and tackle to haul it slowly into each new firing position. After each shot, the gunners swabbed out the greasy residue of powder burn, laid in a new charge, and manhandled the gun back into position before the cannoneer stepped up to aim once more, directing his crew to lever the heavy barrel up or down, left or right, as he squinted down the simple sight-markings on the barrel.

The Louisbourg guns, thirty-six-pounders, twenty-four-pounders, eighteen-pounders, and smaller pieces, all needed crews. Every soldier at Louisbourg had to know something about the guns, for there were usually 120 mounted along the line of defence. Not every embrasure displayed a cannon's muzzle, though, for even the heaviest cannon could be moved to new positions as the need arose. Without becoming a specialist in artillery – Louisbourg first had civilian master gunners, then a company of artillerymen – Sergeant Koller must often have been assigned to the guns, sometimes on the ramparts of the town, occasionally in the bleak isolation of the island battery. He never served at the Royal Battery or in the military outposts elsewhere in Ile Royale, for the Marine officers liked the unfettered

* Actually 36 *livres*, which is closer to 42 pounds or 19 kilograms.

authority of those postings and jealously excluded the Swiss company from the rotation.

In the peaceful 1720s and 1730s no guns were fired in anger, but Koller would still have gained ample experience of the gunner's trade. He could have been part of the crews firing twenty-one guns to salute a royal birthday or fifteen guns in conjunction with a religious celebration. In 1730 he probably helped touch off the general salvo of all the fortress artillery in honour of the newborn royal heir, creating a mighty roar that resounded about the town and left much of it briefly wreathed in smoke. Constantly, winter and summer, gunners at the island scrambled to reply to the signals of fogbound ships groping toward the coast. If these duties did not give the men enough cannon drill, the officers interested in artillery arranged gunnery contests, mounting a target beyond the outerworks and encouraging the men with cash purses. Each year the artillery records noted the consumption of two or three tons of black powder for all these purposes.

Training exercises around the ramparts and assignments to gun duty were highlights of the military routine. Most of the time military duty meant guard duty, a monotonous round of sentry postings enlivened only by occasional civic disturbances. The rhythms of the guard drew officers from their investments to make inspections along the windswept rampart. It took sergeants from their family taverns to organize a crowded guardroom and made soldiers briefly abandon shovels and trowels to present arms at a sentry post. The town's policemen, the sentries also performed a vital defence function. If the guard were maintained with the slightest care – and sentries were court-martialled for minor failings while on duty – there was no chance of a surprise attack breaching the town's defences. The sentry round added the last touch to Vauban's geometry of stone, iron, and men. The enemy who wanted Louisbourg would have to lay formal siege to it or concede it impregnable.

Sentry duty, artillery exercise, training, paperwork – all the mundane rituals of a peacetime garrison occupied Jodocus Koller through the late 1720s and into the 1730s. By then he was a veteran among the Swiss, well into a second term of enlistment. Forgoing discharge or transfer back to Europe may have been a condition of his promotion to sergeant, but it was just one of several sacrifices Koller had made for his rank. His military duties had cost him pay and advancement in his stonemasonry. He had lost many of his friends in the regiment as they departed at the end of their enlistments, leaving Koller as a sergeant and a veteran slightly remote from the newcomers. Yet staying in the regiment gave him no assurance of further progress, for men from the ranks could not aspire to officer's commissions. Like many of the soldiers of Ile Royale, Koller was beginning to find military service a dead end.

There was cause for Koller's dissatisfaction, for it was the sergeants who were made most vividly aware of the paradox of service in Louisbourg. Charged with the daily operations of their troops, sergeants had reason to take pride in their companies, and they expected to apply the blend of stern discipline and regimental solidarity standard throughout the armed services. Constant training was the key to that system, but at Louisbourg there was scarcely time for much more than the minimum of military routines. The real military priority was the construction program, and sergeants who sought to assemble their companies for military exercise were overruled by the staffing needs of the engineers and contractors. When real soldiers would have been drilling together, the men of the Louisbourg garrison were dispersed among individual construction *ateliers* to become stonemasons, limeburners, or woodworkers. Even Koller's Swiss, bigger and stronger than their Marine fellows and judged the best soldiers in the garrison, had little time for military exercises; they did a disproportionate share of fortification work.

A dedicated soldier, taught to put his loyalty and his identity in the military vocation, might have been excused for wondering bitterly if he was a soldier at all as he went through the motions of serving a garrison of day labourers. For a soldier with such doubts, the actions and attitudes of the officer corps of Ile Royale would have become an additional nagging irritant. Indeed, it began to seem to some soldiers that the officers regarded them less as soldiers worthy of the respect accorded men-at-arms than as a collective private estate to be milked endlessly for money.

Officers in eighteenth-century armies were noblemen. War and command were the noble professions, and the few officers not of noble birth knew their commissions gave them cherished entry into the aristocracy. Since military service was a nobleman's vocation rather than his livelihood, officers received only a token wage, adequate for some frugal bachelor ensign, but hardly sufficient to support a properly noble lifestyle. The officer's real income came from the hereditary estates that were a nobleman's birthright.

Military command was only one aspect of the life of a proper young aristocrat. A garrison officer should have studied Vauban in detail and trained himself in field tactics and the command of companies. Those with inquiring minds or great ambitions might collect libraries of mathematics and languages, engineering and military history, and even publish their own writings on military science. Nevertheless, military service was usually only one facet in a life in which court attendance, cultural pursuits, and the management of family interests had equal or greater importance. In peacetime the regiment was something like the estate where an officer's tenants laboured. The owner was expected to maintain a supervisory interest in his military command and his estate, but he would hardly dirty his hands in the running of either.

For the officer corps of Ile Royale, living up to this aristocratic ideal had become a burden. They were noble, but barely so, and those whose titles were not purely colonial usually traced their roots to junior branches of the provincial nobility of southern France. Their families had turned to the colonial service when the prices of commissions in the army or navy proved too high, and many Louisbourg officers were two or three generations removed from ancestors who had come out to serve in the colonies. With each generation their claim on family holdings in France grew more tenuous. Some had acquired new estates in the New World, but unlike small, intensively farmed properties in France, huge colonial landholdings produced little revenue. The landed wealth that formed the underpinning of the noble life no longer supported most of the officers who commanded at Louisbourg.

Some of the Ile Royale officers had other sources of wealth; one was the son of Montréal's wealthiest merchant. But in general the garrison officers were constrained to turn to the local sources of income: fishing, shipping, trade, and property. The fortunate ones had capital to invest with local merchants, and some of them prospered.

The shrewd and well-connected used their authority and their inside knowledge to turn official spending in their direction. Such enterprise contrasted with the image of the land-wealthy aristocrat, but some officers found commerce the best available foundation for their pursuit of prestige and advancement.

Many of the Louisbourg officers were simply poor. If their estates and investments failed them, they lived on their salaries as best as they could, hoping that a royal pension would sustain their families after their death. To economize, they used soldiers as their household servants. As much as they could, they joined the local economy: buying part-ownership of trading vessels, securing contracts to supply the garrison with firewood, investing in fish or timber cargoes. They rented out rooms in their homes. Frequently they married beneath their station: Saint-Etienne de LaTour, great-grandson of a founder of Acadia, married a carpenter's widow, and Louis Loppinot married the daughter of an innkeeper.

The officers never sacrificed their elite prerogatives or their social pretensions, but the aristocratic façade often depended on the generosity of the commanding officers. All the governors entertained lavishly, spending their own fortunes to provide what their officers could not provide themselves. By recommending bonuses and promotions for their subordinates, senior officers enhanced their own prestige and built patronage networks; but patronage was no substitute for money. In a community where merchants and fishing proprietors could rise from obscurity to ease in a decade or two, the poverty of the officer corps was galling to the aristocratic mind, and the officers constantly sought to buttress their social superiority with greater economic security.

Naturally their eyes fell on their troops. Just as an impoverished landowner could squeeze more revenue from his estates, the garrison officers looked for income from the companies they commanded. In an isolated garrison where the officers and Marine officials were linked by common outlook and family ties, there was no one to stand against officers who exploited their men, and over the years the officers' use of their positions for personal gain became blatant.

Exploitation began with the soldiers' pay. A private's monthly pay was scarcely a week's wage for an ordinary labourer, and most of this small amount was deducted to contribute to the cost of his uniform, rations, disability pension fund, and other expenses, but it was still possible for the officers to extort a levy on military wages. By neglecting to distribute goods the men had paid for, or by collecting pay for dead, discharged, or deserted soldiers, the officers made a small revenue – one that was almost a tradition in military organizations all over the world.

More revenue was diverted from the men to the officers through military canteens. Each company ran a small shop to provide drink, tobacco, and personal items such as pipes, combs, and soap to its men. There was a profit for the officers, of course, but the men had little to spend, and the canteen faced the competition of all the other taverns and shops of the town. To increase canteen revenue the officers began to force their men to deal with them. Early in the 1730s, they lobbied to have fortification earnings paid out through the companies. Next they arranged that such wages would be paid just once a year, instead of bi-weekly. Suddenly men awaiting pay for work they had done were obliged to run up bills, often turning to the company canteens for credit. Though the officers failed to enforce an edict forbidding civilian businesses to extend credit to soldiers, they still controlled the men's money almost totally.

Gradually the officers discovered their impunity from correction, and their manipulations became more blatant. Soldiers ordered out to cut firewood found they were doing unpaid work for officers with fuel contracts. Other forms of barely concealed theft appeared. Officers embittered by their inability to live as they believed nobles should – effortlessly, supported by hereditary revenues – turned to their companies as substitute estates.

The revenue milked from the soldiers was not large. The victims were poor to begin with, and the money a company captain extorted from them had to be shared with his junior officers and the general staff. Certainly the officers never grew rich from this source. Years after the exploitative system had been built, senior captains who had no personal income still died with debts outstripping their assets. But the soldiers, compared to whom the poorest officer was a rich and pampered aristocrat, certainly grew poorer. They could still earn money, and there continued to be men like Jodocus Koller who accumulated a respectable nest egg in a decade of service, but the obstacles were much greater in the 1730s than they had been earlier. Only too well aware of an exploitation they were powerless to resist, the soldiers changed their attitude to their officers. Lieutenants and captains who should have been remote figures of stern authority disdaining direct contact with their men instead became closely involved with companies they were eager to milk for funds.

The soldiers concluded that their superiors held them in contempt, valuing them only as slaves to be worked for profit, and in self-defence they developed an exaggerated pride in their status as soldiers. Though their uniforms may have been frayed and their parade-ground performance sloppy from lack of practice, the men continued to proclaim themselves soldiers. A proud claim to the rights due to them as warriors was a salve to their self-respect. It was a defensive rationalization that may have heightened the contempt of their officers, and it probably did not blind Jodocus Koller to the deteriorating position of the private soldier in Ile Royale. Some time early in the 1730s he resolved to quit the service, though not to leave the colony. The professional soldier, trained to abandon all loyalties beyond his regiment, was about to become a colonial pioneer.

III

Koller, almost the only soldier of the Karrer regiment to settle in Ile Royale, planned his retirement with care. As other Swiss soldiers waited for their discharges and whatever future awaited them in Europe, Koller put down roots in Ile Royale, creating a civilian life to replace a military career gone sour.

Koller's assets as he prepared for civilian life were those he had won in a decade of service to the garrison of Ile Royale. He had at least the beginnings of the mason's trade, an asset that would always be useful at Louisbourg. Sergeant's rank, if it had failed to provide the satisfactions of leadership, had given him a measure of respect in a small community where he was now a familiar figure. His economies as a labourer had given him a comfortable nest egg, despite the extortions practised by his officers. The money and the rank might have gone with him to another posting, but the slowly acquired status would not. Koller decided to make the best of what he had in Ile Royale, making his commitment plain in 1728 by becoming the owner of a dilapidated house on Rue Dauphine. A few months later, in February 1729, in a Catholic ceremony on the eve of Lent, Jodocus Koller took a wife.

He was hardly the first Louisbourg soldier to marry. A few of the Swiss brought wives with them, and many sergeants and senior men in the Marine companies found that acquiring a home and family was the best way to blend civilian comforts into the undemanding routine of the peacetime garrison. Several guests at the wedding of Jodocus Koller and Marie-Catherine Auger had successfully made this mix. The bride herself, a woman in her late teens who had spent most of her life in Louisbourg, was the daughter of a retired soldier. Her father, Julien Auger *dit* Grandchamp, had come to North America in the Marine companies. He had married at Montréal while in the garrison there, and his daughter had been born shortly before he was transferred to Ile Royale. At Louisbourg, Auger *dit* Grandchamp had retired to work as a carpenter and to open an inn. The quayside inn had prospered, serving visiting shipowners and merchants as well as thirsty locals, and within a few months of his daughter's marriage, Grandchamp expanded his premises by acquiring the adjoining house from another guest at the wedding, fisherman Jean de Lasson. Grandchamp's late-in-life transformation from soldier to innkeeper should have suggested to Koller the civilian careers available in Louisbourg, and the presence of another wedding guest, his tutor in stonemasonry, Jean Laumonier, testified to an obvious source of income he could tap. Even the military comrades from the regiment who attended his wedding had begun to put down roots. Sergeant Charles-Adam Klem had already purchased a home, as had another guest, the Karrer's second-in-command, Lieutenant the Baron de L'Espérance.

The Baron, gracing with his presence the marriage of one of his subordinates, was one of those oddities who eluded the neat categories of eighteenth-century society. His father was a minor German monarch, Prince Léopold of Montbéliard, his mother one of the four humble sisters who were the royal mistresses. One of twenty-three offspring of this ménage, the Baron received little from his quasi-noble parentage beyond a commission in Colonel Karrer's regiment, into which he seems to have drifted for lack of a more convenient niche – like Jodocus Koller perhaps. A Protestant but French-speaking, L'Espérance fitted easily into the impecunious minor aristocracy of the Louisbourg officer corps, marrying the daughter of Captain Dangeac even before his formal conversion to Catholicism. Their son, the second Baron, followed his father into the Karrer corps, later transferring to the French service to end his career as a colonial governor.

Auger *dit* Grandchamp, Sergeant Klem, the Baron, and many others had cheerfully bridged the gulf between military and civilian life in Ile Royale. With such examples, Koller might perhaps have been expected to stay in the service, placidly raising a family as he awaited a distant retirement and the opening of yet another small tavern. But the opportunities of civilian life outweighed the gloomy prospects of the military, where advancement seemed blocked, achievement unlikely, and exploitation ever greater. Koller decided to have done with the army.

Koller's first acquisition upon his retirement was a grant of land, bestowed with three years' pay upon any soldier who would settle in Ile Royale and help to develop its potential for farming. The land-grant policy had been successful in Canada, where many soldiers had become farmers, but the authorities were naive in expecting similar results in Ile Royale. Agricultural lands could be found, but there was no farming population into which the soldiers could blend, no farmers to instruct them, no farmers' daughters for them to marry. Potential farmers found there were easier ways to earn a living, and few of the soldiers who took a settlement discharge at Louisbourg persevered.

No more a farmer than the other discharged men, Koller followed their example at first. He collected pay for three years after his discharge early in the 1730s, and he accepted a plot of land on the Gabarus shore, but every reference to him in these years confirms that he lived in his home on Rue Dauphine and earned a living as a stone-mason. Freed of military obligations, he had returned to the work that had occupied him in his first years in Ile Royale. The massive fortification project Koller had seen in its infancy was still far from complete. If all went well, the fortress might be substantially complete in the mid-1740s. Even then maintenance and revision would keep many craftsmen employed.

Perhaps Koller still worked alongside the veteran stonemason Jean Laumonier, but in these years when Laumonier was being brought repeatedly into court for beating and abusing his wife, Koller and Marie-Catherine Auger were busy building up a home. Now a well-paid civilian artisan, Koller must have renovated his house, for the property he bought for a pittance in 1728 soon sheltered a growing family. Over fifteen years the Kollers had seven children, of whom three daughters and three sons lived past infancy. By 1734 the Kollers were comfortable enough to add a servant to their expanding household.

The years following Koller's retirement were so peaceful that he almost drops from sight. Only one or two anecdotes illustrate their lives in these years. In 1733 the family was embarrassed by Koller's irascible mother-in-law. Appearing before the high court in a minor legal matter that had already cost the Augers some money, Madame Auger denounced the initial decision, tore up the subpoena, and spoke to the judges in what they considered "scarcely respectable terms." Annoyed, the judges summarily convicted her of contempt and imposed a fine of thirty-three *livres*, to be distributed among the poor of the colony. This minor contretemps was taken seriously in the tight-knit, status-conscious town. People began to taunt all the Auger relatives for the shame they said she had brought her family. The affair would not die down until Madame Auger's sister, the wife of a local merchant captain, begged the judges to announce that the fine was only a pecuniary punishment and not "a note of infamy."

One evening about a year later, when Marie-Catherine Auger was pregnant with the Kollers' third child, some guests visited the Koller home. Talk eventually came around to the sex of the child they were expecting. Since the family already had two girls, a sailor named Jean Darracq predicted the third would surely be a boy. Madame Koller expected another girl. Instantly a wager was on: the loser would pay for a new pair of shoes from Domingo the shoemaker.

It was an incident expressive of the town's love of gambling. People of every station bet spontaneously on unpredictable events: the sex of an unborn child was as good a wager as the arrival date of the first ships of spring. Dice games, backgammon, and billiards provided opportunities for more formal gambling, and card games were particularly favoured by the literate elite. Those who could afford to bet wagered large amounts on their cards – rumour had it that twenty thousand *livres* had changed hands in one session. In a half-hearted attempt to limit gambling, the local authorities banned lotteries and several disapproved games of chance, but wagering retained its popularity in a town poorly provided with other diversions. Madame Koller's bet, typical of the pastimes of the working people of Louisbourg, paid off. After the birth of her third child, Thérèse, she collected her pair of shoes, though the cobbler had later to chase Jean Darracq through the courts for his payment.

Amid these homely instances of family life, what stands out is Jodocus Koller's assimilation into the community. There was no Jodocus Koller *fils* among his children, no Franz or Leopold to recall his Austrian roots. Although his eldest son, Grégoire, was named for Koller's father, all the children bore names that were common in Ile Royale: Marie, Pierre, Josette, Jacques-François, Catherine. Koller kept his friendships among the Swiss troops – a year after his marriage he served as executor of the estate of a well-off young soldier who died in the town hospital, leaving a house and several hundred *livres* to the Church and his fellow soldiers – but he had dropped his foreign background almost as completely as his military career. His home now was Ile Royale, his livelihood the urban crafts of Louisbourg, his family ties those of his wife. Growing up as French as their neighbours, his children must have inherited little of their father's central-European heritage and accent. As in the wager over a pair of shoes, the central figure in his household was probably the woman who was Koller's bond to the local people, his wife Marie-Catherine.

Madame Koller's kitchen was surely the heart of their small and crowded home. Probably the largest room in the Koller house, it would have held a table and benches, locally made or shipped in from New England, with stacked chairs waiting against the walls for guests. Water from the nearest well was stored in a keg or cistern close at hand. Wooden cabinets and hutches probably housed mixed and partial sets of tableware. Complete sets were difficult to obtain and preserve, so most householders assembled a patchwork collection from what was offered in the shops and at auction sales. A kitchen like the Kollers' would have boasted earthenware and pewter dishes, mugs, wine glasses and cups, coffeepots, pepper mills, and sugar bowls to furnish a crowded table. The room would have been dominated by a large stone fireplace and chimney, likely Koller's own handiwork. Perhaps an oven filled one side of the fireplace, but separate coal or wood stoves were uncommon in Ile Royale. The fireplace was at once the house's heating plant and the kitchen's main cooking surface. Its hearth and mantel would have been crammed with frying pans and cooking pots of brass and iron, the fireplace itself equipped with fire irons, pot-hooks, and probably a roasting spit.

Though the fireplace's open flame provided the heat for the Kollers' cooking, the cuisine of the household would hardly have been typified by great chunks of meat roasting over a crackling fire. The food of the people of Louisbourg was more prosaic than that. Few people ate much meat in the eighteenth century, in Ile Royale as elsewhere. What they ate instead was bread – heavy, whole-wheat loaves that gave the colony's people most of the bulk and most of the calories of their daily food consumption. In France, where the mass of the population laboured to produce wheat, savour was added by a little cheap wine and some vegetables, but meat, even in the form of long-preserved, fatty salt pork, was a touch of luxury. Workingmen in the cities of Europe spent half their income to buy bread, about fifteen per cent on all other foods. A family of four would eat six pounds of bread every day of their lives, if they could get it.

Ile Royale knew the same diet. To prove the importance of trade, a local official simply demonstrated that Ile Royale needed five hundred pounds of bread per colonist per year, and produced almost none. Though it grew so little, cultural habit and economic realities kept bread fundamental to Louisbourg diets. The soldier's daily ration included one and a half pounds of bread, freshly baked in the garrison bakery from flour imported each summer from Québec, France, or even New England. The little fish or salt meat added to this ration was more for flavour than for sustenance. The civilians ate similar quantities of bread, baking their own loaves or buying from the bakers and vendors of the town.

A little more affluent than Parisian labourers or peasant farmers, the townspeople of Ile Royale probably enjoyed more diversity in their diet. Meat was not quite so rare as to be a luxury, though it was often a dish eaten in small portions. At Louis Marie's boarding house one evening, a main course (probably bread and soup) was followed by a plate of pickled calves' feet presented by the cook with the words, "Voilà, messieurs, le dessert." One of the guests had seen this dish too often, and his disgusted response provoked the innkeeper's wrath. But in general meat was more appreciated, even endowed with medicinal properties. One man evoked the rarity of meat in the colony by describing the difficulty he had obtaining meat for therapeutic bouillons during a serious illness.

For fresh foods, householders like the Kollers grew herbs and vegetables in their yards, and they often kept chickens or a goat as well. Fish was never scarce. People preferred meat when they could get it, but fresh or dried fish was an important addition to the bread-based diet, and even a substitute for it when stocks of imported flour ran low.

The seasonal rhythms of transport determined meals in a community that imported its dietary habits and most of what it ate. Louisbourg's vegetables were dried peas and beans from Canada, its meat salted and pickled products from France. The local dairy herds were small, but the town imported tubs of heavily salted butter and a range of cheeses. Rum, brandy, and wine never seem to have been lacking. The Kollers, fortunate to live in a well-connected port of trade, would have had a sack of coffee in their attic and probably a barrel of molasses as well. If Koller smoked a pipe, they probably had a few rolls of tobacco and a grater. Indeed, they probably kept bulk quantities of many of the foods they ate, since nearly everything that was imported arrived in preserved and packaged form. To keep the mice out of their stores, the Kollers likely had a cat, and if Koller was a hunter they could also have had a dog.

With so many foods dried, salted, or preserved, a boiled diet had to be basic in Louisbourg's kitchens and dining rooms. Madame Koller would have combined dried vegetables, spices, and fish or meat in soups and stews; there would often have been a big iron *marmite* simmering in the fireplace and filling the Koller home with the aroma of the evening meal. Even the venison and rabbit provided by the hunters would have been best suited to the stewpot. Boiling was probably the customary cooking method for most kinds of foods, and such meals could have been tasty. Sauces based on flour and butter or oil would have enhanced them, baked goods and savouries were common, and certainly every household had its frying pan and roasting spit for meat. Nevertheless, large chunks of dark bread, supplemented by a little soup or stew, were probably the most common mealtime experience of the Koller family and the families in the homes around theirs.

A few years after leaving the service, Jodocus Koller began to see opportunities in Ile Royale's unsatisfied appetite for fresh meat. Over the years a series of official plans to build up cattle herds from imported breeding stock had foundered, partly on the lack of good pastureland. In the mid-1730s Koller began to attack this problem in his own small way. On the piece of land he had received as a retirement bonus, he began to raise hay. At first it was not a business that could have supported a family, so Koller was fortunate to have his mason's work, but he persevered with his land grant and found that fodder commanded a steady market in the town. Perhaps farming satisfied some need Koller had inherited from his rural parentage; certainly it led him into widening areas of enterprise, where he began to display both business acumen and a gambler's instincts. To grow hay he needed to clear forest from his land, and soon he was a vendor of firewood as well as hay. Once he had a substantial pasture under hay, the obvious next step was stock-raising. In 1735 Koller bought a small herd of goats at the auction of Judith Pansart's estate. Five years later he had committed himself to a three-year contract to supply livestock to a new butchery in Louisbourg, mortgaging his house and property to join the venture. One opportunity led to another: by the early 1740s Jodocus Koller, ex-soldier and ex-stonemason, had become an entrepreneur, producing firewood, hay, and livestock for commercial sale.

The sea was the logical way to transport what he produced, and Koller responded to another opportunity. By 1738 he was a boat-owner, and shipping soon became important in his affairs. He could now exploit woodlots and pasturelands further away, and acquire new hay supplies for his herds. He could buy cattle from farmers in Port Toulouse and at the same time bid for a share of the general hauling trade that employed the coastal schooners.

By 1743 and 1744, when Koller filled large firewood orders from the garrison bakery, resource industries seem to have been his exclusive occupations. He may have been on the verge of wealth, his risk-taking rewarded as Canadian crop failures increased the need for local food production. He acquired a second property in the town, and people began to refer to him as a *bourgeois de Louisbourg*, a man of property, a master of men, someone of stature in the town.

Suddenly he had contacts and associates in every corner of the colony. Soldiers and artisans knew him as a comrade who had done well, and his old commanders remembered him with respect; in 1738 Koller rented one of his buildings to the Swiss regiment. With his old garrison friends, his new urban clients for wood and meat, his business partners, and the woodcutters, farmers, and boatmen who worked with him, Koller had built friendship networks well beyond those his marriage had brought him. Still, something of his plain background and original friendships survived. Among his close companions was the scapegrace hunter and sailor Baptiste Guion, next-door neighbour of the innkeeping Augers and probably Koller's mentor in his explorations of the woods and grasslands of Ile Royale.

Above all, Jodocus Koller had put roots into the soil of Ile Royale to a depth few of the colonists could match. His friends in the troops could find a posting elsewhere. Fishermen could catch cod on other shores. The merchants who bought his produce could trade anywhere, and sailors like Jean Lelarge scarcely seemed to need a home. Koller on the other hand was taking his living, an unexpectedly good one, from the woods and waters of Ile Royale. He should have known the island and its resources better than many men born there, and he suffered or prospered with its changing fortunes.

He had developed a new attitude to Ile Royale. As a soldier in the service of France, he had been sworn to fight for Louis XV wherever he was posted, but as a settler of the island named Ile Royale, his loyalty was more specific. From now on his commitment was to the island that had become his home and provider. It was not a commitment he would be able to shirk. Just as he consolidated his success as a colonial settler, fate flung him back to the profession of arms that had brought him to Ile Royale.

IV

Few would have expected a middle-aged ex-soldier like Jodocus Koller to distinguish himself when war came to Louisbourg. Siege warfare rarely made heroes. It was the most impersonal combat known to eighteenth-century man, an engineer's war that pitted iron cannonballs against stone walls and gave few occasions for personal glory. Most soldiers did not object: the shots that battered at walls were less likely to kill the men behind them. A siege could be fought over several months, yet leave a butcher's bill of dead and wounded smaller than the toll of an infantry encounter won and lost in a few minutes.

Yet, whether soldier or civilian, no one in a besieged fortress could escape from the intense human drama of a town under siege. Its fortress in the style of Vauban ensured that Louisbourg would not fall victim to naval raid or sudden assault. Instead, the Vauban fortress would be subjected to a siege in the manner of Vauban. The great engineer had won his reputation attacking fortresses as well as designing them; his plans of attack were as stately and methodical as the geometry of his designs. Under formal siege, the defenders and citizens of a Vauban fortress would find themselves constricted in a vice that tightened inexorably around them, increasing its pressure in carefully orchestrated stages over weeks or months that tested the courage and endurance of every participant. Having laboured to fortify his community according to Vauban, Jodocus Koller was obliged to endure the defence of what he had helped to build. Louisbourg was laid under siege in the spring of 1745, and Jodocus Koller came to the forefront as its people fought for their homes and their lives.

The war had begun a year earlier, in May 1744. At first Ile Royale held the initiative, for thirty years of peace had greatly restored French power in the western Atlantic. Secure against naval raids or petty assaults, its fortifications almost complete, Louisbourg had seven hundred Marine and Swiss troops at its service. Only a peacetime complement, they were still the largest troop concentration in the region, one that was backed by a substantial civilian population and by Indian nations closely allied to France. At sea, the French naval patrols that visited Louisbourg each summer easily outgunned the vessels representing British seapower between Newfoundland and New England, and the French sailors who came to trade and fish at Ile Royale would quickly be transformed into privateers and auxiliaries. Though the latent strength of New England, backed by Britain, was far superior to Ile Royale's, the standing military forces of the British colonies were negligible. The land and sea power that small, well-organized Ile Royale gave France was reason to hope for a reversal of the setbacks France had suffered in the peacemaking of 1713.

Ile Royale went to the attack immediately, led by its commandant Jean-Baptiste Louis LePrévost Duquesnel. A peg-legged veteran in his late fifties, afflicted with painful arthritis and coronary trouble, Duquesnel had come to Ile Royale in 1740 as a reformer, and his short-tempered zeal for correcting the abuses of the military staff had antagonized some colonials, but he had also been preparing his forces for war. Duquesnel understood time was not Ile Royale's ally: the colony's opportunity lay in swift, pre-emptive strikes before New England could convert its schooners into warships and its men into soldiers. A series of successful attacks might throw the enemy on to the defensive, obliging it at least to recover its losses before venturing to attack. Success would rally the Indian allies and give the troops an invigorating taste of victory. Perhaps most important, a bold offensive would force the hand of Duquesnel's superiors in France. The Marine Ministry had always resisted pleas for more troops, arguing there would be time to send reinforcements when they were really needed. If Ile Royale's peacetime garrison managed to carry the war to the enemy, France could hardly fail to reinforce success. Duquesnel would get the ships, men, and arms that would enable Louisbourg to resist an enemy riposte.

At first the offensive went well. An expeditionary force seized the British outpost at Canso Island (Jodocus Koller rented one of his coastal boats to transport the troops) and pushed on to attack Annapolis Royal, the sole remaining British base in Acadia. Success might have swung the ten thousand farmers and woodsmen of Acadia back to the French cause, setting limits to the northern expansion of New England and recovering a valuable colony for the King of France.

But the attack demanded both siege troops and a blockading fleet, and the effort strained the resources of a colony whose supply lines were hostage to enemy privateers. By the time naval aid came to Ile Royale – the powerful sixty-four-gun *Ardent* from France and the newly launched frigate *Caribou* from Québec – American privateers were seizing merchant ships on the coasts of the colony. The naval ships stayed close to Louisbourg all summer to ensure that the colony's provisions got through, and at Annapolis Royal Michel de Gannes de Falaise was forced either to risk a desperate assault without assistance or to lift his siege. De Gannes did not hesitate long. The officer whose cautious retreat from his promise of marriage had saved him from his obligations to Marie-Anne Carrerot fifteen years earlier had little inclination for a glorious death on the walls of Annapolis Royal. He prudently raised his siege, and then, finding the wary Acadians unwilling to support his troops all winter, retreated toward Louisbourg.

De Gannes's retreat late in October 1744 marked the end of Ile Royale's advantage; time had caught up with Duquesnel's offensive. Though the colony's successes on land and sea had moved Bishop Dubreuil in Québec to institute services of thanksgiving, there would be little more to celebrate in Louisbourg. Knowing that a thoroughly roused New England would take the offensive, Ile Royale inspected its resources. Louisbourg still had only its peacetime garrison, enough to man the ramparts but not to undertake a really active defence. The *corsaires* had done well, and the supply lines had been kept open, but privateering had also frittered away food and ammunition in an unwinnable war of attrition against an ever-growing enemy fleet. Though careful rationing would sustain the colony all winter, the prospects for 1745 were serious.

To calculate the dangers for 1745, Ile Royale no longer had the leader who had ordered the offensives of 1744. Commandant Duquesnel's shaky health had failed, and he died suddenly in mid-October, just before de Gannes returned from Acadia. The combat veteran and reformer was succeeded by the senior garrison officer, a man with little combat experience and long involvement in the malpractice of the local officer corps. Sixty-six-year-old Louis DuPont

Duchambon had come to Ile Royale with its founding garrison and had served nowhere else in the intervening years. His command included his three sons and four of his nephews, a closely knit and influential clan in a corps of officers to which Duchambon had ties of blood, marriage, and shared experience. Though the well-to-do DuPont clan may have had less need than many to abuse its soldiers, Duchambon shared interests and outlook with the officers most dependent on manipulations of the military paychest. This group had suffered under the reforming governors sent in from the navy. Now it looked to Duchambon to restore old privileges.

Duchambon's accession provoked disaffection among the soldiers, to whom Duquesnel's reforms and the early successes of the war had brought new pride and optimism. Duquesnel had held the troops in no special affection, but his campaign against exploitation encouraged their claim to the respect due to soldiers. Canso gave them victory, and in Acadia they performed well, making long wilderness marches in good order and pinning down a sizeable enemy garrison for more than a month. Evidently garrison self-respect had soared. The diggers and masons were growing into soldiers again, and Duquesnel had encouraged their enthusiasm by promising them shares in the plunder of Canso and Annapolis Royal.

In these circumstances the promotion of Duchambon was a disaster for the men. The new commander gave no sign that he shared the soldiers' high opinion of themselves. He stood by while the officers reinstated old abuses. Prize money won at Canso went undistributed. Within months of the change in command the troops were embittered and angry.

The mid-winter imposition of rationing was the final straw. As civilians began to buy food from the military stores, the soldiers were issued what was left over: often spoiled, rotten, inedible rations they had already paid for in payroll deductions. A wave of resentment flared through the garrison, apparently among the Swiss most of all. Just before Christmas some of the men drew up a petition to Duchambon, asking that he be their friend and protector against the abuses of others. But the petition went unpresented, for the French and Swiss companies in the barracks decided on more extreme action.

In an army that meted out death sentences for minor breaches of discipline, mutiny could only have exploded from desperation and fury; but their act of mutiny did not reduce the soldiers to an orderless mob. In the cold early morning of December 27, virtually the whole garrison assembled, fully armed, entirely officerless, in formal parade-order on the courtyard of the King's Bastion, displaying the utmost in military bearing even in the act of revolt. Lieutenants and captains rushing to the citadel to remonstrate, then to parley, heard furious talk of killing all the officers – even of burning the town. Seeing that an ill-chosen word or an accidental shot would precipitate murder, the powerless officers restrained their anger, and the mutineers preserved their discipline. Even when they commanded the town, the troops held to their formations, as if aware that violence could transform them into a formless mob. They limited themselves to a simple list of demands for the redress of their grievances. When Duchambon helplessly accepted, the garrison acknowledged the authority of its officers once more, ending the revolt before noon the same day, as if eager to recover the normal state of obedience.

The mutineers presented their morning of mutiny merely as a blow for legitimate claims, but neither the troops nor their officers could ever have taken such fundamental disobedience lightly. Tension in the garrison must have been slow to dissipate, and feelings must have run high among townspeople like Jodocus Koller. As an ex-soldier Koller knew the enlisted men's grievances, but the revolt of the troops jeopardized the colony in which he had staked his future. Koller could hardly have welcomed the mutiny: he must have been relieved by its swift and peaceful conclusion. The presence of men like him, with friendships and interests on both sides, may even have helped to resolve the hostilities. There were no further consequences of the mutiny that winter.

As the new year began, the loyalty of the troops was only one worry for the people of Louisbourg. Duchambon still had only his peacetime garrison (even if he could rely on it), and the campaigns of 1744 had left the colony with reduced ammunition stores and barely adequate stocks of food. Already there was disquieting intelligence about New England's plans for the spring. Joannis Dolabaratz, the privateer captured in June and returned to Louisbourg in a prisoner exchange, reported that Boston was abuzz with talk of an attack on Ile Royale. Dolabaratz was scornful of the danger posed by such talk, but his information confirmed that the initiative no longer lay with Ile Royale. Forced to guess what form the American threat would take, the colony had to rely on the strategic thinking that had produced the massive fortifications of Louisbourg.

Fundamental to French strategy was the rule that fortresses were vulnerable only to what Vauban had called a *siège en forme*, a slow, methodical attack by a large army and a blockading fleet. Such forces, reckoned the French, could only be sent against Louisbourg from Britain, for there were neither troops nor naval bases in the Thirteen Colonies. Minister Maurepas in France, Commandant Duchambon in Louisbourg, and amateur strategists such as Dolabaratz all recognized that New England's privateers would attempt a strangling blockade of Ile Royale and perhaps even set raiding parties ashore. Just to break the blockade would be a taxing assignment, but all the French planners united in the belief that whatever militia forces New England might muster against the fortress would shatter on Louisbourg's ditches and ramparts and be blown apart by the defenders' cannon. Lacking a regular army and navy, New England was judged incapable of mounting the *siège en forme* that might succeed against the isolated, undermanned, and understocked fortress. Since military intelligence reported no signs that Britain was preparing a major expedition for North America, the danger of a formal siege in 1745 seemed remote. Such a judgment sustained Duchambon in March and April when enemy vessels began ranging the icebound shore of Ile Royale. It sustained Maurepas early in 1745 when he decided not to reinforce Louisbourg immediately. Perhaps the same judgment comforted Jodocus Koller and his neighbours as they faced the spring of 1745.

Unfortunately the judgment was wrong.

The colonial officials of France were used to a closely centralized administration, in which decisions were made and implemented through networks of patronage and clientage that spanned the Atlantic. They found it difficult to take seriously the politics of the British colonies. Though the Thirteen Colonies had powerful governors, vigorous legislatures, and enormous resources of wealth and population, French officials expected that London would take all major military decisions and that the British regular forces would implement them. The autonomy of the British colonies seemed merely to confer an advantage on Ile Royale, allowing it to strike even before New England knew it was at war. Duquesnel would have seen danger no better than Duchambon: the high command in Louisbourg and France was unable to see a threat in the enthusiastic militias and amateur commanders of the northern British colonies.

Planning to triumph through superior discipline, Ile Royale was about to be confronted by a remarkable feat of military organization. In January 1745, when Duchambon was agonizing over measures to counter the blockade he expected that spring, the legislators of Massachusetts were furiously debating the merits of an expedition against Louisbourg. In February, as Maurepas dispatched the lone frigate he judged sufficient for Ile Royale's protection in the early spring,* the Massachusetts legislature approved the expedition by a one-vote majority. By April, when Duchambon wrote to notify a military patrol headed overland from Canada to Acadia that he would not need its assistance, the New England colonies had enlisted and armed four thousand volunteers. Many were absolute amateurs, promised by their chaplains that faith in God would carry them irresistibly to victory, but the militia also possessed a nucleus of trained military men and many experienced shipboard artillerymen. Even more professional was a British naval squadron from the West Indies that sailed at the last minute to join the colonials' assault on Ile Royale. Braced against the privateers' blockade and the threat of raiding parties, Louisbourg was about to be confronted by the formal siege that could be its downfall.

In April and May, onshore winds kept the floating ice crushed tightly against the shore of Ile Royale. From the ramparts, masts could be seen out beyond the ice. Were these friendly ships seeking entry, or enemies preparing the blockade?

Finally the wind changed, the ice began to disperse, and on May 7 the Basque fishing boat *Saint-Domingue* struggled into port to tell of a running fight against warships it had finally evaded the night before.

---

* Thwarted first by ice and then by enemy vessels, it never reached Ile Royale.

The enemy was out in strength, and Duchambon guessed that the blockade he had expected was falling into place. He had already mustered the sailors, fishing crews, and men of the town into militia companies, and now he sent troops and militiamen by ship and shore to reconnoitre south of Louisbourg. On May 10 he dispatched a ship to France. Escaping in night and fog, it would report that Louisbourg was blockaded, but siege dangers would not be mentioned.

In the early hours of May 11, between three and four in the morning, a hundred sail rose gently over the southern horizon. In the succeeding hours, with day breaking clear and fine, cannon and pealing bells roused the soldiers and citizens of Ile Royale as transport ships escorted by men-of-war moved steadily into Gabarus Bay. By nine the invasion fleet was lowering scores of boats. Instead of six months' notice of siege, Louisbourg had a couple of hours, for the landing of several thousand New Englanders a few miles from the fortress would begin a battle that both sides sought to make a classic *siège en forme*.

The New England militia had come to Ile Royale with plans for surprise attack and swift victory, but Vauban and his fellow theorists had influenced British military writing as much as French, and when New England's General Pepperrell confronted the regular fortifications of Louisbourg, he immediately ordered his army into the first stage of a formal siege. Vauban had designated the first stage of a siege as the period when the attacker surrounded his intended victim and organized a methodical attack. For Pepperrell the logistics were challenging. He had first to land his men and equipment from small boats on steep, icy, surf-washed gravel beaches. Then, as his skirmishers pushed back the defenders and attempted to occupy a huge area of unknown ground, Pepperrell had to set up his supply lines, lay out and build siege camps, and put in roads and supply depots and ammunition dumps, all in terrain newly cleared of snow but still boggy and soft where it was not covered with tangled thickets of spruce.

In Louisbourg, Duchambon and his corps of officers also prepared for a formal siege. In a fortress, even staff officers aged in decades of peace were imbued with Vauban's principles of siegecraft, and honour demanded that the corps prove its professionalism by conducting a defence on those principles. Largely lacking in siege experience, the

Louisbourg officers were nevertheless well aware of Vauban's precepts for the opening stages of a defence. Vauban recommended that a besieged town conduct an aggressive defence as the enemy struggled to organize his siege. In defence of one of his fortresses, Vauban gave up ground with the utmost reluctance, always delaying the time when he would have to rely solely on his walls. He advised defenders to fan out from their fortifications, to harass the enemy in his preparations, to raid his forward posts, and to skirmish with his troops. Luck and determination could stretch the preliminaries of the siege for weeks, even against a numerically superior enemy.

Despite Vauban, Duchambon decided virtually to concede the preliminary stage of the siege. Amazed and delighted, the New Englanders took the defenders' inactivity as proof of cowardice or incompetence – "these scoundellous French dogs, they dare not stay to fight," cried one – but the French commander had his reasons. Ill-informed about his foe, Duchambon could hope the enemy was an unusually large raiding party, seeking to capture Louisbourg by over-whelming the defenders in immediate battle. Even as it became obvious that a siege was beginning, manpower problems restrained Duchambon from vigorous harassing operations. Louisbourg should have been reinforced before facing a formal siege: seven hundred troops and about as many militiamen were barely enough to man the ramparts and outer works. The more men Duchambon sent beyond the walls, the fewer he would have when the preliminary skirmishing sooner or later gave way to the vital later stages of the siege. Already his scouting parties were cut off from Louisbourg and would have to straggle back in small groups. Instead of sending more men after them, Duchambon began to retrench, trusting to the walls that twenty-five years of work had raised around the town.

A major decision in the strategy of withdrawal was the sacrifice of the Royal Battery, the isolated coastal defence-work facing the harbour entrance from the north shore of the port. Against an attempt to force warships into the port, the Royal Battery could have given valuable service, but when the enemy raised the stakes by initiating land siege, outlying posts became a liability. Duchambon and his council of war probably knew the military dictum on coastal defences: the only way to silence one is to attack it by land, an approach nearly always successful. Instead of leaving the two or three hundred soldiers and militiamen gathered at the Royal Battery to inevitable capture, Duchambon brought them into the fortress, ordering them first to remove the stores and disable the cannon by spiking.

No matter how sensible, Duchambon's strategy of retrenchment held a serious flaw – one soon uncovered in the evacuation of the Royal Battery. The general retreat before this sudden and ill-understood invasion *looked* cowardly, not only to the invaders but also to soldiers withdrawn from the battery, fishermen ordered to abandon their fishing properties, and civilians obliged to desert their homes. Told to flee to the fortress, everyone feared the worst, and the evacuation of the Royal Battery was achieved in haste that verged on panic. Though there was no immediate danger, valuable supplies were left behind, so that several return trips were required. No attempt was made to remove the heavy artillery, and the cannon were not even disabled properly. The battery itself, a mile from the town, would be of little use to the besiegers, but they would find its cannon very useful indeed.

Not everyone in Louisbourg favoured the defensive strategy of the professional soldiers. One anonymous diarist, already ill-disposed to the officers, thought the surrender of the Royal Battery madness, for like many armchair strategists he could not accept that the imposing shore battery was of little use when the threat shifted from sea to land. Others were eager for any kind of aggressive action. Proud of their community and keen to defend their stake in it, some civilians resented the uncontested surrender of all the valuable land and property beyond the outer earthworks. Unlike the officer corps, they had no professional code to restrain their sense of territorial violation, and the sight of an invading rabble come to sack their homes roused many to seek an immediate, angry confrontation with the foe.

The strongest advocate of immediate confrontation was Jean-René Cruchon's old friend Pierre Morpain. Morpain's views carried weight: he held naval rank as port captain and was influential in a militia that included many sailors. An emotional man who inspired strong loyalties, Morpain drew his military ideas from privateering, where the headlong frontal assault had served him well. As the invasion fleet entered Gabarus Bay on May 11, Morpain urged that the garrison and militia be sent forth to meet the enemy in the open field instead of cowering inside the town. It was a plan likely to play into the enemy's hands, but Duchambon did authorize a token force to meet the landings. Morpain took fifty or sixty militiamen, backed by half a Marine company under Duchambon's son, and crossed Gabarus Plain to meet the enemy whose boats were reaching shore.

The fate of Morpain's sortie confirmed the professionals' reservations about risking their forces in open ground. Few as they were, Morpain's men drove off the boats approaching them, but other boats made an easy landing further down the shore, and Morpain was quickly outflanked. There was an exchange of musketry. Almost surrounded, Morpain's men retreated through the woods in ones and twos, leaving several dead and several prisoners. A larger force would have held out longer, but it would just as surely have been outflanked and outnumbered by soldiers landing from the fast-moving boats. Continued fighting would inevitably weaken the small French forces more than the large New England one. Instead, Duchambon's caution had preserved his men to defend the walls. Wounded and angry, Morpain was helped back to Louisbourg by two slaves who had accompanied him. His faith in aggressive tactics scarcely shaken by the debacle, he would argue for the rest of his life that an immediate confrontation would have saved the fortress on the first day.

Had Jodocus Koller been in Louisbourg on May 11, he would surely have been part of Morpain's force, for his own military ideas mirrored the port captain's. In the aftermath, it might have been Koller's body that moved a New Englander to write, "It is an awful thing to see men wounded and wallowing in their own blud and breething oute their last breths." But Koller was not in Louisbourg when the enemy landed. He had been in Port Toulouse for weeks, supervising his woodcutters. One of his boats, squeezing through gaps in the ice to reach Louisbourg late in March, had brought early news of enemy ships off the coast. Koller himself left Port Toulouse for Louisbourg soon after the New England landings, coming overland to visit his farm on the way.

The visit proved remarkable. Koller's farm, the discharge bonus that had been the making of his fortune, lay close beside the landing beaches where the New Englanders had come ashore. The invaders had built their camps on land Koller had cleared, and they had rounded up and slaughtered the cattle he kept there. But whatever his shock at finding an enemy army encamped on his quiet woodland farm, Koller quickly recovered his old military instincts.

Unseen, he reconnoitred, and the dispositions of these alien troops struck him as highly unprofessional. The thousands of New England volunteers had been leaderless and uncontrolled for most of their first days ashore. Ranging far and wide, they had confirmed that no enemy lurked close by, and relief and the hope of plunder began to replace military concerns in many of them. Each night there was feasting and singing in the camp as the invaders consumed plundered food and liquor to celebrate their landing. Though the New Englanders were armed and ready for action, camp discipline was lax, and Koller easily evaded the sentries to penetrate right into their quarters. The camp was large and well equipped – stacks of scaling ladders particularly impressed him. The troops impressed him less: "scum and children" he would later describe them. Partly for bravado, partly to prove the story he would tell, Koller stole a pot from one of the enemy tents, then carefully withdrew from the camp and headed for Louisbourg. Crossing no man's land by night, he came home at four in the morning of May 17, almost a week after the landings.

Koller reached Louisbourg in time to see the concluding phases of the general withdrawal. He was not the last straggler to come through the tightening enemy blockade. For several days scouts from Michel Daccarrette's party and other men caught outside the fortress came in. One man managed to steal a grey horse and made a bold sight galloping in to safety. Two others came in at a dead run, chased by enemy soldiers until grapeshot from the ramparts halted the pursuit. To reach safety, Koller and the other fugitives crossed a devastated landscape. For several days Michel de Gannes de Falaise's company had been demolishing or burning homes and sheds that might assist the enemy's approach to the walls. Further off, where the French could no longer venture, New Englanders had been burning and looting the fishing properties of the north shore, gathering plunder and making sure that if their siege failed they would leave devastation behind them.

Even the northern half of the port had been abandoned. Gilles Girard Lacroix, a sea captain from Québec who had brought in an essential cargo of Canadian flour late in 1744, arose before dawn on May 11 to refloat his ship, pulled ashore for the winter at the top of the harbour and blocked by ice floes until that day. The next day, with the enemy certain to occupy the harbour shore, Lacroix went out in a shallop to scuttle his ship. He saved its logbook, which became more a personal diary of the siege than a ship's record. Across the water, Jean Lelarge was sinking *Tempête*, the coast-guard corvette he had yet to take to sea. Only the ships pulled up close to the guns of the quay could be spared. All over the northern harbour, captains and shipowners were sacrificing their schooners and fishing boats.

In the fortress Duchambon disposed his forces. As the troops were posted around the defence perimeter, each company of seventy regulars was bolstered by militiamen, for the defenders would not only man the ramparts and the guns on them but would also defend the outerworks and the *glacis* around the clock. Louis Loppinot, now an ensign, married and the father of several legitimate children, took up duties with his company at the King's Bastion. De Thierry's company, newly withdrawn from the Royal Battery, was assigned the important duty of the Dauphin Gate and Bastion. Captain Schönherr's company of tough Swiss was assigned to *les meurtrières*, a long, low wall facing the ocean in the southeast part of the town. The wall had been loopholed for musket fire against boat attack, but wave action had piled a ramp of gravel almost to the top of the wall. Accurately estimating that the enemy might consider storming this weak section of his defences, Duchambon reinforced the Swiss company with Jean Lelarge's privateering crew of seventy men, who quickly got to work raising a stockade behind the vulnerable wall. When Koller made his nocturnal entry to the fortress, troops were at their posts all around the ramparts. The largest part of the defending army was outside the walls, camping in the ditch, manning the covered way, watching the *glacis* for enemy raids. The garrison and the militia would maintain this watch in rotation, night and day throughout the battle.

Tension was great. One night Duchambon was called urgently to the *meurtrières*, where two boats had been seen bobbing up and down behind the waves. The defenders prepared to resist an attack, but the boats held their distance, and the tension turned to hilarity when dawn revealed the two boats were a pair of rocks emerging from a falling tide.

With the troops in place, Duchambon and his staff made circuits of inspection. Despite the disconcerting retreats of the first few days and the humiliation of being fired upon when the enemy's smiths repaired the cannon abandoned to them at the Royal Battery, morale seemed high. Now that the men who had mutinied to protest their unmilitary treatment were being given a chance to prove their martial prowess, their dissatisfaction faded. None deserted during operations beyond the walls, and their conduct would elicit praise from all close observers of the siege. Messengers had been sent to bring Canadian troops and Indians from Acadia, and naval reinforcement was expected from France, perhaps powerful enough to scatter the four British men-of-war blockading the harbour. The beleaguered garrison determined to hold out until help arrived.

A week after the landing, both sides were ready for a formal siege. In a few busy days the New Englanders had occupied the Royal Battery, looted and burned the nearby settlements, and rounded up most of the stragglers in the woods. General Pepperrell's commanders had begun to impose order on their troops, and though many wild proposals for attack were entertained, they focussed their efforts on preparations for directing artillery fire against the walls of Louisbourg. The Royal Battery, though it could lob shots across the mile of water to the town, was irrelevant to these preparations, for only fire at very close range could threaten a fortress as substantial as Louisbourg. Gangs of New Englanders struggled to bring cannon, powder, and shot ashore and across the wild rock-and-bog expanse of Gabarus Plain. After some errors, a serviceable gun battery was erected about a thousand yards from the Dauphin Gate. The siege was ready to begin.

The preliminary stage of the siege of Louisbourg ended May 18 with a brief negotiation between besieged and besieger. Having built their first siege battery and fired a few shots at the ramparts, the New England commanders called a ceasefire and sent a messenger to Louisbourg under flag of truce. Now that the town of Louisbourg was formally besieged, did the defenders wish to discuss a surrender? It was a ritual known to every student of siegecraft, and Duchambon was ready with a lively rejection: "Our only reply to your demand shall come from the mouths of our cannon." The exchange of notes served notice that both sides were ready and willing for a *siège en forme*. The artillery duel could begin.

Artillery, the weapon that had forced fortification to the technical advances eventually codified by Vauban, was still basic to siege warfare in 1745, for defences in the style ordained by Vauban's geometry posed a nearly impregnable barrier to infantry seeking to come to grips with the forces within. Foot soldiers foolhardy enough to make the attempt found themselves obliged to climb up and jump down a series of ramps and walls tall and steep enough to disable every man who fell from them. To get to and through these obstacles, the attackers had to venture across several hundred feet of ground absolutely naked to carefully prepared interlocking fire from cannon and musketry. The thing was virtually impossible, as the professionals in the New England high command knew. An inspection convinced the amateurs, whose early successes had inspired them to propose an immediate assault. The invaders would only find and fight their foe after sustained cannonfire had dismounted the defenders' guns and hammered the ditches and walls of Louisbourg into rubble that armed men might cross at a trotting pace. Pepperrell turned to his gunners.

Their challenge was to select the weakest point in the long circuit of defences that formed the fortress of Louisbourg. A frontal attack had been rendered impossible at every potential site: naval attack was blocked by the big guns of the Island Battery; boat attack from the ocean faced the eastern bastions and the *meurtrières*; and troops like Pepperrell's who landed down the shore and struggled overland confronted the landward bastions. Yet when every direct entry was closed, artillery could still be applied to the place where a breach could most efficiently be made and invaded. Searching for this weak spot, the New Englanders' eyes fell on the Dauphin Bastion. It was protected by wall, ditch, and outerworks, and strongly defended with cannon and musketry, but it offered certain attractions to the New England gunners. Forming a corner where the line of defence turned sharply from the land to the harbour, the Dauphin could be bombarded from two directions: from directly west of the Dauphin Gate, and from the north shore, an acceptably short cannonshot across the harbour. The gunners noted how the bastion lay on ground sloping down to the shore from the central ridge crowned by the King's Bastion, where the lie of the land might permit cannonfire to angle in over the earthworks intended to screen the stone walls. On the harbour side, the walls of the Dauphin fell sheer into the water of the port, without intervening earthworks to protect against fire from across the harbour. Few other points offered such targets, and though breaching stone walls was a slow and arduous process, frontal assault was out of the question. The Dauphin offered the best prospect for eventual success.

It was not simply a matter of setting up guns and firing away, for the defenders were alive to the threat of artillery. Lacking the man-power to hold the ground in front of the Dauphin earthworks, they relied on their firepower to carry the battle for them. Every gun the besiegers set up would be a target for the cannoneers of the Dauphin and King's bastions, and every enemy gun crew a target for the musketry of soldiers and militiamen. Their fire would force the besiegers into the ground to work their way forward in protective trenches.

Here again Vauban, theorist of attack as well as defence, had calculated the optimum angles, and though terrain and inexperience disrupted his carefully measured progression of siege trenches, a few skilled siegemasters and a mass of willing volunteers carried out the essence of his siege program. The New Englanders' first guns had been cautiously set up nearly a mile west of the ramparts, and their limited use soon became obvious: many shots failed to reach the walls. The second battery did no great damage to the defences, but its fire enabled Pepperrell to end the preliminaries with his ritual demand for surrender. Then ten days of trenching began in earnest. Working mostly by night, the diggers pushed recklessly on to within 250 yards of the Dauphin Gate, partly by trench, partly behind an earthen ramp. As the diggers advanced, labouring gangs brought cannon from the camp and the captured Royal Battery. Finally, late in May, the besiegers took advantage of two days of thick fog to drive through the final section of their trench. On May 29 their advanced battery on Francoeur's hill stood ready to fire at the Dauphin Gate. The owner of that hill was among the defenders watching the preparations. François Lessenne *dit* Francoeur, a civilian gunner who had taught many of the garrison cannoneers, was stationed at the Dauphin Bastion.

Captain Joseph Sherburne, commander of the New Englanders' advanced battery, had difficulty recruiting gun crews from among the volunteer army, for the risks of gun duty were daunting. If the first gun mounted at the advanced battery could survive and be joined by others, the hazards could be divided and then reduced as the defenders' gun positions were battered systematically. But the first gun mounted would be subject to the full fury of the musketry and close-range cannonfire of the defenders, who might even make an infantry sortie against this harbinger of destruction. Odds against the survival of the first men at the guns were fearsome, but Sherburne found some brave volunteers. On May 29, a Saturday eighteen days after the landing, they went up the trench to where a pair of eighteen-pounders awaited them in the narrow pit. Even with its forward side reinforced with barrels of earth, the battery was much exposed to the Dauphin gunners facing it and the King's Bastion gunners further off on the right flank.

Sherburne and his gunners levered their first cannon into place between the hogsheads and adjusted the aim for the Dauphin Gate 230 yards ahead. They had no cartridges, so the gunners packed loose powder down the barrel before ramming in a wad and a cannonball. The master gunner put a fuse down the touchhole and the cannon was ready to fire.

At the Dauphin and the King's, French gunners were following the same sequence, loading, wadding, aiming the heavy guns, their target the lonely eighteen-pounder and the men around it. Soldiers on the ramparts were at the extremes of musket range, but there were closer muskets lining the outerworks.

In the advanced battery, master gunner William Coomes touched his smouldering match to the fuse. It fizzed and sparkled, and then the tightly packed powder exploded with a roar. Choking on sulphur fumes, their view blotted out by billowing white smoke, the men cowering in the trench peeped out for a look, then set about swabbing out the hot barrel with water, making it cool and clean for a second shot and a third and a fourth.

Somewhere along the outerworks, covered by the back wall of the *glacis* as he observed the enemy gunners, a Marine soldier held his Charleville musket in his left hand as his right hand dug a cartridge out

of the wood-and-leather case on his belt. He had prepared the cartridges before going on duty: they were slim paper tubes rolled around
a musketball and an ounce of black powder, then glued or folded shut.
Now he tore the cartridge open with his teeth and sprinkled powder
into the small pan at the root of the musket barrel. Closing the pan, he
reversed his musket, standing it on butt end to drop the cartridge down
the barrel. He removed the ramrod from its clamps beneath the barrel,
packed the cartridge tightly in place, then sheathed the ramrod again.
Raising his musket, resting the long barrel on the turf of the *glacis*, he
watched the wind carry away the smoke of the enemy gun's fourth
shot. The officer behind him ordered free firing.

In the advanced battery William Coomes leaned forward along
the gun barrel, ignoring heavy French fire as he sighted for a fifth shot.

In the outerworks, the Marine soldier sighted down the slim, polished barrel. It was a longish range, and the smoothbore musket did
not offer a sharpshooter's accuracy, but many muskets were firing and
not every shot could miss. He squeezed the trigger and powder flared
in the pan by his face.

Hit by a musket ball, William Coomes fell dead beside his gun.
As the body was removed, Joseph Merell stepped up to take over.

Duchambon had already reinforced the Dauphin Gate with cut
stone, bundled wood, and piled earth to make a wall eighteen feet
thick, but the New Englanders at the advanced battery could see their
cannonballs exploding stone shards from the face of the rampart. They
fired as often as they could, for a long, steady pounding of the gate
would be required. Despite French fire smashing at the entrenchment
protecting them, the besiegers soon mounted a second cannon and
began to return fire against the rampart artillery. Tired, powder-
grimed, and in danger for his life, Joseph Merell began to warm to
his work. He leapt forward when one of his shots went astray. He
cried, "God damn me if I don't strike the gate this time!"

The right flank of the King's Bastion, designed to cover the
sloping ground in front of the Dauphin, had a clear line of fire into
one end of the advanced battery. The rampart artillery stood on
wheeled carriages, and the crews could roll their guns back from the
embrasures to clean and load in some safety. A gun crew loaded, then
ran its big gun back into firing position. Aiming carefully to conserve

powder, a red-coated cannoneer touched match to fuse and leaned away from the explosion as his gun recoiled. Beating away powder smoke, he heard the cheers of the nearby crews.

The cannonball carried away most of Joseph Merell's head, and he died instantly. Beside him Captain Joshua Pierce took the shot in the stomach. He lived for a quarter-hour, and according to one soldier "was able to speak many things." Another remembered "It's hard to die" as Pierce's last words.

By the end of the first day the two guns at the advanced battery had been fired, cleaned, reloaded, and fired again fifty-six times, under a rain of musket balls and cannonading from the defenders. Many of the first crews were dead or disabled, but the start of a breach had appeared in the Dauphin Gate and the shattered stonework of several gun embrasures convinced the besiegers they had exacted some revenge for their losses. That night there was a lull, the French scrambling to shore up the gate, the New Englanders deepening their trench and hauling up two more cannon.

As the duel reopened on Sunday morning the attackers were slightly less exposed. Their losses shrank as four cannon hammered the Dauphin gun embrasures, killing two civilian gunners and wrecking three embrasures. The Dauphin's fire began to slacken, but the unchallenged guns on the King's Bastion still swept the siege battery with fire. Near midday, Sherburne went back in search of ammunition, missing the arrival of a supply team bringing several barrels. The new team loaded a double charge, hoping for the greatest possible effect and ignoring the deadly physics of artillery. Their shot strained the gun beyond endurance and it exploded like a bomb, dismounting the adjacent cannon and blowing up several powder barrels to kill two men and wound several others. Again night fell, and both sides turned to the work of repair. Duchambon ordered new embrasures to replace those dismantled at the Dauphin. Sherburne began work on a battery that would shield his men from the King's Bastion and return some fire against it.

French losses were still slight, but the power of the enemy artillery continued to grow. On May 31, the day the arch of the Dauphin Gate fell in, the New Englanders opened the second half of their attack on the Dauphin, digging out Titcomb's battery on Pierre Martissans's fishing property to fire across eight hundred yards of water against the harbour wall of the gateway. Major Titcomb's gunners opened fire on June 2, and soon they were accepted as the most serious threat, for their fire toppled a substantial breach beside and behind the Dauphin Gate. New guns were mounted to fire on Titcomb's battery, but the damage from the besiegers' fire was becoming cumulative.

The artillery duel was reaching a deadly balance. The besiegers continued to lose men to defenders' fire and to exploding cannon, but they had weathered the most dangerous days, and the French had failed to destroy the most exposed siege batteries. Occasionally a gun was dismounted or a crew blown up, but both sides had learned the limited value of musketry against well-protected foes at long range, so the vigour of the battle seemed less intense. The rampart gunners fired sparingly, while the besiegers kept up battering fire as steadily as their powder stores allowed. Though it was vital to the success or failure of the siege, the artillery battle became the competition of a few specialists, methodical and unspectacular. Men began to call back and forth across no man's land, offering a bowl of punch or an introduction to the pretty girls of the town before closing the discussion with a derisive exchange of musketry.

As the gunners of Titcomb's and the advanced battery worked to open a breach around the Dauphin Gate, their fellows further back were subjecting the town itself to steady and indiscriminate bombardment. Batteries too distant to batter the walls effectively could lob cannonballs high into the air to crash down among the streets and houses, and no part of the town was spared from their terror. The Royal Battery pounded the quayfront properties, the battery on Rabasse's hill swept all the east-west streets, and the advanced battery lofted one shot over the entire town to lodge in the Maurepas Gate. A lucky gunner shot away the bell in the citadel tower, and soon the barracks chapel was an abandoned ruin, its roof gone and its walls shattered. Part of the Marine offices on the quay collapsed. Cannonballs plunged into inns and storehouses and homes, spraying rubble to cause further damage. The New Englanders added mortar fire, hurling hollow iron spheres packed with black powder on a high, arching trajectory. Their fuses spluttering like fireworks, well-timed mortars exploded just before they landed, showering death and destruction below. For a few days the besiegers used red-hot shot, firing cannonballs heated in ovens to ignite the wooden buildings of the town. The defenders' fire parties limited the damage, and soon the New England high command decided that the use of red-hot shot against civilians was dishonourable.

Under shot and shell the life of the town began to collapse. The widow Cruchon and her teenaged daughters huddled in their home. Louise Samson awaited the imminent birth of the Lelarges' fourth child. Marie-Catherine Auger tried to protect the six young Kollers and her widowed mother while her husband worked in the defences. The retired merchant Claude Morin could remember action as a militia leader in the successful 1709 attack on St. John's, before he and his family had evacuated Plaisance. Now his two sons held militia commissions in the defence of Louisbourg. Sharing the risks of the soldiers, people such as these could do little but try to keep the rhythms of life going. The Récollets offered daily mass and benediction in the hospital chapel, while the courts and the notary held their usual sessions for urgent and even routine business. Occasionally small boats went out under cover of darkness to fish beyond the harbour, and a few men ventured across no man's land to bring back spruce boughs for *sapinette*. Despite the naval blockade and fire from the Royal Battery, a few merchant ships reached the town. Jean Lelarge went out in a boat to pilot one of these to the quayside, and the defenders eagerly added its guns and supplies to their arsenal. A few days later the enemy tried to burn this vessel, but the sailors of Louisbourg easily isolated the fireship sent against them, and it burned itself out harmlessly.

Working at all hours, men had to sleep under the artillery barrage, then return to risk their lives in the long defence line or in repair parties about the town. Their losses were still small, but the struggle strained the resources of soldiers and militiamen. Pierre Morpain was magnificent, on the move night and day to exhort the militia. Duchambon spent every night in the defences, directing repairs and watching for signs of an attack. Sometimes he sent scouts forward, and diarist Girard Lacroix came back from one of these hazardous missions claiming to have heard the enemy in the trenches planning an assault. The possibility kept the outerworks alert, and each night bonfires blazed on the *glacis* to expose any movement, but the invaders were not yet ready to confront the unbreached walls, and the over-worked defenders refrained from sorties.

When an attack came, it was not directed against the town, and neither Duchambon nor Morpain could help to repel it. In the New England camp, keen amateur soldiers, emboldened by their success against outlying settlements and undefended outposts, had proposed an attack on the fortified island that still protected the harbour from the British naval squadron outside. Naval commander Peter Warren vigorously supported them, for as time passed he feared being trapped on the coast by a powerful French relief squadron. With nervousness and impatience eating at morale, the New Englanders approved a plan of attack, hoping that success would allow the navy to enter the port and join their attack on the town.

At the island, Captain d'Ailleboust commanded a company of Marine regulars, a squad of cannoneers and over a hundred militia-men. Apart from exchanges with Warren's ships and duels against the distant Royal Battery, they had seen little action, but they were not a target ripe for plucking. A self-contained masonry fort mounting thirty-six guns, the battery covered most of the small island, drop-ping ten-foot walls to a shoreline difficult of access. When four hundred New Englanders crossed the harbour after midnight on June 7, rowing whaleboats they had dragged from Gabarus Bay, the defenders stood ready to give a textbook demonstration of the perils of assaulting regular fortifications.

In the town, Duchambon learned of the attack from an explo-sion of musketry and artillery across the water. The safety of the town hung in the balance as the firing continued, and so did the life of his eldest son, second-in-command at the island, but there was no way to help. Towards dawn the firing slackened and a boat came across with news. With the loss of only two or three men, the island had routed its invaders. A few had come ashore and had even planted ladders, but they had been decimated by the battery's firepower. Captain d'Ailleboust had leapt into an embrasure to direct the fire, only to be pulled back by soldiers arguing that the risk was unneces-sary. Musketry and grapeshot swept the boats wallowing offshore and drove back the survivors. By morning at least sixty bodies lay on the shore or drifted in the water, and over one hundred New Englanders had survived by asking for quarter. The battery stood undamaged in the morning light as shallops brought the prisoners into the town.

The New Englanders sacrificed at the island were not the only men who had been eager to come to grips with the foe. Inside the fortress the militia's enthusiasm for confrontation had been dampened only temporarily by Morpain's rebuff at the landings. With the enemy cannon battering their homes and families, they renewed their call for action. Though a council of officers had ruled out sorties across the outerworks, Duchambon yielded to militia pressure. During the foggy days at the end of May he organized a boat expedition to slip through the naval blockade and land about a hundred men at Petit Lorembec for an irregular campaign against the rear of the New England lines.

Command of the militia party went to Philippe LeNeuf de Beaubassin, an ex-officer of the Marine garrison. His father had been town major of Louisbourg, and his brother commanded a company during the siege, but Beaubassin had resigned his commission in 1741 after a quarrel with his superiors. Marriage to a daughter of Michel Daccarrette ensured him a commercial career, and he had privateered in 1744. In his thirties, a dissatisfied aristocrat with an inherited tradition of leadership, Beaubassin was a logical choice for the mission. He probably took command with the hope of proving himself to the professional soldiers who had called his resignation "no great loss to the service."

Another volunteer was Jodocus Koller, still eager for action and perhaps bored by the prospect of endless repair work on the fortress masonry. Before the boats sailed, Koller was named second-in-command. He balanced the aristocratic Beaubassin, and his actions in the expedition would display the tenacity and fighting spirit that had raised this man of obscure background and precarious social standing into his position of leadership.

The expedition landed safely, and in the thick bush behind Lighthouse Point, Beaubassin met the enemy several times, only to see each fight degenerate into a confused melee. In these woodland encounters between equally determined skirmishers, superior numbers gave the only real advantage. The New Englanders committed more men to each clash, and the sortie became another demonstration of the futility of Morpain's aggressive strategy. Beaubassin fell back to Lorembec, where he was joined in a desperate holding action by a band of allied Indians. Here he was wounded and evacuated to Louisbourg with other casualties, leaving command to Koller. Instead of taking to the boats as ammunition ran low, Koller successfully disengaged his survivors from the battle and made a long overland retreat to the Miré Valley. In the escape an Indian named Petit-Jean was shot. There was no time to bury him, but the men covered his body with brush before they fled. So blanketed, Petit-Jean recovered consciousness, and he amazed the militiamen by rejoining them a few days later.

Koller probably hoped to reverse his expedition's fortunes at the Miré, for it was a likely rendezvous at which to join the troops expected from Canada. They had not arrived, but after putting the river between him and his pursuers, Koller sent word of his position to Louisbourg, dispatching a shallop that once more evaded the blockade. Duchambon sent back a boatload of ammunition, for he shared Koller's hopes for a junction of forces behind the enemy lines.

Koller's friend, the woodsman and sailor Jean-Baptiste Guion, piloted the ammunition up the coast to the Miré, only to find the Canadians were still not there and the Indians were returning to their villages. As the action moved elsewhere, Guion and two others were left to guard the cache of ammunition. Guion did not complain – being far from the beleaguered fortress suited his pacific temperament. Lacking the ardour of his friend Koller, he eventually made his way to Niganiche at the far north of the island, there to sit out the battle in all possible tranquillity. Though privateers had looted and burned here near the start of the siege, carrying out a policy of destroying the Ile Royale fishery, Guion would not be disturbed.

Koller had taken over Guion's shallop and ferried the remaining members of the expedition back to Louisbourg in mid-June, arriving to discover a town in ruins from a month of bombardment. Duchambon later reported that no property had escaped damage, so the Koller home had probably been hit – by blast and flying rubble if not by a direct impact. By this time most of the townspeople were crowded into the bombproof shelters of the bastions, so Koller presumably found his family here, though his nine-year-old son may have been old enough to have joined the boys carrying powder to the guns. The casemates, chambers in the fortress walls, offered safety, but anyone venturing out of them risked sudden death. Diarist Lacroix saw a pregnant woman dismembered at the door of a shelter and a Basque fisherman killed running down the street.

Two weeks of cannonading from Titcomb's and the advanced battery had pounded the Dauphin Bastion and part of the King's into shattered remnants of the ramparts Koller had helped to build. With the Dauphin gateway crumbling, Morpain and Verrier directed a militia work-party that dug out a second line of defence behind the entrance. Jean Lelarge and eight others, alerted to the danger of boat attack by the fight at the island, volunteered to barricade the water-front with a floating boom of chained masts. Achieved under heavy fire from across the harbour, the job took a day. But these efforts were makeshift substitutes, for the contest of artillery was going against the defenders. The breach was growing, the repair work falling behind. Weeks of toil and the destruction of their homes strained everyone's endurance, while casualties from gunfire and flying masonry slowly increased. Now the relief forces the defenders had been awaiting were urgently needed. Koller's trip to the Miré had shown that the Canadian troops in Acadia, warned too late, were still far distant. Now he learned the most eagerly awaited succour for the town had been decisively checked while he was in the woods.

Weeks before the siege began, the French navy had dispatched the sixty-four-gun ship of the line *Vigilant* to provision Louisbourg and sweep away the privateers expected to be harassing its supply lines. Under a naval officer familiar with Ile Royale, *Vigilant* made a fast crossing and sighted Louisbourg on May 29, just as the artillery duel opened at the Dauphin Bastion. Warren's small squadron and the larger privateers, often evaded by the small boats of the townspeople, were ready for the big man-of-war. Unaware of the enemy hidden in coastal fog close to the harbour, Captain de Maisonfort turned from his route to attack the one vessel he saw. Then, keeping between *Vigilant* and the harbour, Warren gave chase, as the people on Louisbourg's ramparts watched and cursed their misfortune. A running battle began within sight of the town, and as night fell the gunfire over the horizon gave way to ominous silence.

The capture of *Vigilant* denied Louisbourg essential supplies and reinforcements. The larger squadron being outfitted in France would not arrive in time, and the besiegers gained new confidence and new ammunition supplies from their victory. In the next few days the blockade around Louisbourg was strengthened by new naval vessels. As the defenders' supplies ran low, transports from New England brought the besiegers new men, more weapons and ammunition, and abundant supplies of food. In the town, hope for relief faded.

With defeat looming, old tensions broke out. Two Swiss soldiers were the first to give up the fight, leaping from their places in the Dauphin outerworks to sprint across to the New England lines. Soon afterwards, a Marine soldier was persuaded by the American prisoners he was guarding to cross the lines with a letter describing the desperate condition of the town. Discovered before he could desert, the soldier was summarily hanged, but smouldering fears about the once-mutinous troops were fanned.

The possibility of defeat provoked bitterness among the civilians, particularly those who had wanted a more aggressive resistance. On June 17 Pierre Morpain fought with Captain d'Ailleboust, newly replaced at the island by Michel de Gannes. Morpain's claim to command wherever the militia served provoked the quarrel, and when Morpain pressed his case, a council of war dismissed him from command. Irked by the amateur strategist's growing opposition, the professionals had humiliated a man whose fiery determination had kept all the militiamen at peak performance. Civilians murmured that Morpain was better qualified to lead than some they could name. Diarist Girard Lacroix, who was sympathetic to Morpain, probably joined "all the honest men" who paid their respects to the port captain at his home. Jodocus Koller, newly returned from his demonstration of belief in aggressive tactics, was presumably in that crowd as well.

Striving to resolve the split between the professionals and the militia, d'Ailleboust negotiated with another influential militia leader, Michel Daccarrette. Deep in conversation, the two circled the ramparts and were returning to d'Ailleboust's post when a cannonball plunging down struck Daccarrette, cutting him in half and leaving d'Ailleboust unharmed beside him. With negotiation for a reconciliation so brutally interrupted, Pierre Morpain did not return to service, but the militiamen he had inspired stayed at their posts, standing with the regulars in an increasingly hopeless defence.

At the Dauphin Bastion, the battle of the breach grew desperate. By mid-June most of the gun embrasures along its rampart had been battered in, and newly cut ones gave the gunners little more protection than the advanced battery had given its first volunteers. The first Marine officer to die at the guns was Ensign Louis Loppinot, whose leg was blown off by cannonfire. A week passed and another ensign was killed along with two of his gunners, living just long enough for a brief confession. Much of the bastion was rubble. Steady fire from the advanced battery dismounted gun after gun, while Major Titcomb's battery pounded the causeway from the Dauphin Gate to the quay. The breach was nearly passable to infantry.

By Vauban's rules, the third stage of a formal siege began once the battering of the walls and guns eliminated most of the advantages offered by fortification. An intact wall and defensive artillery kept the besieger at a distance; a breached wall and dismounted guns allowed the troops to pour in. Late in June, as the siege artillery completed its arduous demolition work, General Pepperrell's commanders saw they could gain the help of Warren's growing naval squadron if a gun battery at Lighthouse Point could do what boat assault had failed to do: silence the island battery. The new battery was quickly erected, and for several days de Gannes's troops submitted to a ferocious bombardment that crumbled the battery around them. Soon Warren was planning to risk entry to the harbour, and assault preparations were laid by land and sea.

This culminating stage would have to be an all-out assault. The breach battered into the Dauphin Gate was rough and jagged and backed by a second defence line, but the New Englanders would have to storm it whatever their losses. The assault troops would load their muskets before breaking from cover around the advanced battery, but they would have no time to reload in the charge. Their bayonets would have to carry them forward to clear the outworks, seize the breach, and break into the town, against the surviving artillery on the ramparts and the muskets and bayonets of desperate defenders. Even if they failed to hold the breach, their assault had to pin down the defenders of the King's–Dauphin line, for as they launched themselves across the battered *glacis*, whaleboats and barges would be pushing out from the north shore, rowing for the quay.

What gave both groups of assault troops hope was the firepower of the British fleet, now grown to eleven men-of-war averaging more than fifty guns each. If they forced their way into the port, their close-range fire would devastate the Louisbourg waterfront before the boat attack landed. Though Warren's wooden ships were sure to be mauled by the shore guns, a combined assault might overwhelm the battered defences of the town.

After all the punishment they had taken, the fortifications of Louisbourg remained formidable. The attackers' losses were certain to be great, and despite an encouraging distribution of rum and a flood of martial oratory, many New Englanders must have had the disaster at the island in mind as they confronted the walls. Balancing such fears, however, were the consequences of a successful storming. The rules of war were clear: a besieged town that refused capitulation when threatened with a general assault could expect no mercy if the attack succeeded. If the besiegers successfully broke through the Dauphin breach and swarmed in over the quay wall, the vanquished troops could be denied quarter, the townspeople pillaged and plundered to the limits of their resources.

The defenders knew the rules, and as they watched the enemy preparing the assault, the benefits of a capitulation on terms began to be mooted among soldiers and civilians alike. Duchambon asked his captains to report. Engineer Verrier summarized the perilous state of the walls. Captain de Sainte-Marie, the artillery commander, outlined his serious losses in cannon and mortars and confirmed that the magazines held less than a tenth of the 75,000 pounds of powder on hand at the opening of the battle. There was no likelihood of imminent rescue by any means. The council of war agreed that the enemy's assault was likely to succeed.

The people were coming to the same conclusion. Active in defence of their homes and livelihoods, they had frequently resented the officers' cautious by-the-book defence of the town, but they too could estimate the odds against repelling an attack in which they, their homes, and their families were likely to be destroyed. At last the militia and the professionals were in agreement. Though surrender was likely to mean exile from Ile Royale and the loss of all they had built in three decades, no voice was raised against the decision to seek terms. Supported by a petition of citizens, Duchambon sent out a courier on June 26, proposing a ceasefire and negotiations.

With no bargaining chips beyond his offer to spare the besiegers from a bloody assault, Duchambon could ask for little but the preservation of his town from pillage. Sending out his proposals in the morning of June 27, he received immediate counter-demands and held out for only one concession. He wanted the professional pride of his officer corps assuaged by the honours of war; the defeated garrison must be allowed to yield the town with flags flying, drums beating, and muskets shouldered. With that point granted, the embattled town surrendered that evening. The New England militia who had conquered a Vauban fortress by their own version of a Vauban siege marched into Louisbourg.

Jodocus Koller, the expatriate mercenary who had committed everything to Ile Royale, lost everything in the defeat. Spared from pillage, the townspeople would not be permitted to remain in their home. Soldiers and civilians alike were deported to France. What they could carry went with them; all else was sold or simply abandoned to the victors. Crammed aboard ship with other colonists of every sort – soldiers, tradesmen, widows, priests, fishermen, merchants, infants – Koller and his family left Louisbourg some time that summer.

Koller almost came back. In 1748, after four years of inconclusive warfare on land and sea, Britain and France were ready for peace – or at least a truce. Each agreed to return what had been conquered since 1744, and so the summer of 1749 saw the colonists of Ile Royale preparing to return from discontented exile to take up their interrupted lives. The renewal of fishing and trade, the return of an enlarged garrison, and renovation of the battered town and fortifications quickly revived the fortunes of Ile Royale. New immigrants came to join the returned exiles, filling the old homes and properties and spilling out beyond the rebuilt Dauphin Gate to the siege-shattered *faubourg* along the harbour shore. By 1755 a visitor could report Louisbourg "considerably grown in homes and people . . . even more populous than it was before the war."

The visitor was François Bigot, one of the pre-war residents who had not returned to settle. Bigot had moved on to Québec, promoted to the Intendancy of New France. Commandant Duchambon had retired with a pension in 1746 and settled at his ancestral home in Saintonge, where he lived to the age of ninety-five. One of a few colonists to build lasting careers in France during the exile, Jean Lelarge settled his family in the naval town of Rochefort. Pierre Morpain was among several senior men of the colony who had died during the years of exile. In Louisbourg their sons and successors were coming to the fore.

The Kollers were among those missing from the reborn community. Aliens in France, Jodocus Koller and his family had spent the years there among a community of Louisbourg refugees in Rochefort. There, in the early months of 1749, the treaty documents already signed, the family was caught in a brief, virulent epidemic that set the seal on their misfortunes. Jodocus Koller and Catherine Auger fell victim in February, and four of their children died with them. Only five-year-old Catherine and thirteen-year-old Grégoire would see Louisbourg again – and not in order to inherit their parents' once-prosperous livelihood. For the Kollers the disastrous consequences of siege had almost been total. The children went back to eke out a living as orphan wards of their widowed grandmother Auger.

Epilogue

Among a very few townspeople of Louisbourg who evaded deportation in 1745 was Jean-Baptiste Guion, whose venture out of the fortress to aid Jodocus Koller had removed him from the besiegers' grasp. Sheltering in the ruins of Niganiche until the siege was over, Guion emerged after the surrender as noncombative as ever and made his own peace with the victors of the siege. By making himself useful to the occupation troops who would be Louisbourg's only population for several years, he won tolerance for his continued presence. He even agreed to pilot the victors' warships along the local coasts, and on to Québec if they desired. Newly widowed, Guion remarried without benefit of clergy in 1746, making a private exchange of vows at Scatary with another fugitive from deportation. His life seemed almost uninterrupted by siege and conquest.

Staying on while his fellows were exiled was part of the Guion style; his behaviour had often gone against the colonial grain. In the busy commercial town, Baptiste Guion had always been unambitious, even something of a ne'er-do-well. He had scraped a living from Ile Royale's woods and waters, done some hunting, piloted loads of freight down the coast, and laid stone with the fortification labourers if he had to. His family took in boarders, and one way or another enough money came in, but the Guion career suggests little of the common striving to found and preserve a secure family estate.

Such purposelessness had offended the authorities of the colony. Brusquely issuing paternal assessments of whose behaviour served the colony and whose did not, they pegged Guion as an idle fellow trying to live as a hunter, as if he were no better than the vagabonds and masterless fishermen who lived in the woods under chronic suspicion of all manner of crime.

Such disparagement failed to cow Baptiste Guion. In 1742, when the authorities of Ile Royale tried to expropriate his town lot for the benefit of some more-enterprising colonist, Guion strongly and successfully defended his property rights. His home in the town, his circle of relatives and friends, his growing family – all the ties that made the authorities more vexed to see him live like the rootless runaways in the woods – sustained him in his resistance. And Guion had a unique claim to a place in the community, one that seemed to absolve him from the immigrant newcomer's obsession with security. Through his father, Baptiste Guion could claim to be part of Ile Royale's founding family, one settled there before the imperious authorities had arrived, even before the island bore that name.

Certainly the Guion experience in the region was long-standing. Guions had already been in Canada several generations when Baptiste's father Joseph and uncle François went seeking fortune in Acadia in the 1680s. Tiny Acadia, too close to New England to be securely French, was the scene of nearly constant struggles for coastal supremacy, and François and Joseph Guion became privateers, raiding English shipping, scattering the enemy's fishing fleets, and ravaging coastal settlements in Maine. They seem to have enjoyed several runs of good fortune, but François Guion, the elder brother and the leader of their ventures, died about 1701, not yet forty, and Joseph Guion's fighting spirit evidently died with him. There would be another decade of sea battles and shore raids before New England subjugated Acadia, but Joseph Guion was not one of the warriors to win renown in the fight. At the dawn of the new century Joseph Guion dropped out of sight. He married an Acadian and started a family – his son Baptiste was born in these years – but neither his marriage nor the baptisms of his offspring were recorded in the registers of any Canadian or Acadian parish.

The Guions may have spent some of these years in one of the isolated inlets of western Nova Scotia, for, after 1710, when Joseph Guion established a residence in Québec, he retained close ties to the Micmac bands of this coast. Veteran small-boat sailors, the Micmacs had taken over the Guions' privateering role, and in 1710 Guion collected some of their prizes at Havre-à-l'Anglois on Cape Breton Island for delivery to Canadian purchasers. In 1713, when France was about to colonize Cape Breton Island in place of ceded Acadia and Newfoundland, Joseph Guion, then hauling freight between Québec and Plaisance, was generally acknowledged as the pilot most familiar with Cape Breton's shores and harbours.

At Plaisance Commandant de Costebelle, soon to be governor of the new colony, arranged to interview the expert, but Guion's advice dismayed him. The colonizers' eye had already fallen on Havre-à-l'Anglois, which was soon to be renamed Louisbourg, but Guion dismissed that harbour contemptuously, reporting that only the smallest vessels could cross the shallows at the entrance to the harbour. Instead, Guion recommended St. Anne's Bay, which he described enthusiastically and in detail.

There were no shallows at Havre-à-l'Anglois. Costebelle's deputy founded Louisbourg there that fall, after a survey that downgraded St. Anne's Bay and reported the entire island population to be thirty migrant Indian families and a single, unnamed Frenchman. Undaunted by the rejection of Guion's advice, the Guion family followed the settlers to Louisbourg, where Joseph Guion died late in 1714.

There is an inventory of Joseph Guion's meagre estate that suggests why he lied about Havre-à-l'Anglois and promoted St. Anne's Bay. It points to the identity of the single Frenchman already on Cape Breton Island in 1713 and hints at the wellsprings of Baptiste Guion's future attachment to the island.

The inventory shows that Joseph Guion owned a house at Québec, newly acquired and unpaid for, but he also had a second home. This second home, either incomplete or partly collapsed when the inventory was taken, stood at St. Anne's Bay. Guion had stayed there before 1713, it appears, and perhaps his distortions about Havre-à-l'Anglois had been inspired by the hope of bringing a rush of settlers to land he could claim to own. It is possible, at least, that Baptiste Guion was a true child of Ile Royale, born there at St. Anne's in his parents' wilderness years, before the advent of the governors, soldiers, and merchants who had built a colony and been brought down in 1745. For his part, Guion planned to stay.

In avoiding the colonial war of 1745, Baptiste Guion seems to have been following the instincts that had guided his father in 1701, and he was even more adept at regaining a place in society when peace returned. The return of Guion's old friends and neighbours to Ile Royale in 1749 posed a problem, for his collaboration with the enemy was widely suspected. Guion protested that his co-operation had been forced, however, and in the absence of proof his claim had to be accepted.

Guion was almost the only colonist to have profited from the enemy occupation. Besides paying him for piloting services, the English had built a new house on his quayside lot, and when the occupying troops left Ile Royale, Guion triumphantly reclaimed both his property and the new house on it. He and his wife regularized their unorthodox marriage at the chapel and soon added two new children to the large families they each had. Soon the elder Guion children were married and settling in the community.

The authorities may have retained their doubts about Guion, but the townspeople evidently did not. In 1749, though questions about his collaboration were still fresh, Guion was elected one of the guardians of the children of his old friend Jodocus Koller. By his initiative on their behalf, we have a last glimpse of the Koller family.

By 1752 young Grégoire Koller had gone from Ile Royale, perhaps apprenticed and sent off with a small patrimony from his parents' few belongings. Young Catherine Koller continued to live with her elderly grandmother in the Auger inn next door to the Guions. Madame Auger, who had displayed a prickly disposition in her courtroom encounter years before, evidently found the care of her young ward burdensome, and gradually the neighbours became concerned by her treatment of the seven-year-old girl. In May 1752, Jean-Baptiste Guion challenged Madame Auger's guardianship in the courts, charging that she gave Catherine Koller daily beatings but no education.

In the crowded town there were many witnesses. Several people had seen the poor child beaten, left unfed, put outdoors in winter storms, and generally abused and neglected. They testified in righteous anger, but other witnesses said Madame Auger had worked to teach the child prayers and catechism and had punished her quite

appropriately when she failed to learn. In the end the judge felt unable
to break Madame Auger's guardianship, but he seems to have grasped
her unsuitability as a foster parent. By court order Catherine Koller was
sent that summer to be enrolled at the Ursuline sisters' convent school
in Québec, and the last of the unfortunate Kollers left Louisbourg.

By the end of Catherine Koller's school years, there was no
Louisbourg left to which she might have returned. The brief
Anglo–French truce broke down in 1755, and Britain entered the war
with a new strategy. Instead of fighting in continental Europe, Britain
aimed to strike at France's seapower and its colonial holdings around
the world. The sea war began that summer on the Grand Banks, and
the people of Louisbourg saw their home become an armed camp
under annual threat of blockade. With the "useless mouths" of the
colony evacuated to France, Ile Royale's supply lines were kept open
against enemy attack by naval men like Jean Lelarge, by privateers,
and by blockade-running merchant captains from Louisbourg and
France. In 1757 a French fleet warded off a British attempt to attack
Louisbourg. In the spring of 1758, thirty-five hundred soldiers and a
fleet of ten ships gathered to defend the fortress, but after three seasons
of war the growing British seapower was beginning to tell. Forty ships
blockaded the colony; more than 13,000 army troops prepared to land
and besiege.

Governor Drucour could spare more men to defend the shore of
Gabarus Bay than could Duchambon thirteen years before, but when
the British assault-landing succeeded early in June, Drucour fell back
to a classic defence of his walls, knowing defeat was largely a matter
of time. The British force was overwhelming, and General Amherst
applied unrelenting pressure, again focussing the attack at the
Dauphin Bastion. By the end of July capitulation could no longer be
delayed. Once more the colony was emptied of its people. Québec
fell the next year, Montréal the next, and the colony's future rested in
British hands.

Since 1749 Halifax had been rising to serve the British much as
Louisbourg had served the French, and the victors hardly needed both
ports. In 1760, with global victory not yet confirmed and peace negotiations looming, the British cabinet decided to raze Louisbourg's
defences but to leave the half-empty town standing. That summer

gangs of miners exploded the slowly built and twice-assaulted ramparts, leaving the town encircled by long mounds of rounded rubble.

Peace confirmed British sway over North America, and a few years later Louisbourg's British garrison sailed away, followed by most of the small civil population. Inside the circle of demolished walls abandoned houses began to crumble and disappear, until only the grass-green ruin of the fortifications remained, still tracing Vauban's military geometry around the once-embattled peninsula.

Some of the Louisbourg exiles eventually became the founders of France's foothold on the fishery, the little colony of Saint-Pierre and Miquelon. Some went out to Louisiana, the Caribbean, South America, even the Far East. Others stayed in France to find new careers in the port cities or to subsist for years on royal pensions. Some died in the French Revolution, some thrived in it, and slowly they rejoined the mainstream of French society.

But Jean-Baptiste Guion was there to see Louisbourg's walls demolished. His experiences during the second siege of his town went unrecorded, but he had once more contrived to remain on his home island when everyone else was shipped away. In 1768 the last records of the dying town mention "Monsieur Dion a french pilot" settled in a house that had once been his mother's.

The Guions, there before the soldiers ever came, still there after the soldiers left, are probably still near by, and whether Jean-Baptiste really was born on the island scarcely matters. In his steady devotion to his home, his self-sufficient disregard for constituted authority, and his absolute commitment to not going down the road, he makes a curious personal link from Louisbourg's era to later ones, a true survivor.

Afterword to the 2000 Edition

Not long after *Louisbourg Portraits* was published in 1982, I interviewed a historian who had written a biography of an emperor, and then about the life of an obscure family of peasants. I asked him about the difference between these books, expecting he would refer to the rising importance of social history and the broad shifts in what historians study.

He said instead that when he wrote about the emperor, he had recently obtained a good degree and a chair at Yale. Issues of power and status were interesting to him. Later, when he was married and raising children, it was the situations and emotions of ordinary life that intrigued him most. For the first time, I contemplated the ghosts of autobiography that may attend a book, even one about a subject far away in time and space.

Looking back at *Louisbourg Portraits* after some twenty years, I now note in its pages its striving, eager young men, seeking with varying degrees of success to make futures for themselves. I see echoes of the things that preoccupied me when I was writing of Jacques Rolland and Jean Lelarge.

Louisbourg Portraits was my first book, my attempt to find a place for myself in the world of writing. Finding ways to understand these eighteenth-century lives, so open but so mysterious, seemed both the hardest and the most satisfying thing I had ever done. Finding a language in which to write about them was a slow, private struggle. I knew almost nothing about publishing and bookselling in 1982, and I hardly believed what I was writing could be published. Devoting my time to these lives and stories sometimes seemed as quixotic and ill-fated as any venture of Rolland or Louis Davory.

Another part of my mind, however, presumed there must be an audience who would take an interest in the stories that I found so compelling. Indeed there was. *Louisbourg Portraits* found a publisher relatively easily. In the years since, it has sold steadily and never fallen out of print. It began making friends at once, and the warmth of the reception it received opened for me just about the career I hoped it would. I have been writing on historical subjects ever since, and I continue to be grateful for the interest readers have shown. We are constantly being told that interest in history is dead or dying. In the years since *Louisbourg Portraits* was published, it has never seemed so to me.

I followed no particular model. I was already at work when I read Emmanuel Le Roy Ladurie's remarkable *Montaillou* – though, indeed, that wonderful book about the people of a small village in the Pyrenees caught up in the Inquisition against the Cathar heresy about 1300 AD did inspire me to continue. Other books about the intimate lives of ordinary people appeared not long after *Louisbourg Portraits*: Natalie Davis's *The Return of Martin Guerre*, and in Canada, Sandra Gwyn's beautifully constructed *The Private Capital: Ambition and Love in the Age of Macdonald and Laurier*. All these works and others like them certainly drew on the long historical shift away from political and national history toward the rhythms of personal and private life. But each of those books followed its own inspiration. Mine was inspired by the particular historical sources that existed in such abundance at Louisbourg, and by my good fortune in being able to immerse myself in them over several years, before beginning to write.

Inspired also, and above all, by the lives and stories I encountered in those sources. I no longer much fear living out some milder, modern version of the misfortunes of Jacques Rolland or Louis Davory. But their experiences and what they made of them still intrigues me, as does the life of Jodocus Koller (whose story may have some echo of my own father, also an adaptable immigrant and ex-soldier turned family man), and of Jean Lelarge, and all the others.

It is not just because I now have daughters that Marie-Louise Cruchon, the one subject of *Louisbourg Portraits* who says barely a word on her own behalf, now strikes me as the emotional centre of the book. For there was always more than simply projections of self in these episodes.

"An immense and indispensable advantage of history," wrote the American critic Paul Goodman, "is that it continually presents to us many other possible human ways of being." A glimpse of other ways of being does indeed seem to be the gift the people of eighteenth-century Louisbourg left to us in the historical record they created. I do not expect to write any other book quite like *Louisbourg Portraits* (recently, indeed, I have turned to neglected fields of national political history). But I remain grateful that I once was able to.

There have been some new books and Web sites that dedicated readers might seek out about Louisbourg, but I have left the suggested readings and the text itself essentially untouched. My debt to Louise remains as great as when I wrote the preface.

A Note on the Sources

"They must have left remarkable diaries!" – the comment of an audience given a taste of the kind of history the Ile Royale sources make possible.

But only about three Louisbourg diaries are known, and none goes far beyond a chronicle of siege. To portray Louisbourg and its people, one needs a different sort of source produced by another impulse entirely.

Eighteenth-century France was, for its time, a centralized state, and keeping the central authority informed demanded paperwork. Colonial authorities routinely compiled dossiers on every aspect of their responsibilities, not only by written reports but also in maps, plans, censuses, and statistical tables. They made copies of everything, for their careers might depend on what they wrote. Under royal persuasion, officials outside the administrative hierarchy acquired the same habit: notaries routinely kept copies of the legal agreements they witnessed, priests diligently compiled their registers of baptisms and marriages and burials, and the law courts preserved verbatim transcripts even of trivial cases. Record-keeping was in the nature of the society. As a result, seventeenth- and eighteenth-century French colonies in Canada are often more abundantly documented than nineteenth-century British ones, where the impulse to document and file was less insistent.

At once a rather small community and a fully-fledged royal colony, Ile Royale was particularly well-documented. With fewer people in their purview, the record-keepers could be more detailed than usual, and with clerks, courts, and notaries close at hand, people availed themselves of the services offered.

Louisbourg ended not in pillage and flames but in orderly capitulation, so its records went into exile with the record-keepers. They eventually found their way to what became the National Archives of France. In the twentieth century the advent of microfilm photography made them easily available in Canada. The result: though most of the people of Ile Royale were illiterate, and though there survive very few diaries and almost no personal correspondence, most individuals who lived in eighteenth-century Louisbourg for any length of time can today be named and identified, even (in varying degree of detail) described.

Such sources made *Louisbourg Portraits* possible. By attending to them I have not had to invent a single character, episode, or event. *Louisbourg Portraits* is history: there is no line of dialogue that is not taken from a document, and I have not had to transpose events in time or place. Events described in *Louisbourg Portraits* happened; the people to whom they occurred existed; and the records have long been available to scholars. Where I have speculated on motivation or attitude or emotion, I have tried to make plain both the speculation and the historical evidence that supports it.

I have not burdened the text of *Louisbourg Portraits* with endless references to these sources, though a page-by-page annotation of the text may be consulted at the Archives of Fortress of Louisbourg National Historic Park or through my publishers. The notes that follow suggest in a general way the interplay between text and sources, and they credit important historical writings on a variety of topics.

My former colleagues of the research staff of Fortress of Louisbourg National Historic Park have produced a library of closely detailed research reports that have informed my account of many aspects of the town and colony, but most of these remain unpublished. Among published works, the book that dominates any list of readings is J. S. McLennan's *Louisbourg from Its Foundation to Its Fall* (Macmillan, 1918). The principal work of an amateur historian, and first published in 1918, it remains a remarkably detailed and fair narrative of the colony's history. Biographies of many important figures in Louisbourg's history appear in Volumes II, III, and IV of the *Dictionary of Canadian Biography* (University of Toronto Press, 1967, 1974, 1980). *Fortress of Louisbourg* by John Fortier and Owen

Fitzgerald (Oxford University Press, 1979) is a beautiful words-and-photos study of the reconstructed town. However, nothing can substitute for a visit to Fortress of Louisbourg National Historic Park.

Louis Davory's Crime

The chapter mentions *greffier* Laurens Meyracq at the keeping of the court's transcripts, and it is on those transcripts that the chapter is built. The record of the case, including the verbatim testimony of each witness, filled several fat handwritten dossiers which now repose in file boxes labelled as Volumes 186 and 196 of the series of papers catalogued as "G2" in the Section "Outre-Mer" of the Archives Nationales on Rue des Francs-Bourgeois in Paris, France. From Sergeant Bellefond's account of his nocturnal patrol to the freeing of Louis Davory, and including such peripheral details as the drowning of Pierre Barrau and the wintry conditions of the citadel jail cells, the case has been reconstructed from the original record. Biographical data and supplementary material come from administrative correspondence, court transcripts, shipping registers, and the parish registers of Louisbourg.

The Marriage of Marie-Louise Cruchon

Again, the essence of the story comes from judicial records, this time from the suits and counter-suits of the embattled Cruchon–Rolland family. Their angry denunciations provide such details as the widow's forgery of parental consent and Rolland's gambling losses during Carnaval. The legal consequences offer valuable documents – the detailed inventory of Rolland's shop, the auction of his goods – and the notarial files preserve the marriage contract and the agreements with Mervin.

The challenge is not to find evidence but to interpret it, for the sources offer no flat explanation of why the marriage took place or why it ended. Fortunately the nature of the family and of family relations in past societies has become the subject of systematic historical attention in recent years, and I have benefited from some of the methods and findings of this work. Edward Shorter, *The Making of the Modern Family* (Basic Books, 1975), offers an engaging introduction to family history. The account of what happened to the Cruchons and Rolland is my own, however, and might be interpreted differently by other students of the case.

Business is the other subject of the chapter. Louisbourg's commerce is abundantly documented, but details about the Mervin firm and Rolland's career in France are sparse; my account here is a general portrait of French merchant-trade of that period. So much of the history of eighteenth-century Canada has been written in essentially military terms that even the existence of a French commercial world has rarely been recognized. The notion of a commercial aspect to Louisbourg has been particularly unwelcome. The men of Rolland's intensely business-oriented milieu would have been surprised by such a verdict upon them.

Charles Renaut's Letter

The letter itself is one of the very few pieces of personal correspondence left by any of the people of Ile Royale. The letter and the inventory taken after his death, although almost the sum of the evidence about him, nevertheless tell more than is known about most of his fellow migrant fishermen.

Historians are just beginning to appreciate the economic importance and human drama of the enormous industry that linked the cod stocks of eastern Canada to the markets of Europe. The brief account here builds on the range of Ile Royale sources, on my own researches in eighteenth-century economic history, and from written accounts such as Charles de La Morandière, *Histoire de la Pêche Française de la Morue dans l'Amérique Septentrionale* (Maisonneuve et Larose, 1962).

Trade with the Indians was less important to Ile Royale than to most Canadian colonies of its time. The best summary of the subject is Olive Dickason, *Louisbourg and the Indians* (Parks Canada, 1976). On the Basques, William J. Douglass and Jon Bilbao, *Amerikanuak:*

Basques in the New World (University of Nevada Press, 1975), stands out in a very limited historical literature.

The Sea and Jean Lelarge

To my knowledge, the remarkable and in some ways important career of Jean-François Lelarge has never before been noted by historians.

Louisbourg Admiralty records provide most of the account of Lelarge's commercial sailing. Court records cover his spectacular marriage, and once he joined the navy – one of several sailors from New France to achieve naval rank – a Marine Ministry personnel file followed his career.

Some of Lelarge's seafights are described only in a petition to the Marine Ministry written by his brother-in-law (the precise relationship remains unclear, but a remarriage – either by Lelarge or by Louise Samson – seems possible). As a family record, the petition may sometimes exaggerate Lelarge's feats, but its overall accuracy is confirmed by independent sources, and it is surely true to the spirit of the man.

The account of housebuilding and the carpenter's trade draws on Peter Moogk, *Building a House in New France* (McClelland and Stewart, 1977), and on the architectural research program of the Fortress of Louisbourg.

Sergeant Koller in Peace and War

With the siege of 1745, *Louisbourg Portraits* approaches terrain covered by many other historical studies, but the availability of earlier studies has not much simplified the task.

The 1745 siege has always been presented as a moral struggle more than a military one, with willpower and enthusiasm taken to be the decisive factors. The first histories were written in New England soon after the event to stress the achievement of gallant amateurs and citizen armies. Most historians have followed this tack, neglecting important French sources and taking for granted that if the victors were heroic amateurs, the vanquished must have been cowardly incompetents. Fortification has usually been mentioned only to create gothic images of mossy battlements and medieval decay; there has been almost total neglect of the principles of siegecraft that governed the conflict. Scholarly stress on morale has encouraged more thoroughly romanticized and erroneous accounts of the battle in popular history and fiction.

I have attempted instead to base a realistic siege narrative in the context of Vaubanian warfare. Vauban's own text *On the Attack and the Defence of Fortified Places* is the essential source on fortification and siegecraft, but Christopher Duffy, *Fire and Stone: The Science of Fortress Warfare, 1660–1860* (David and Charles, 1975), is an excellent introduction for modern readers. My account also differs from most in presenting the defenders' viewpoint at least as thoroughly as the attackers'. Concerning the attackers, George Rawlyk, *Yankees at Louisbourg* (University of Maine Press, 1967), makes a useful guide to New England sources and siege journals. The Girard Lacroix journal of the siege, edited by Julian Gwyn and myself, is published in *La Chute de Louisbourg* (Editions de l'Université d'Ottawa, 1978).

Sergeant Koller's career in Louisbourg before the siege is pieced together from reference to him in censuses, notarial registers, and parish records. His death is reported in an estate inventory filed at Louisbourg in 1749.

Chronology of Events

1701

Opening stages of the War of Spanish Succession, which will dominate European diplomacy for the next dozen years as the expansion of French influence is resisted by the other powers.

Louis XIV rules at Versailles. France, with twenty million people, is the largest, most powerful nation of Europe. French power in North America is expanding. New France includes: Canada, established for nearly a century and growing rapidly, with fifteen thousand people living by agriculture and the fur trade; Acadia, with a few thousand farming settlers; Plaisance, a fishing base on the south coast of Newfoundland; and newly founded Louisiana. Other French overseas interests include Martinique, the principal French Caribbean colony, outposts in India, the African slave trade, and a growing foreign trade.

In Britain, the Protestant monarchy has been confirmed with the exile of the Stuart dynasty (1688) and the coronation of William and Mary. British colonial interests (the Thirteen Colonies, Newfoundland, Jamaica and other Caribbean islands, and trade to India) compete with those of France.

1702

Death of William of Orange, coronation of Queen Anne of England.

1704

Battle of Blenheim. British capture Gibraltar. Canadian raids into New England.

1705

Famines and war reverses in France.

1706

French attack St. John's and other English settlements in Newfound-land from Plaisance (p. 129). Intendant Raudot of New France proposes post-war colonization of Cape Breton Island. Pierre Morpain begins privateering career in West Indies (p. 59).

1707

Act of Union unites England and Scotland. Death of Sebastien LePrestre de Vauban, age seventy-four (p. 186). British siege fails to capture Port Royal in Acadia.

1708

Battle of Oudenarde, allies push into France. Death of François de Laval, first Bishop of Québec.

1709

French from Plaisance capture St. John's and burn other English settlements in Newfoundland (p. 129)

1710

British capture Port Royal in Acadia. Birth of future Louis XV. Pierre Lelarge settles in Plaisance (p. 129).

1711

British naval expedition against Québec wrecked in St. Lawrence.

1712

Births of Jean-Jacques Rousseau, Marquis de Montcalm, Jean Lelarge (p. 128).

1713

Peace of Utrecht ends War of Spanish Succession. Late victories enable Louis XIV to salvage a peace, partly by colonial concessions. France yields Hudson Bay, Acadia, Newfoundland to Britain and prepares to settle Cape Breton Island. Joseph de Saint-Ovide de Brouillan takes possession of Louisbourg harbour and founds the colony of Ile Royale with a detachment of troops.

1714

Death of Queen Anne, coronation of King George I.
  About seven hundred civilians from Plaisance, Acadia, Québec, and France settle at Louisbourg and its outports to begin fishing and trade.

1715

Death of Louis XIV, age seventy-two. Coronation of Louis XV under the Regency of the Duc d'Orléans.
  Jacobite rising in Scotland falls to restore Stuart dynasty. Birth of Louise Samson (p. 158).

1717

Governing institutions of Ile Royale established. Saint-Ovide de Brouillan succeeds de Costebelle as governor.

1718

Louisbourg confirmed as capital of Ile Royale.

1719

Census of Ile Royale reports Louisbourg population 853, Ile Royale 2,262.

1720

Twenty-five-year fortification project begins at Louisbourg. Birth of Jacques-François Rolland (p. 49).

1721

Robert Walpole becomes British prime minister. Bach completes Brandenburg Concertos.

1722

Ile Royale garrison increased to 350 men with first detachment of Karrer Regiment to Louisbourg (p. 185).

1723

Louis XV reaches age of majority. Comte de Maurepas appointed French Minister of Marine, responsible for naval and colonial affairs.

1725

Marriage of Louis XV. Death of Peter the Great, Tsar of Russia.
    Etienne Verrier appointed chief engineer at Louisbourg (p. 185). Wreck of the *Chameau* (p. 139).

1726

Cardinal Fleury heads French government. Like Walpole, Fleury follows a peace policy.

Census of Ile Royale reports Louisbourg population 1,296, Ile Royale 3,950. Jean-René Cruchon brings his family to Louisbourg (p. 56).

1727

Death of King George I, coronation of George II. Death of Bishop Saint-Vallier, Bishop of Québec, 1688–1727. Sisters of Charity found school at Louisbourg (p. 69). Death of Isaac Newton.

1729

Marriage of Jodocus Koller and Marie-Catherine Auger (p. 206). Birth of Marie-Louise Cruchon (p. 67).

1730

Deaths of Charles and Mathurin Renaut (p. 126). Marriage of Jeanne Lelarge and Pierre Chouteau (p. 135).

1731

Record fish catch in Ile Royale as Louisbourg exports 167,000 quintals of dried cod to Europe. Jeanne Crosnier seeks separation from Jean Laumonier (p. 26).

1732

Outbreak of smallpox in Louisbourg (p. 68). Birth of George Washington. Benjamin Franklin publishes *Poor Richard's Almanack*.

1733

War of Polish Succession threatens Anglo–French conflict. Smallpox kills Pierre Lelarge and many other Louisbourg citizens (p. 149).

1734

Ile Royale census reports Louisbourg population 1,616, Ile Royale 4,527, garrison strength 580. Louisbourg lighthouse completed. Joseph Lartigue appointed judge of Louisbourg *bailliage* (p. 7). Jean Lelarge wins master's certificate from Louisbourg Admiralty (p. 150).

1735

Private betrothal of Jean Lelarge and Louise Samson (p. 159).

1737

Ile Royale census reports Louisbourg population 1,963, Ile Royale 5,181, garrison strength 580. Quayside fire destroys several buildings. Marriage of Jean Lelarge and Louise Samson (p. 160).

1738

Mandatory retirement of Governor Saint-Ovide. Death of Jean-René Cruchon (p. 61). Birth of Jean-Aimable Lelarge (p. 166).

1739

Britain declares war on Spain. Naval officer Isaac de Forant named governor of Ile Royale (p. 11). Ile Royale fish catch begins five-year decline (p. 122).

1740

War of Austrian Succession. With French support, Frederick the Great, newly crowned King of Prussia, opposes the claims of Maria Theresa, Queen of Hungary and Bohemia, Archduchess of Austria. Death of de Forant, appointment of Louis LePrévost Duquesnel. Louis Davory arrested and tried for theft (p. 5).

1741

France enters War of Austrian Succession.
    Death of Julien Auger *dit* Grandchamp (p. 207). Jacques Rolland visits Louisbourg (p. 52).

1742

Fall of Walpole and peace party in Britain. Jacques Rolland settles in Louisbourg and marries Marie-Louise Cruchon (p. 65).

1743

Death of Cardinal Fleury; Louis XV begins personal rule. Death of Joseph Lartigue (p. 47). Jean Lelarge visits Boston (p. 154). Separation of Jacques Rolland and Marie-Louise Cruchon (p. 98).

1744

France declares war on Britain. Louisbourg troops seize Canso and besiege Annapolis Royal in Acadia. Privateers active on the coast of Ile Royale. Death of Duquesnel; Louis DuPont Duchambon acting governor.

1745

First siege and capture of Louisbourg. Colonists of Ile Royale exiled to France (p. 243).
    Marshal de Saxe wins Battle of Fontenoy. Jacobite rising in Scotland. Madame de Pompadour installed at Versailles as the accepted royal mistress.

1746

Duc d'Anville's naval expedition fails to recover Louisbourg. Jean Lelarge given naval duties. French capture Madras in India. Jacobite rising crushed at Culloden.

1748

Treaty of Aix-la-Chapelle ends War of Austrian Succession. Britain and France return their conquests.

Montesquieu publishes *Esprit des Lois*.

1749

France reoccupies Ile Royale. Governor Desherbiers lands at Louisbourg with an enlarged garrison and the exiled civilian population.

Britain establishes Halifax, Nova Scotia. Comte de Maurepas dismissed as Minister of Marine. Deaths in the Koller family (p. 244).

1751

Army officer Comte de Raymond appointed governor of Ile Royale. Battle of Arcot begins British territorial expansion in India. Diderot and d'Alembert begin *Encyclopédie*, key work of the French Enlightenment.

1752

Census of Ile Royale reports Louisbourg population 4,174, Ile Royale 8,814, garrison strength 1,250. Britain adopts modern Gregorian calendar.

1753

Anglo–French military tension mounts in North America and India. Jean Lelarge visits Louisbourg (p. 175).

1755

French regular troops reinforce Ile Royale and Canada, and British troops sent to Thirteen Colonies. British navy attacks French fleet off Newfoundland.

Acadians deported. Rigaud de Vaudreuil appointed governor general of New France.

Ile Royale goes on war footing as garrison increases to 2,300.

1756

Seven Years War. British leader William Pitt plans to attack France by attacking its colonies and foreign trade. Marquis de Montcalm takes command of French troops in Canada. Birth of Mozart.

1757

British fail to lay siege to Louisbourg; naval action on coast of Ile Royale. Battle of Plassey confirms British control of India.

1758

Second siege and capture of Louisbourg. Colonists and troops exiled to France.

Birth of Horatio Nelson, Maximilien Robespierre.

1759

Siege of Québec and battle of Plains of Abraham. British capture Guadeloupe. Voltaire publishes *Candide*. Death of Handel.

1760

Battle of Montréal and fall of New France. Fortifications of Louisbourg demolished. Death of George II, coronation of George III.

1761

Death of Jean Lelarge (p. 178).

1762

France captures St. John's, Newfoundland. Britain captures Grenada and Martinique. Rousseau publishes *Le Contrat Social*. Catherine the Great crowned Empress of Russia.

1763

Treaty of Paris ends Seven Years War. British possession of Canada, Ile Royale, India confirmed. France retains fishing rights in Newfoundland, recovers Martinique, acquires Saint-Pierre and Miquelon, cedes Louisiana to Spain.

1768

Last British troops withdrawn from Louisbourg.

1774

Death of Louis XV.

1775

American Revolution begins.

1783

Treaty of Paris confirms American independence. Loyalist exiles begin resettlement of Cape Breton Island.

1789

French Revolution begins.

1804

Napoleon Bonaparte crowned Emperor of France.

Louisbourg Portraits, first published in 1982, was Christopher Moore's first book. It won the Gevernor General's Literary Award and has continued to delight readers ever since.

Christopher Moore has gone on to become one of Canada's most versatile writers of history. His other books include the bestselling photographic history *Canada: Our Century*; the young people's history called *The Story of Canada* (with Janet Lunn), which won the Mister Christie Award; and *1867: How the Fathers Made a Deal*, which Dalton Camp called "just about the best book on our history I've ever read." He has written widely about Canadian history in many media, including a long-running column in *The Beaver: Canada's History Magazine* and many contributions to CBC Radio's "Ideas." In 1999–2000, he was national chair of The Writers' Union of Canada.

Christopher Moore lives in Toronto.